Apache Spark for Data Science Cookbook

Overinsightful 90 recipes to get lightning-fast analytics with Apache Spark

Padma Priya Chitturi

BIRMINGHAM - MUMBAI

Apache Spark for Data Science Cookbook

First published: December 2016

Production reference: 1161216

Published by Packt Publishing Ltd.
Livery Place
35 Livery Street
Birmingham
B3 2PB, UK.
ISBN 978-1-78588-010-0

www.packtpub.com

Credits

Author

Padma Priya Chitturi

Reviewer

Roberto Corizzo

Commissioning Editor

Akram Hussain

Acquisition Editors

Vinay Argekar

Manish Nainani

Content Development Editor

Sumeet Sawant

Technical Editor

Deepti Tuscano

Copy Editor

Safis Editing

Project Coordinator

Shweta H Birwatkar

Proofreader

Safis Editing

Indexer

Mariammal Chettiyar

Graphics

Disha Haria

Production Coordinator

Arvindkumar Gupta

About the Author

Padma Priya Chitturi is Analytics Lead at Fractal Analytics Pvt Ltd and has over five years of experience in Big Data processing. Currently, she is part of capability development at Fractal and responsible for solution development for analytical problems across multiple business domains at large scale. Prior to this, she worked for an Airlines product on a real-time processing platform serving one million user requests/sec at Amadeus Software Labs. She has worked on realizing large-scale deep networks (Jeffrey dean's work in Google brain) for image classification on the big data platform Spark. She works closely with Big Data technologies such as Spark, Storm, Cassandra and Hadoop. She was an open source contributor to Apache Storm.

First, I would like to thank the Packt Publishing team for providing a great opportunity for me to take part in this exciting journey and would like to express my special thanks and gratitude to my family, friends and colleagues who has been very supportive and helped me in finishing this project within time.

About the Reviewer

Roberto Corizzo is a PhD student at the Department of Computer Science, University of Bari, Italy. His research interests include Big Data analytics, data mining, and predictive modeling techniques for sensor networks. He has been involved as technical reviewer for Packt's *Learning Hadoop 2* and *Learning Python Web Penetration Testing* video courses.

www.PacktPub.com

For support files and downloads related to your book, please visit `www.PacktPub.com`.

Did you know that Packt offers eBook versions of every book published, with PDF and ePub files available? You can upgrade to the eBook version at `www.PacktPub.com` and as a print book customer, you are entitled to a discount on the eBook copy. Get in touch with us at `service@packtpub.com` for more details.

At `www.PacktPub.com`, you can also read a collection of free technical articles, sign up for a range of free newsletters and receive exclusive discounts and offers on Packt books and eBooks.

`https://www.packtpub.com/mapt`

Get the most in-demand software skills with Mapt. Mapt gives you full access to all Packt books and video courses, as well as industry-leading tools to help you plan your personal development and advance your career.

Why subscribe?

- Fully searchable across every book published by Packt
- Copy and paste, print, and bookmark content
- On demand and accessible via a web browser

Customer Feedback

Thank you for purchasing this Packt book. We take our commitment to improving our content and products to meet your needs seriously – that's why your feedback is so valuable. Whatever your feelings about your purchase, please consider leaving a review on this book's Amazon page. Not only will this help us, more importantly it will also help others in the community to make an informed decision about the resources that they invest in to learn. You can also review for us on a regular basis by joining our reviewers club. **If you're interested in joining, or would like to learn more about the benefits we offer, please contact us**: customerreviews@packtpub.com.

Table of Contents

Preface

In recent years, the volume of data being collected, stored, and analyzed has exploded, in particular in relation to the activity on the Web and mobile devices, as well as data from the physical world collected via sensor networks. While previously large-scale data storage, processing, analysis, and modeling was the domain of the largest institutions such as Google, Yahoo!, Facebook, and Twitter, increasingly, many organizations are being faced with the challenge of how to handle a massive amount of data.

With the advent of big data, extracting knowledge from large, heterogeneous, and noisy datasets requires not only powerful computing resources, but the programming abstractions to use them effectively. The abstractions that emerged in the last decade blend ideas from parallel databases, distributed systems, and programming languages to create a new class of scalable data analytics platforms that form the foundation for data science at realistic scales.

The objective of this book is to get the audience the flavor of challenges in data science and addressing them with a variety of analytical tools on a distributed system such as Spark (apt for iterative algorithms), which offers in-memory processing and more flexible for data analysis at scale. This book introduces readers to the fundamentals of Spark and helps them learn the concepts with code examples. It also talks in brief about data mining, text mining, NLP, machine learning, and so on. The readers get to know how to solve real-world analytical problems with large datasets and are made aware of a very practical approach and code to use analytical tools that leverage the features of Spark.

What this book covers

Chapter 1, *Big Data Analytics with Spark*, introduces Scala, Python and R can be used for data analysis. It also details about Spark programming model, API will be introduced, shows how to install, set up a development environment for the Spark framework and run jobs in distributed mode. I will also show working with DataFrames and Streaming computation models.

Chapter 2, *Tricky Statistics with Spark*, shows how to apply various statistical measures such as generating sample data, constructing frequency tables, summary and descriptive statistics on large datasets using Spark and Pandas

Chapter 3, *Data Analysis with Spark,* details how to apply common data exploration and preparation techniques such as univariate analysis, bivariate analysis, missing values treatment, identifying the outliers and techniques for variable transformation using Spark.

Chapter 4, *Clustering, Classification and Regression,* deals with creating models for regression, classification and clustering as well as shows how to utilize standard performance-evaluation methodologies for the machine learning models built.

Chapter 5, *Working with Spark MLlib,* provides an overview of Spark MLlib and ML pipelines and presents examples for implementing Naive Bayes classification, decision trees and recommendation systems.

Chapter 6, *NLP with Spark,* shows how to install NLTK, Anaconda and apply NLP tasks such as POS tagging, Named Entity Recognition, Chunker, Sentence Detector, Lemmatization using Core NLP and Stanford NLP over Spark.

Chapter 7, *Working with Sparkling Water - H2O,* details how to integrate H2O with Spark and shows applying various algorithms such as k-means, deep learning and SVM and also show developing applications –spam detection and crime detection with Sparkling Water.

Chapter 8, *Data Visualization with Spark,* show the integration of widely used visualization tools such as Zeppelin, Lightning Server and highly active Scala bindings (Bokeh-Scala) for visualizing large data sets.

Chapter 9, *Deep Learning on Spark,* shows how to implement deep learning algorithms such as RBM, CNN for learning MNIST, Feed-forward neural networks with the tools Deep Learning4j, TensorFlow using Spark.

Chapter 10, *Working with SparkR,* provides examples on creating distributed data frames in R, various operations that could be applied in SparkR and details on applying user-defined functions, SQL queries and machine learning in SparkR.

What you need for this book

Throughout this book, we assume that you have some basic experience with programming in Scala, Java, or Python and have some basic knowledge of machine learning, statistics, and data analysis.

Who this book is for

This book is intended for entry-level to intermediate data scientists, data analysts, engineers and practitioners who want to get acquainted with solving numerous data science problems using a distributed computing framework like Spark. The readers are expected to have knowledge on statistics, data science tools like R, Pandas and understanding on distributed systems (some exposure to Hadoop).

Sections

In this book, you will find several headings that appear frequently (Getting ready, How to do it, How it works, There's more, and See also).

To give clear instructions on how to complete a recipe, we use these sections as follows:

Getting ready

This section tells you what to expect in the recipe, and describes how to set up any software or any preliminary settings required for the recipe.

How to do it...

This section contains the steps required to follow the recipe.

How it works...

This section usually consists of a detailed explanation of what happened in the previous section.

There's more...

This section consists of additional information about the recipe in order to make the reader more knowledgeable about the recipe.

See also

This section provides helpful links to other useful information for the recipe.

Conventions

In this book, you will find a number of text styles that distinguish between different kinds of information. Here are some examples of these styles and an explanation of their meaning.

Code words in text, database table names, folder names, filenames, file extensions, pathnames, dummy URLs, user input, and Twitter handles are shown as follows: "Both spark-shell and PySpark are available in the `bin` directory of `SPARK_HOME`, that is, `SPARK_HOME/bin`"

A block of code is set as follows:

```
from pyspark
import SparkContext

stocks = "hdfs://namenode:9000/stocks.txt"

sc = SparkContext("<master URI>", "ApplicationName")
data = sc.textFile(stocks)

totalLines = data.count()
print("Total Lines are: %i" % (totalLines))
```

Any command-line input or output is written as follows:

```
$SPARK_HOME/bin/spark-shell --master <master type>
Spark context available as sc.
```

Warnings or important notes appear in a box like this.

Tips and tricks appear like this.

Reader feedback

Feedback from our readers is always welcome. Let us know what you think about this book-what you liked or disliked. Reader feedback is important for us as it helps us develop titles that you will really get the most out of.

To send us general feedback, simply e-mail `feedback@packtpub.com`, and mention the book's title in the subject of your message.

If there is a topic that you have expertise in and you are interested in either writing or contributing to a book, see our author guide at `www.packtpub.com/authors`.

Customer support

Now that you are the proud owner of a Packt book, we have a number of things to help you to get the most from your purchase.

Downloading the example code

You can download the example code files for this book from your account at `http://www.packtpub.com`. If you purchased this book elsewhere, you can visit `http://www.packtpub.com/support` and register to have the files e-mailed directly to you.

You can download the code files by following these steps:

1. Log in or register to our website using your e-mail address and password.
2. Hover the mouse pointer on the **SUPPORT** tab at the top.
3. Click on **Code Downloads & Errata**.
4. Enter the name of the book in the **Search** box.
5. Select the book for which you're looking to download the code files.
6. Choose from the drop-down menu where you purchased this book from.
7. Click on **Code Download**.

You can also download the code files by clicking on the **Code Files** button on the book's webpage at the Packt Publishing website. This page can be accessed by entering the book's name in the **Search** box. Please note that you need to be logged in to your Packt account.

Once the file is downloaded, please make sure that you unzip or extract the folder using the latest version of:

- WinRAR / 7-Zip for Windows
- Zipeg / iZip / UnRarX for Mac
- 7-Zip / PeaZip for Linux

The code bundle for the book is also hosted on GitHub at `https://github.com/ChitturiP adma/SparkforDataScienceCookbook`. We also have other code bundles from our rich catalog of books and videos available at `https://github.com/PacktPublishing/`. Check them out!

Errata

Although we have taken every care to ensure the accuracy of our content, mistakes do happen. If you find a mistake in one of our books-maybe a mistake in the text or the code-we would be grateful if you could report this to us. By doing so, you can save other readers from frustration and help us improve subsequent versions of this book. If you find any errata, please report them by visiting `http://www.packtpub.com/submit-errata`, selecting your book, clicking on the **Errata Submission Form** link, and entering the details of your errata. Once your errata are verified, your submission will be accepted and the errata will be uploaded to our website or added to any list of existing errata under the Errata section of that title.

To view the previously submitted errata, go to `https://www.packtpub.com/books/conten t/support` and enter the name of the book in the search field. The required information will appear under the **Errata** section.

Piracy

Piracy of copyrighted material on the Internet is an ongoing problem across all media. At Packt, we take the protection of our copyright and licenses very seriously. If you come across any illegal copies of our works in any form on the Internet, please provide us with the location address or website name immediately so that we can pursue a remedy.

Please contact us at `copyright@packtpub.com` with a link to the suspected pirated material.

We appreciate your help in protecting our authors and our ability to bring you valuable content.

Questions

If you have a problem with any aspect of this book, you can contact us at `questions@packtpub.com`, and we will do our best to address the problem.

1
Big Data Analytics with Spark

In this chapter, we will cover the components of Spark. You will learn them through the following recipes:

- Initializing SparkContext
- Working with Spark's Python and Scala shells
- Building standalone applications
- Working with the Spark programming model
- Working with pair RDDs
- Persisting RDDs
- Loading and saving data
- Creating broadcast variables and accumulators
- Submitting applications to a cluster
- Working with DataFrames
- Working with Spark Streaming

Introduction

Apache Spark is a general-purpose distributed computing engine for large-scale data processing. It is an open source initiative from AMPLab and donated to the Apache Software Foundation. It is one of the top-level projects under the Apache Software Foundation. Apache Spark offers a data abstraction called **Resilient Distributed Datasets** (**RDDs**) to analyze the data in parallel on top of a cluster of resources. The Apache Spark framework is an alternative to Hadoop MapReduce. It is up to 100X faster than MapReduce and offers the best APIs for iterative and expressive data processing. This project is written in Scala and it offers client APIs in Scala, Java, Python, and R.

Initializing SparkContext

This recipe shows how to initialize the `SparkContext` object as a part of many Spark applications. `SparkContext` is an object which allows us to create the base RDDs. Every Spark application must contain this object to interact with Spark. It is also used to initialize `StreamingContext`, `SQLContext` and `HiveContext`.

Getting ready

To step through this recipe, you will need a running Spark Cluster in any one of the modes that is, local, standalone, YARN, or Mesos. For installing Spark on a standalone cluster, please refer to `http://spark.apache.org/docs/latest/spark-standalone.html`. Install Hadoop (optional), Scala, and Java. Please download the data from the following location:

`https://github.com/ChitturiPadma/datasets/blob/master/stocks.txt`

How to do it...

Let's see how to initialize SparkContext:

1. Invoke spark-shell:

```
$SPARK_HOME/bin/spark-shell --master <master type>
Spark context available as sc.
```

2. Invoke PySpark:

```
$SPARK_HOME/bin/pyspark --master <master type>
SparkContext available as sc
```

3. Invoke SparkR:

```
$SPARK_HOME/bin/sparkR --master <master type>
Spark context is available as sc
```

4. Now, let's initiate `SparkContext` in different standalone applications, such as Scala, Java, and Python:

Scala:

```
import org.apache.spark.SparkContext._
import org.apache.spark.SparkConf
```

```scala
object SparkContextExample {
  def main(args: Array[String]) {
   val stocksPath = "hdfs://namenode:9000/stocks.txt"
   val conf = new SparkConf().setAppName("Counting
    Lines").setMaster("spark://master:7077")
   val sc = new SparkContext(conf)
   val data = sc.textFile(stocksPath, 2)
   val totalLines = data.count()
   println("Total number of Lines: %s".format(totalLines))
  }
}
```

Java:

```java
import org.apache.spark.api.java.*;
import org.apache.spark.SparkConf;
import org.apache.spark.api.java.function.Function;

public class SparkContextExample {
   public static void main(String[] args) {
      String stocks = "hdfs://namenode:9000/stocks.txt";
      SparkConf conf = new SparkConf().setAppName("Counting
      Lines").setMaster("spark://master:7077");
      JavaSparkContext sc = new JavaSparkContext(conf);
      JavaRDD<String> logData = sc.textFile(stocks);

      long totalLines = stocks.count();
      System.out.println("Total number of Lines " + totalLines);
   }
}
```

Python:

```python
from pyspark
import SparkContext

stocks = "hdfs://namenode:9000/stocks.txt"

sc = SparkContext("<master URI>", "ApplicationName")
data = sc.textFile(stocks)

totalLines = data.count()
print("Total Lines are: %i" % (totalLines))
```

How it works...

In the preceding code snippets, `new SparkContext(conf)`, `new JavaSparkContext(conf)`, and `SparkContext("<master URI>", "ApplicationName")` initialize SparkContext in three different languages: Scala, Java, and Python. SparkContext is the starting point for Spark functionality. It represents the connection to a Spark Cluster, and can be used to create RDDs, accumulators, and broadcast variables on that cluster.

There's more...

SparkContext is created on the driver. It connects with the cluster. Initially, RDDs are created using SparkContext. It is not serialized. Hence it cannot be shipped to workers. Also, only one SparkContext is available per application. In the case of Streaming applications and Spark SQL modules, StreamingContext and SQLContext are created on top of SparkContext.

See also

To understand more about the SparkContext object and its methods, please refer to this documentation page: `https://spark.apache.org/docs/1.6.0/api/scala/index.html#org.apache.spark.SparkContext`.

Working with Spark's Python and Scala shells

This recipe explains the spark-shell and PySpark command-line interface tools from the Apache Spark project. Spark-shell is the Scala-based command line interface tool and PySpark is the Python-based command-line tool used to develop Spark interactive applications. They are already initialized with SparkContext, SQLContext, and HiveContext.

How to do it...

Both spark-shell and PySpark are available in the `bin` directory of SPARK_HOME, that is, SPARK_HOME/bin:

1. Invoke spark-shell as follows:

```
$SPARK_HOME/bin/spark-shell [Options]

$SPARK_HOME/bin/spark-shell --master <master type> i.e., local,
spark, yarn, mesos.
$SPARK_HOME/bin/spark-shell --master
spark://<sparkmasterHostName>:7077

Welcome to
      ____              __
     / __/__  ___ _____/ /__
    _\ \/ _ \/ _ `/ __/  '_/
   /___/ .__/\_,_/_/ /_/\_\   version 1.6.0
      /_/

Using Scala version 2.10.5 (Java HotSpot(TM) 64-Bit Server VM, Java
1.7.0_79)
Type in expressions to have them evaluated.
Type :help for more information.
16/01/17 20:05:38 WARN Utils: Your hostname, localhost resolves to
a loopback address: 127.0.0.1; using 192.168.1.6 instead (on
interface en0)
SQL context available as sqlContext.

scala> val data = sc.textFile("hdfs://namenode:9000/stocks.txt");
data: org.apache.spark.rdd.RDD[String] = MapPartitionsRDD[1]
textFile at <console>:27

scala> data.count()
res0: Long = 57391

scala> data.first()
res1: String = NYSE    CLI    2009-12-31   35.39 35.70 34.50 34.5
                890100          34.12

scala> data.top(2)
res5: Array[String] = Array(NYSE CZZ    2009-12-31   8.77  8.77  8.67
    8.70   694200     8.70, NYSE   CZZ    2009- 12-30  8.71  8.80
    8.46    8.68   1588200      8.68)

scala> val mydata = data.map(line => line.toLowerCase())
```

```
mydata: org.apache.spark.rdd.RDD[String] = MapPartitionsRDD[3] at
map at <console>:29

scala> mydata.collect()
res6: Array[String] = Array(nyse cli 2009-12-31 35.39 35.70
34.50 34.57 890100 34.12, nyse cli 2009-12-30 35.22 35.46
34.96 35.40 516900 34.94, nyse cli 2009-12-29 35.69 35.95
35.21 35.34 556500 34.88, nyse cli 2009-12-28 35.67 36.23
35.49 35.69 565000 35.23, nyse cli 2009-12-24 35.38 35.60
35.19 35.47 230200 35.01, nyse cli 2009-12-23 35.13 35.51
35.07 35.21 520200 34.75, nyse cli 2009-12-22 34.76 35.04
34.71 35.04 564600 34.58, nyse cli 2009-12-21 34.65 34.74
34.41 34.73 428400 34.28, nyse cli 2009-12-18 34.11 34.38
33.73 34.22 1152600 33.77, nyse cli 2009-12-17 34.18 34.53
33.84 34.21 1082600 33.76, nyse cli 2009-12-16 34.79 35.10
34.48 34.66 1007900 34.21, nyse cli 2009-12-15 34.60 34.91
34.39 34.84 813200 34.39, nyse cli 2009-12-14 34.21 34.90
33.86 34.82 987700 34.37, nyse cli 200...)
```

2. Invoke PySpark as follows:

```
$SPARK_HOME/bin/pyspark [options]
$SPARK_HOME/bin/pyspark --master <master type> i.e., local,
spark, yarn, mesos
$SPARK_HOME/bin/pyspark --master spark://
sparkmasterHostName:7077

Python 2.7.6 (default, Sep  9 2014, 15:04:36)
[GCC 4.2.1 Compatible Apple LLVM 6.0 (clang-600.0.39)] on darwin
Type "help", "copyright", "credits" or "license" for more
information.
Using Spark's default log4j profile: org/apache/spark/log4j-
defaults.properties
16/01/17 20:25:48 INFO SparkContext: Running Spark version 1.6.0
...

Welcome to
      ____              __
     / __/__  ___ _____/ /__
    _\ \/ _ \/ _ `/ __/  '_/
   /__ / .__/\_,_/_/ /_/\_\   version 1.6.0
      /_/

Using Python version 2.7.6 (default, Sep  9 2014 15:04:36)
SparkContext available as sc, HiveContext available as sqlContext.

>>> data = sc.textFile"hdfs://namenode:9000/stocks.txt");
```

```
>>> data.count()
57391
>>> data.first()
NYSE      CLI    2009-12-31   35.39 35.70 34.50 34.57 890100
34.12
>>> data.top(2)
['NYSE   CZZ    2009-12-31   8.77  8.77  8.67  8.70   694200    8.70',
 'NYSE   CZZ    2009-12-30   8.71  8.80  8.46  8.68   1588200   8.68' ]

>>> data.collect()

['NYSE CLI 2009-12-31 35.39 35.70 34.50 34.57 890100 34.12,
 'NYSE CLI 2009-12-30 35.22 35.46 34.96 35.40 516900 34.94,
 'NYSE CLI 2009-12-29 35.69 35.95 35.21 35.34 556500 34.88',
 'NYSE CLI 2009-12-28 35.67 36.23 35.49 35.69 565000 35.23',
 'NYSE CLI 2009-12-24 35.38 35.60 35.19 35.47 230200 35.01',
 'NYSE CLI 2009-12-23 35.13 35.51 35.07 35.21 520200 34.75',
 'NYSE CLI 2009-12-22 34.76 35.04 34.71 35.04 564600 34.58',
 'NYSE CLI 2009-12-21 34.65 34.74 34.41 34.73 428400 34.28',
 'NYSE CLI 2009-12-18 34.11 34.38 33.73 34.22 1152600 33.77',
 'NYSE CLI 2009-12-17 34.18 34.53 33.84 34.21 1082600 33.76',
 'NYSE CLI 2009-12-16 34.79 35.10 34.48 34.66 1007900 34.21',
 'NYSE CLI 2009-12-15 34.60 34.91 34.39 34.84 813200 34.39',
 'NYSE CLI 2009-12-14 34.21 34.90 33.86 34.82 987700 34.37',
 'NYSE CLI 200...
```

How it works...

In the preceding code snippets, Spark RDD transformations and actions are executed interactively in both Spark-shell and PySpark. They work in **Read Eval Print Loop** (**REPL**) style and represent a computer environment such as a Window console or Unix/Linux shell where a command is entered and the system responds with an output in interactive mode.

There's more...

Both Spark-shell and PySpark are better command-line interfaces for developing Spark applications interactively. They have advanced features for application prototyping and quicker development. Also, they have numerous options for customizing them.

See also

The Apache Spark documentation offers plenty of examples using these two command-line interfaces; please refer to this documentation page:
`http://spark.apache.org/docs/latest/quick-start.html#interactive-analysis-with-the-spark-shell`.

Building standalone applications

This recipe explains how to develop and build Spark standalone applications using programming languages such as Scala, Java, Python, and R. The sample application under this recipe is written in Scala.

Getting ready

Install any IDE tool for application development (the preferred one is Eclipse). Install the SBT build tool to build the project. Create the Scala project and add all the necessary libraries to the `build.sbt` file. Add this project to Eclipse. SBT is a build tool like Maven for Scala projects.

How to do it...

1. Develop a Spark standalone application using the Eclipse IDE as follows:

```
import org.apache.spark.SparkContext
import org.apache.spark.SparkContext._
import org.apache.spark.SparkConf

object SparkContextExample {
def main(args: Array[String]) {
val file="hdfs://namenode:9000/stocks.txt"
val conf = new SparkConf().setAppName("Counting
        Lines").setMaster("spark://master:7077")
val sc = new SparkContext(conf)
val data = sc.textFile(file, 2)
val totalLines = data.count()

println("Total number of Lines: %s".format(totalLines))}}
```

2. Now go to the project directory and build the project using `sbt assembly` and `sbt package` manually or build it using eclipse:

```
~/SparkProject/ SparkContextExample/sbt assembly
~/SparkProject/ SparkContextExample/sbt package
```

How it works...

`sbt assembly` compiles the program and generates the JAR as `SparkContextExample-assembly-<version>.jar`. The `sbt package` generates the jar as `SparkContextExample_2.10-1.0.jar`. Both the jars are generated in the path `~/SparkProject/SparkContextExample/target/scala-2.10`. Submit `SparkContextExample-assembly-<version>.jar` to the Spark cluster using the `spark-submit` shell script under the `bin` directory of `SPARK_HOME`.

There's more...

We can develop a variety of complex Spark standalone applications to analyze the data in various ways. When working with any third-party libraries, include the corresponding dependency jars in the `build.sbt` file. Invoking `sbt update` will download the respective dependencies and will include them in the project classpath.

See also

The Apache Spark documentation covers how to build standalone Spark applications. Please refer to this documentation page:
https://spark.apache.org/docs/latest/quick-start.html#self-contained-applications.

Working with the Spark programming model

This recipe explains the fundamentals of the Spark programming model. It covers the RDD basics that is, Spark provides a **Resilient Distributed Dataset (RDD)**, which is a collection of elements partitioned across the nodes of the cluster that can be operated in parallel. It also covers how to create and perform transformations and actions on RDDs.

How to do it...

1. Let's create RDDs and apply a few transformations such as map and filter, and a few actions such as count, take, top, and so on, in Spark-shell:

```
scala> val data = Array(1, 2, 3, 4, 5)
scala> val rddData = sc.parallelize(data)
scala> val mydata = data.filter(ele => ele%2==0)
mydata: org.apache.spark.rdd.RDD[String] =
MapPartitionsRDD[3]    at
filter at <console>:29
scala> val mydata = data.map(ele => ele+2)
mydata: org.apache.spark.rdd.RDD[String] =
MapPartitionsRDD[3]    at
filter at <console>:30
scala> mydata.count()
res1: Long = 5
scala> mydata.take(2)
res2:Array[Int] = Array(1,2)
scala> mydata.top(1)
res2:Array[Int] = Array(5)
```

2. Now let's work with the transformations and actions in a Spark standalone application:

```
object SparkTransformations {
def main(args:Array[String]){
val conf = new SparkConf
        conf.setMaster("spark://master:7077")
val sc = new SparkContext(conf)
val baseRdd1 =
sc.parallelize(Array("hello","hi","priya","big","data","hub",
"hub","hi"),1)
val baseRdd2 =
sc.parallelize(Array("hey","ram","krishna","priya"),1)
val baseRdd3 =  sc.parallelize(Array(1,2,3,4),2)
val sampledRdd = baseRdd1.sample(false,0.5)
val unionRdd = baseRdd1.union(baseRdd2).repartition(1)
val intersectionRdd = baseRdd1.intersection(baseRdd2)
val distinctRdd = baseRdd1.distinct.repartition(1)
val subtractRdd = baseRdd1.subtract(baseRdd2)
val cartesianRdd = sampledRdd.cartesian(baseRdd2)
val reducedValue = baseRdd3.reduce((a,b) => a+b)
val collectedRdd = distinctRdd.collect
collectedRdd.foreach(println)
val count = distinctRdd.count
```

```
val first = distinctRdd.first
println("Count is..."+count); println("First Element
is..."+first)
val takeValues = distinctRdd.take(3)
val takeSample = distinctRdd.takeSample(false, 2)
val takeOrdered = distinctRdd.takeOrdered(2)
takeValues.foreach(println)
println("Take Sample Values..")
takeSample.foreach(println)
val foldResult = distinctRdd.fold("<>")((a,b) => a+b)
println(foldResult) }}
```

How it works...

Spark offers an abstraction called an RDD as part of its programming model. The preceding code snippets show RDD creation, transformations, and actions. Transformations such as `union`, `subtract`, `intersection`, `sample`, `cartesian`, `map`, `filter`, and `flatMap` when applied on a RDD result in a new RDD, whereas actions such as `count`, `first`, `take(3)`, `takeSample(false, 2)` and `takeOrdered(2)` compute the result on the RDD and return it to the driver program or save it to external storage. Although we can define RDDs at any point, Spark computes them in lazy fashion, that is, the first time it is used in any action.

There's more...

There are a few transformations, such as `reduceByKey`, `groupByKey`, `repartition`, `distinct`, `intersection`, `subtract`, and so on, which result in shuffle operation. This shuffle is very expensive as it involves disk I/O, data serialization, and network I/O. Using certain configuration parameters, shuffle can be optimized.

See also

The Apache Spark documentation offers a detailed explanation about the Spark programming model. Please refer to this documentation page:
`http://spark.apache.org/docs/latest/programming-guide.html`.

Working with pair RDDs

This recipe shows how to work with RDDs of key/value pairs. Key/value RDDs are often widely used to perform aggregations. These key/value RDDs are called pair RDDs. We'll do some initial ETL to get the data into a key/value format and see how to apply transformations on single-pair RDDs and two-pair RDDs.

Getting ready

To step through this recipe, you will need a running Spark cluster either in pseudo distributed mode or in one of the other distributed modes, that is, standalone, YARN, or Mesos. It could be run in local mode as well.

How to do it…

1. We can create a pair RDD from a collection of strings in the following way:

```
val baseRdd =
sc.parallelize(Array("this,is,a,ball","it,is,a,cat","john,is,
in,town,hall"))
val inputRdd = sc.makeRDD(List(("is",2), ("it",2), ("cat",8
("this",6),("john",5),("a",1)))
val wordsRdd = baseRdd.flatMap(record => record.split(","))
val wordPairs =  wordsRdd.map(word => (word, word.length))
val filteredWordPairs = wordPairs.filter{case(word, length) =>
length >=2}
```

2. Also, pair RDDs can be created from the hdfs input files. Let's take a text file which contains stocks data as follows:

```
IBM,20160113,133.5,134.279999,131.100006,131.169998,4672300
GOOG,20160113,730.849976,734.73999,698.609985,700.559998,
2468300
MSFT,20160113,53.799999,54.07,51.299999,51.639999,66119000
MSFT,20160112,52.759998,53.099998,52.060001,52.779999,35650700
YHOO,20160113,30.889999,31.17,29.33,29.440001,16593700
```

3. Now, creating pair RDDs for the preceding data looks like this:

```
val textFile = sc.textFile("hdfs://namenodeHostName:8020
/data/stocks.txt")
val stocksPairRdd = textFile.map{record => val colData =
record.split(",")
(colData(0),colData(6))}
```

4. Let's apply transformations on pair RDDs as follows:

```
val stocksGroupedRdd = stocksPairRdd.groupByKey
val stocksReducedRdd = stocksPairRdd.reduceByKey((x,y)=>x+y)
val subtractedRdd = wordPairs.subtractByKey(inputRdd)
val cogroupedRdd = wordPairs.cogroup(inputRdd)
val joinedRdd = filteredWordPairs.join(inputRdd)
val sortedRdd = wordPairs.sortByKey
val leftOuterJoinRdd = inputRdd.leftOuterJoin(filteredWordPairs)
val rightOuterJoinRdd = wordPairs.rightOuterJoin(inputRdd)
val flatMapValuesRdd = filteredWordPairs.flatMapValues(length =>
1 to 5)
val mapValuesRdd = wordPairs.mapValues(length => length*2)
val keys = wordPairs.keys
val values = filteredWordPairs.values
```

How it works...

The usage of various pair RDD transformations is given as follows:

- groupByKey groups the values of the RDD by key.
- reduceByKey performs aggregation on the grouped values corresponding to a key.
- subtractByKey removes tuples in the first RDD whose key matches with the other RDD.
- join groups all the values pertaining to a particular key in both the RDDs.
- cogroup does the same job as join but in addition it first groups the values in the first RDD and then in the other RDD.
- leftOuterJoin and rightOuterJoin work similarly to join with a slight variation that is, leftOuterJoin includes all the records from left RDD and if there is no matching record found in the right RDD, the corresponding values are represented as none and vice versa for rightOuterJoin.

- `mapValues` transformation applies a function to each of the values of the pair RDD without changing the key.
- The functioning of `flatMapValues` is typical. It applies the function which returns an iterator to each value of a pair RDD, and for each element returned, a key/value entry is produced with the old key.
- `keys` and `values` transformations return respectively all keys and all values of a pair RDD.

There's more...

There are other pair RDD transformations, such as, `foldByKey`, `combineByKey`, and `aggregateByKey`, and actions such as `countByKey` and `countByValue` along with the available regular actions such as `count`, `first`, `take`, and so on. Any pair RDD transformation would involve a shuffle operation which shuffles the data across the partitions. To know more about the working of the shuffle operation and its performance impact, please refer to `http://spark.apache.org/docs/latest/programming-guide.html #working-with-key-value-pairs`.

See also

The *Working with the Spark programming model* and *Working with Spark's Python and Scala shells* recipes explain how to work with RDDs and how to make use of Spark shell for testing the application logic.

Persisting RDDs

This recipe shows how to persist an RDD. As a known fact, RDDs are lazily evaluated and sometimes it is necessary to reuse the RDD multiple times. In such cases, Spark will re-compute the RDD and all of its dependencies, each time we call an action on the RDD. This is expensive for iterative algorithms which need the computed dataset multiple times. To avoid computing an RDD multiple times, Spark provides a mechanism for persisting the data in an RDD.

After the first time an action computes the RDD's contents, they can be stored in memory or disk across the cluster. The next time an action depends on the RDD, it need not be recomputed from its dependencies.

Getting ready

To step through this recipe, you will need a running Spark cluster either in pseudo distributed mode or in one of the distributed modes, that is, standalone, YARN, or Mesos.

How to do it...

Let's see how to persist RDDs using the following code:

```
val inputRdd =
sc.parallelize(Array("this,is,a,ball","it,is,a,cat","julie,is,in,the,church
"))
val wordsRdd = inputRdd.flatMap(record => record.split(","))
val wordLengthPairs = wordsRdd.map(word before code=> (word, word.length))
val wordPairs = wordsRdd.map(word => (word,1))
val reducedWordCountRdd = wordPairs.reduceByKey((x,y) => x+y)
val filteredWordLengthPairs = wordLengthPairs.filter{case(word,length) =>
length >=3}
reducedWordCountRdd.cache()
val joinedRdd = reducedWordCountRdd.join(filteredWordLengthPairs)
joinedRdd.persist(StorageLevel.MEMORY_AND_DISK)
val wordPairsCount =  reducedWordCountRdd.count
val wordPairsCollection = reducedWordCountRdd.take(10)
val joinedRddCount = joinedRdd.count
val joinedPairs = joinedRdd.collect()
reducedWordCountRdd.unpersist()
joinedRdd.unpersist()
```

How it works...

The call to `cache()` on `reducedWordCountRdd` indicates that the RDD should be stored in memory for the next time it's computed. The `count` action computes it initially. When the `take` action is invoked, it accesses the cached elements of the RDD instead of re-computing them from the dependencies.

Spark defines levels of persistence or `StorageLevel` values for persisting RDDs. `rdd.cache()` is shorthand for `rdd.persist(StorageLevel.MEMORY)`. In the preceding example, `joinedRdd` is persisted with storage level as `MEMORY_AND_DISK` which indicates persisting the RDD in memory as well as in disk. It is good practice to un-persist the RDD at the end, which lets us manually remove it from the cache.

There's more…

Spark defines various levels of persistence, such as MEMORY_ONLY, MEMORY_AND_DISK, MEMORY_AND_DISK2, and so on. Deciding when to cache/persist the data can be an art. The decision typically involves trade-offs between space and speed. If you attempt to cache too much data to fit in memory, Spark will use the LRU cache policy to evict old partitions. In general, RDDs should be persisted when they are likely to be referenced by multiple actions and are expensive to regenerate.

See also

Please refer to http://spark.apache.org/docs/latest/programming-guide.html#rdd-persistence to gain a detailed understanding of persistence in Spark.

Loading and saving data

This recipe shows how Spark supports a wide range of input and output sources. Spark makes it very simple to load and save data in a large number of file formats. Formats range from unstructured, such as text, to semi-structured, such as JSON, to structured, such as SequenceFiles.

Getting ready

To step through this recipe, you will need a running Spark cluster either in pseudo distributed mode or in one of the distributed modes, that is, standalone, YARN, or Mesos. Also, the reader is expected to have an understanding of text files, JSON, CSV, SequenceFiles, and object files.

How to do it…

1. Load and save a text file as follows:

```
val input =
sc.textFile("hdfs://namenodeHostName:8020/repos/spark/README.md")
val wholeInput =
sc.wholeTextFiles("file://home/padma/salesFiles")
```

```
val result = wholeInput.mapValues{value => val nums = value.split
(" ").map(x => x.toDouble)
nums.sum/nums.size.toDouble}
result.saveAsTextFile("/home/Padma/outputFile.txt")
```

2. For loading a JSON file, the `people.json` input file is taken from the `SPARK_HOME` folder whose location is `/spark-1.6.0/examples/src/main/resource/people.json`. Now, loading and saving a JSON file looks like this:

```
// Loading JSON file
import com.fasterxml.jackson.module.scala.DefaultScalaModule
import com.fasterxml.jackson.module.scala.
experimental.ScalaObjectMapper
import com.fasterxml.jackson.databind.ObjectMapper
import com.fasterxml.jackson.module.databind.
    DeserializatiuonFeature
...
case class Person(name:String, age:Int)
...
val jsonInput =
sc.textFile(""hdfs://namenode:9000/data/people.json")
val result = jsonInput.flatMap(record => {
try{Some(mapper.readValue(record, classOf[Person]))
}
catch{
case e:Exception => None
}} )
result.filter(person =>
person.age>15).map(mapper.writeValueAsString(_)).
saveAsTextFile(output File)
```

3. To load and save a CSV file, let's take the stocks data:

```
IBM,20160113,133.5,134.279999,131.100006,131.169998,4672300
GOOG,20160113,730.849976,734.73999,698.609985,700.559998,2468300
MSFT,20160113,53.799999,54.07,51.299999,51.639999,66119000
MSFT,20160112,52.759998,53.099998,52.060001,52.779999,35650700
YHOO,20160113,30.889999,31.17,29.33,29.440001,16593700
.
.
import java.io.StringReader
import au.com.bytecode.opencsv.CSVReader
...
case class Stocks(name:String, totalPrice:Long)
...
val input = sc.textFile("hdfs://namenodeHostName:8020
```

```
/data/stocks.txt")
val result = input.map{line => val reader = new CSVReader(new
StringReader(line))
reader.readAll().map(x => Stocks(x(0), x(6)))
}
result.map(stock => Array(stock.name, stock.
totalPrice)).mapPartitions {stock =>
val stringWriter = new StringWriter
val csvWriter = new CSVWriter(stringWriter)
csvWriter.writeAll(people.toList)
Iterator(stringWriter.toString)
}.saveAsTextFilehdfs://namenode:9000/CSVOutputFile")
```

4. Now, let's see the way sequenceFile is loaded and saved:

```
val data = sc.sequenceFile(inputFile, classOf[Text],
classOf[IntWritable]).map{case(x,y) => (x.toString, y.get())}
val input = sc.parallelize(List(("Panda",3),("Kay",6),
("Snail",2)))
input.saveAsSequenceFilehdfs://namenode:9000/
sequenceOutputFile")
```

How it works...

The call to textFile() on the SparkContext with the path to the file loads the text file as RDD. If there exists multiple input parts in the form of a directory then we can use SparkContext.wholeTextFiles(), which returns a pair RDD with the key as the name of the input file. Well, for handling JSON files, the data is loaded as a text file and then it is parsed using a JSON parser. There are a number of JSON libraries available, but in the example we used the Jackson (http://bit.ly/17k6vli) library as it is relatively simple to implement.

 Please refer to other JSON libraries, such as this one: http://bit.ly/1xP 8JFK

Loading CSV/TSV data is similar to JSON data, that is, first the data is loaded as text and then processed. Similar to JSON, there are various CSV libraries, but for Scala, we used opencsv (http://opencsv.sourceforge.net). Using CSVReader, the records are parsed and mapped to case class structure. While saving the file, CSVWriter is used to output the file.

When coming to `SequenceFile`, it is a popular Hadoop format composed of a flat file with key/value pairs. This sequence file implements Hadoop's writable interface. `SparkContext.sequenceFile()` is the API to load the sequence file in which the parameters `classOf[Text]` and `classOf[IntWritable]` indicate the `keyClass` and `valueClass`.

There's more...

As Spark is built on the ecosystem of Hadoop, it can access data through the `InputFormat` and `OutputFormat` interfaces used by Hadoop MapReduce, which are available for many common file formats and storage systems (for example, S3, HDFS, Cassandra, HBase, and so on).

> For more information, please refer Hadoop InputFormat (`http://hadoop.apache.org/docs/stable/api/org/apache/hadoop/mapred/InputFormat.html`) and SequenceFiles (`http://hadoop.apache.org/docs/current/api/org/apache/hadoop/mapred/SequenceFileInputFormat.html`).

Spark can also interact with any Hadoop supported formats (for both old and new Hadoop file APIs) using `newAPIHadoopFile`, which takes a path and three classes. The first class represents the input format. The next class is for our key and the final class is the class of our value. The Spark SQL module provides a more efficient API for structured data sources, which includes JSON and Hive.

See also

For more details on Hadoop input and output formats and `SequenceFiles` input format, please refer to the following:

- `http://spark.apache.org/docs/latest/programming-guide.html#external-datasets`
- `http://commons.apache.org/proper/commons-csv`
- `http://hadoop.apache.org/docs/current/api/org/apache/hadoop/mapred/SequenceFileInputFormat.html`
- `http://hadoop.apache.org/docs/current/api/org/apache/hadoop/mapred/InputFormat.html`
- `http://wiki.apache.org/hadoop/SequenceFile`

Creating broadcast variables and accumulators

This recipe shows how to use accumulators and broadcast variables. **Accumulators** are used to aggregate values from worker nodes back to the driver program. One of the most common uses of accumulators is to count events that occur during job execution for debugging purposes. The other type of shared variable is the broadcast variable, which allows the program to efficiently send a large, read-only value to all the worker nodes for use in one or more Spark operations. Such variables are used in cases where the application needs to send a large, read-only lookup table to all the nodes.

Getting ready

To step through this recipe, you will need a running Spark cluster either in pseudo distributed mode or in one of the distributed modes, that is, standalone, YARN, or Mesos.

How to do it…

1. The log file of workers from Spark log `$SPARK_HOME/logs` is taken, whose filename looks like this: `spark-padma-org.apache.spark.deploy.worker.Worker-1-blrrndtipdl19`. Place this file in HDFS. This log file contains Spark log information with different trace levels, such as `DEBUG`, `INFO`, `WARN`, and `ERROR`. The sample data looks as follows:

```
16/01/14 16:28:33 INFO worker.Worker: Registered signal handlers for [TERM, HUP, INT]
16/01/14 16:28:34 WARN util.NativeCodeLoader: Unable to load native-hadoop library for your platform... us
16/01/14 16:28:34 INFO spark.SecurityManager: Changing view acls to: dl01
16/01/14 16:28:34 INFO spark.SecurityManager: Changing modify acls to: dl01
16/01/14 16:28:34 INFO spark.SecurityManager: SecurityManager: authentication disabled; ui acls disabled;
16/01/14 16:28:35 INFO util.Utils: Successfully started service 'sparkWorker' on port 59565.
16/01/14 16:28:35 INFO worker.Worker: Starting Spark worker 172.22.225.174:59565 with 6 cores, 18.6 GB RAM
16/01/14 16:28:35 INFO worker.Worker: Running Spark version 1.6.0
16/01/14 16:28:35 INFO worker.Worker: Spark home: /home/dl01/bigdata/spark-1.6.0
16/01/14 16:28:40 INFO server.Server: jetty-8.y.z-SNAPSHOT
16/01/14 16:28:40 INFO server.AbstractConnector: Started SelectChannelConnector@0.0.0.0:8081
16/01/14 16:28:40 INFO util.Utils: Successfully started service 'WorkerUI' on port 8081.
16/01/14 16:28:40 INFO ui.WorkerWebUI: Started WorkerWebUI at http://172.22.225.174:8081
```

2. Let's work with an accumulator now:

```
val sc = new SparkContext
val logFile =
sc.textFile("hdfs://namenodeHostName:8020/data/spark-
```

```
worker-Worker1.out")
val errorLines = sc.accumulator(0)
val debugLines = logFile.map{line =>
if(line.contains("ERROR"))
errorLines +=1
if(line.contains("DEBUG"))line
}
debugLines.saveAsTextFile("hdfs://namenodeHostName:8020/data
/out/
debugLines.txt")
println("ERROR Lines: "+ errorLines.value)
```

3. Now create a broadcast variable and use it in the workers as follows:

```
val sc = new SparkContext
val broadCastedTemperatures = sc.broadcast(Map("KOCHI" ->
22,"BNGLR" -> 22, "HYD" -> 24, "MUMBAI" -> 21, "DELHI" -> 17,
"NOIDA" -> 19, "SIMLA" -> 9))
val inputRdd = sc.parallelize(Array("BNGLR",20), ("BNGLR",16),
("KOCHI",-999), ("SIMLA",-999), ("DELHI",19), ("DELHI",-999),
("MUMBAI",27), ("MUMBAI",-999), ("HYD",19), ("HYD",25),
("NOIDA",-999) )
val replacedRdd = inputRdd.map{case(location, temperature) =>
val standardTemperatures = broadCastedTemperatures.value
if(temperature == -999 && standardTemperatures.get(location) !=
None) (location, standardTemperatures.get(location).get) else
if(temperature != -999) (location, temperature )
}
val locationsWithMaxTemperatures =
replacedRdd.reduceByKey{(temp1,
temp2) => if (temp1 > temp2) temp1 else temp2}
```

How it works...

Initially, when working with accumulators, we created `Accumulator[Int]`, called `errorLines`, and added 1 to it whenever we saw a line that contained `ERROR`. We will see the correct count for `errorLines` only after the `saveAsTextFile()` action runs because the transformation `map()` is lazy, so the side-effect, incrementing the accumulator happens only when the `map()` is forced to occur by `saveAsTextFile()`. The return type of the accumulator would be the `org.apache.spark.Accumulator[T]` object where `T` is the type of the value.

Well, coming to broadcast variables, `SparkContext.broadcast` creates a broadcast variable of type `Broadcast[T]`. T is of any type and it should be serializable. The value of the broadcast variable is accessed using the `value` property. The variable is sent to each node only once and is read-only.

There's more...

Spark has support for custom accumulator types. They need to extend `AccumulatorParam`.

For additional information on this, please visit: `http://spark.apache.org/docs/latest/programming-guide.html#accum ulators-a-nameaccumlinka`.

Also, when working with broadcast variables, it is essential to choose a serialization format which is fast and compact.

For more information on broadcast variables, please refer: `http://spark.apache.org/docs/latest/programming-guide.html#broad cast-variables`.

See also

Please visit the earlier *Working with the Spark programming model*, *Working with Spark's Python and Scala shells*, and *Working with pair RDDs* recipes to get familiar with Spark.

Submitting applications to a cluster

This recipe shows how to run an application on distributed clusters. An application is launched on a set of machines using an external service called a **cluster manager**. There is a wide variety of cluster managers such as Hadoop YARN, Apache Mesos, and Spark's own built-in standalone cluster manager. Spark provides a single tool for submitting jobs across all cluster managers, called **spark-submit**. Through various options, spark-submit can connect to different cluster managers and control how many resources your application gets.

Getting ready

To step through this recipe, you will need a running Spark cluster either in pseudo distributed mode or in one of the distributed modes, that is, standalone, YARN, or Mesos.

How to do it...

1. Let's create a word count application:

```
package org.apache.spark.programs
object WordCount{
def main(args:Array[String]) {
val conf = new SparkConf
conf.setAppName("WordCount")
val sc = new SparkContext(conf)
val input =
sc.parallelize(Array("this,is,a,ball","it,is,a,cat","john,is,
in,town,hall"))
val words = input.flatMap{record => record.split(",")}
val wordPairs = words.map(word => (word,1))
val wordCounts = wordPairs.reduceByKey{(a,b) => a+b}
val result = wordCounts.collect
println("Displaying the WordCounts:")
result.foreach(println)
```

2. Submit the application to Spark's standalone cluster manager:

```
spark-submit --class org.apache.spark.programs.WordCount --master
spark://master:7077 WordCount.jar
```

3. Submit the application to YARN:

```
spark-submit --class org.apache.spark.programs.WordCount --master
yarn WordCount.jar
```

4. Submit the application to Mesos:

```
spark-submit --class org.apache.spark.programs.WordCount --master
mesos://mesos-master:5050 WordCount.jar
```

How it works...

When `spark-submit` is called with the `--master` flag as `spark://master:7077` submits the application to Spark's standalone cluster. Invoking with the `--master` flag as `yarn` runs the application in the YARN cluster, whereas specifying the `--master` flag as `mesos://mesos-master:5050` runs the application on `Mesos` cluster.

There's more...

Whenever `spark-submit` is invoked, it launches the driver program. This driver program contacts the cluster manager and requests resources to launch executors. Once the executors are launched by the cluster manager, the driver runs through the user application. It delegates the work to executors in the form of tasks. When the driver's `main()` method exits, it will terminate the executors and releases resources from the cluster manager. `spark-submit` provides various options as well to control specific details.

See also

For more information on submitting applications to a cluster and the various options provided by Spark-submit, please visit:
`http://spark.apache.org/docs/latest/submitting-applications.html`. Also, for detailed information about the different cluster managers, please refer to the following:

Also, to learn in details about the different cluster managers, please refer:

- `http://spark.apache.org/docs/latest/spark-standalone.html`
- `http://spark.apache.org/docs/latest/running-on-mesos.html`
- `http://spark.apache.org/docs/latest/running-on-yarn.html`

Working with DataFrames

Spark SQL is a Spark module for structured data processing. It provides the programming abstraction called **DataFrame** (in earlier versions of Spark, it is called **SchemaRDD**) and also acts as distributed SQL query engine. The capabilities it provides are as follows:

- It loads data from a variety of structured sources (for example, JSON, Hive, and Parquet)

- It lets you query data using SQL, both inside a Spark program and from external tools that connect to Spark SQL through standard database connectors (JDBC/ODBC), such as BI tools like Tableau.
- Spark SQL provides rich integration between SQL and regular Python/Java/Scala code, including the ability to join RDDs and SQL tables, expose custom functions in SQL, and more.

A DataFrame is an RDD of row objects, each representing a record. It is also known as a **schema of records**. These can be created from external data sources, from results of queries, or from regular RDDs. The created DataFrame can be registered as a temporary table and apply SQLContext.sql or HiveContext.sql to query the table. This recipe shows how to work with DataFrames.

Getting ready

To step through this recipe, you will need a running Spark cluster either in pseudo distributed mode or in one of the distributed modes, that is, standalone, YARN, or Mesos.

How to do it...

1. Let's see how to create a DataFrame from a JSON file:

```
import org.apache.spark.sql._
import org.apache.spark.sql.SQLContext
import org.apache.spark.SparkConf
import org.apache.spark.SparkContext

object JSONDataFrame {
def main(args:Array[String])
{
val conf=new SparkConf
conf.setMaster("spark://master:7077")
conf.setAppName("sql_Sample")
val sc=new SparkContext(conf)
val sqlcontxt=new SQLContext(sc)
val df = sqlContext.read.json("/home/padma/Sparkdev/spark-
1.6.0/examples/src/main/resources/people.json")
df.show
df.printSchema
df.select("name").show
df.select("name","age").show
df.select(df("name"),df("age")+4).show
```

```
df.groupBy("age").count.show
df.describe("name,age")  }  }
```

2. Now create a DataFrame from a text file and query on the DataFrame:

```
object DataFrames {
case class Person(name:String, age:Int)
def main(args:Array[String])
{
val conf = new SparkConf
conf.setMaster("spark://master:7077")
conf.setAppName("DataFramesApp")
val sc = new SparkContext(conf)
val sqlContext = new SQLContext(sc)
import sqlContext.implicits._
val peopleDf = sc.textFile("/home/padma/Sparkdev/spark-
1.6.0/examples/src/main/resources/people.txt").
map(line => line.split(",")).map(p =>
Person(p(0),p(1).trim.toInt)).toDF
peopleDf.registerTempTable("people")
val teenagers = sqlContext.sql("select name, age from people
where age >=13 AND name in(select name from people where age=
30)")
teenagers.map(t => "Name: " + t(0)).collect().foreach(println)
  }
}
```

3. Here is the code snippet to show how to create a DataFrame from a parquet file:

```
val sc = new SparkContext(conf)
val sqlContext = new SQLContext(sc)
import sqlContext.implicits._
val df1 = sc.makeRDD(1 to 5).map(i =>
(i,i*2)).toDF("single","double")
df1.write.parquet("/home/padma/Sparkdev/SparkApp/
test_table/key=1")
val df2 = sc.makeRDD(6 to 10).map(i =>
(i,i*4)).toDF("single","triple")
df2.write.parquet("/home/padma/Sparkdev/SparkApp/
test_table/key=2")
val df3 = sqlContext.read.parquet("/home/padma/Sparkdev/
SparkApp/test_table")
df3.show
```

How it works...

Initially, the JSON file is read, which is the DataFrame, and the API such as `show()`, `printSchema()`, `select()`, or `groupBy()` can be invoked on the data frame. In the second code snippet, an RDD is created from the text file and the fields are mapped to the case class structure `Person` and the RDD is converted to a data frame using `toDF`. This data frame `peopleDF` is converted to a table using `registerTempTable()` whose table name is `people`. Now this table `people` can be queried using `SQLContext.sql`.

The final code snippet shows how to write a data frame as a parquet file using `df1.write.parquet()` and the parquet file is read using `sqlContext.read.parquet()`.

There's more...

Spark SQL in addition provides HiveContext, using which we can access Hive tables, UDFS, SerDes, and also HiveQL. There are ways to create DataFrames by converting an RDD to a DataFrame or creating them programmatically. The different data sources, such as JSON, Parquet, and Avro, can be handled and there is provision to directly run `sql` queries on the files. Also, data from other databases can be read using JDBC. In Spark 1.6.0, a new feature known as **Dataset** is introduced, which provides the benefits of Spark SQL's optimized execution engine over RDDs.

See also

For more information on Spark SQL, please visit:
`http://spark.apache.org/docs/latest/sql-programming-guide.html`. The earlier *Working with the Spark programming model, Working with Spark's Python and Scala shells*, and *Working with pair RDDs* recipes covered the initial steps in Spark and the basics of RDDs.

Working with Spark Streaming

Spark Streaming is a library in the Spark ecosystem which addresses real-time processing needs. Spark's batch processing executes the job over large datasets at once, where as Streaming aims for low latency (in hundreds of milliseconds), as data becomes available, it is transformed and processing is done in near real time.

Spark Streaming functions by running jobs over the small batches of data that accumulate in small intervals. It is used for rapid alerting, for supplying dashboards with up-to-date information, as well as for scenarios that need more complex analytics. For example, a common use case in anomaly detection to run K-means clustering on small batches of data and trigger an alert if the cluster center deviates from what is normal.

For more information, please visit: `http://spark.apache.org/docs/late st/streaming-programming-guide.html`.

This recipe shows how to work with Spark Streaming and apply stateless transformations and Windowed transformations.

Getting ready

To step through this recipe, you will need a running Spark cluster either in pseudo distributed mode or in one of the distributed modes, that is, standalone, YARN, or Mesos.

How to do it...

1. There are two types of transformations supported in Spark Streaming: stateless and stateful (windowed). Let's apply the stateless transformations:

```
import org.apache.spark.SparkConf
import org.apache.spark.SparkContext._
import org.apache.spark.streaming._
import org.apache.spark.streaming.StreamingContext._
import org.apache.spark.streaming.dstream._
import org.apache.spark.SparkConf

object StatelessTransformations {
def main(args:Array[String]) {
val conf= new SparkConf
conf.setMaster("spark://master:7077").setAppName("StreamingApp")
val sc = new SparkContext(conf)
val ssc = new StreamingContext(sc, Seconds(5))
val spamInfoRDD = ssc.sparkContext.textFile("/path/fileName", 2)
val lines = ssc.socketTextStream("172.22.225.174", 7777)
val mapLines = lines.map(ele => ele+"<<<>>>")
val mapLines2 = lines.map(ele => (ele,1))
val errorLines = lines.filter(line =>line.contains("Padma"))
```

```
val flatMapLines = lines.flatMap(ele => ele.split(","))
val reduceByKeyLines = mapLines2.reduceByKey((a,b) => a+b)
val groupByKeyLines = mapLines2.groupByKey().mapValues(names =>
names.toSet.size)
val unionedDstreams = mapLines.union(flatMapLines)
val joinedDstream = reduceByKeyLines.join(groupByKeyLines)
val cogroupedDStream = reduceByKeyLines.cogroup(groupByKeyLines)
val transformLines = lines.transform(rdd =>
{rdd.union(spamInfoRDD).filter(_.contains("Padma"))})
errorLines.print
mapLines.print
flatMapLines.print
reduceByKeyLines.print
groupByKeyLines.print
joinedDstream.print
cogroupedDStream.print
unionedDstreams.print
ssc.start
ssc.awaitTermination
ssc.stop
 }
}
```

2. Now let's apply windowed/stateful transformations:

```
object StatefulTransformations {
def updateRunningSum(values:Seq[Long], state:Option[Long])
Some(state.getOrElse(0L) + values.size)
def main(args:Array[String])
{
val conf = new SparkConf
conf.setMaster("spark://master:7077").setAppName("
Stateful_transformations")
val sc = new SparkContext(conf)
val ssc = new StreamingContext(sc, Seconds(1))
val lines = ssc.socketTextStream("172.25.41.66", 7777)
val windowedLines = lines.window(Seconds(4),Seconds(2))
val mapLines = lines.map(ele => (ele,1L))
val windowCounts = windowedLines.count
val countByWindowLines = lines.countByWindow(Seconds(4),
Seconds(2))
val reducedLines = lines.reduce(_+_)
val updateDStream = mapLines.updateStateByKey
(updateRunningSum _)
val mapLines = lines.map(ele => (ele,1))
val reducedKeyWindow  = mapLines.reduceByKeyAndWindow({(x,y)=>
x+y}, {(x,y) => x-y}, Seconds(4), Seconds(2))
 windowedLines.print
```

```
windowCounts.print
reducedKeyWindow.print
countByWindowLines.print
updateDStream.print
reducedLines.print
ssc.checkpoint("/home/padma/StreamingCheckPoint/")
ssc.start
ssc.awaitTermination
    }
}
```

3. It's also possible to apply DataFrames, that is, SQL operations on streaming data. The following code snippet shows SQL operations over streams of data:

```
import org.apache.spark.streaming.StreamingContext._
import org.apache.spark.streaming.kafka._
import org.apache.spark.sql._
import org.apache.spark.sql.SQLContext
...
object StreamingSQL {
  case class Words(wordName:String, count:Int)
 def main(args:Array[String])
 {
 val conf = new SparkConf
 conf.setAppName("StreamingSQL").setMaster
 ("spark://master:7077")
    val sc = new SparkContext(conf)
    val ssc = new StreamingContext(sc,Seconds(4))
    val kafkaParams = Map("test-consumer-group" -> 1)
    val topicMap = Map("test" -> 1)
    val kafkaLines =
    KafkaUtils.createStream(ssc,"blrovh:2181",
    "test-consumer-group",topicMap)
    val words = kafkaLines.map{tuple => tuple._2}
    val wordPairs = words.map(word => (word,1))
    val reduceWords = wordPairs.reduceByKey((a,b) => a+b)
    reduceWords.foreachRDD{
    rdd =>
    {
      val sqlContext = new SQLContext(rdd.sparkContext)
      import sqlContext.implicits._
      val df = rdd.map(record => Words(record._1, record._2))
      val dfNew = sqlContext.createDataFrame(df)
      dfNew.registerTempTable("Words")
      val data = sqlContext.sql("select wordName from Words")
      data.foreach(row => println(row.toString))
      }
    }
```

```
ssc.start
ssc.awaitTermination   } }
```

How it works...

The `new StreamingContext(SparkContext, Seconds(1))` line instantiates the `StreamingContext`, which takes `SparkContext` and batch interval as parameters. `StreamingContext.socketTextStream(<ip>,<port-number>)` initializes a socket stream, which listens on the specified port for messages. This creates a DStream (discretized stream) which is a sequence of RDDs, being generated for each batch.

When working with windowed/stateful transformations, `lines.window(Seconds(4),Seconds(2))` creates a window of 4 seconds and a sliding duration of 2 seconds on the incoming DStream lines. The window-based transformations such as `reduceByKeyAndWindow` and `countByWindow` use data or intermediate results from previous batches to compute the results of the current batch. The `updateStateByKey` transformation constructs DStream (key, state) pairs by the specified function, where this function indicates how to update the state for each key given new values.

In the case of applying SQL operations on streaming data, `KafkaUtils.createStream` initializes a DStream from Kafka. It takes `StreamingContext`, zookeeperhostname (`blrovh`), `port-number` of zookeeper (`2181`), `consumer-group name` (**test-consumer-group**) and `topic map (Map("test" -> 1))` as parameters. The `new` SQLContext line creates SQLContext and `SQLContext.createDataFrame` creates a data frame for each RDD of the DStream. Using the DataFrame, the SQL queries are executed.

There's more...

Spark Streaming uses a **micro-batch** architecture, where the streaming computation is a continuous series of batch computations on small batches of data. For each input source, Spark Streaming launches receivers, which are long-running tasks within an application executor, collects the data, replicates it to another executor for fault tolerance, and saves it as RDDs. Using the Kafka Direct Streaming approach, the Dstream is created as `KafkaUtils.createDirectStream[String, String, StringDecoder, StringDecoder](ssc, kakfaParams, topicSet)`. To address the fault tolerance, check-pointing is done, which periodically saves the state to a reliable filesystem.

Also, when running SQL queries on streaming data, there is a method for retaining the data for a specific duration before the query can complete. As in Spark batch processing, streams of data can be persisted either in memory or in disk. In the case of stateful operations, the data is, by default, persistent in memory.

See also

For more details on Spark Streaming, internal architecture, check-pointing, performance tuning, and receiver parallelism, please refer to the following:

- `http://spark.apache.org/docs/latest/streaming-programming-guide.html`
- `http://www.michael-noll.com/blog/2014/10/01/kafka-spark-streaming-integration-example-tutorial/`

Tricky Statistics with Spark

2

In this chapter, you will learn the following recipes:

- Working with Pandas
- Variable identification
- Sampling data
- Summary and descriptive statistics
- Generating frequency tables
- Installing Pandas on Linux
- Installing Pandas from source
- Using IPython with PySpark
- Creating Pandas DataFrames over Spark
- Splitting, slicing, sorting, filtering and grouping DataFrames over Spark.
- Implementing co-variance and correlation using DataFrames over Spark.
- Concatenating and merging operations over DataFrames
- Complex operations over DataFrames.
- Sparkling Pandas

Introduction

Statistics refers to the mathematics and techniques with which we understand data. It is a vast field which plays a key role in the areas of data mining and artificial intelligence, intersecting with the areas of engineering and other disciplines. Statistics helps in describing data, that is, descriptive statistics reveals the distribution of the data for each variable. Also, statistics is widely used for the purpose of prediction.

In this chapter, we'll see how to apply various statistical measures and functions on large datasets using Spark.

Working with Pandas

Pandas is an open source Python library for highly specialized data analysis. It is the reference point that all professionals using the Python language need to study and analyze data sets for statistical purposes of analysis and decision-making. Pandas arises from the need to have a specific library for the analysis of the data which provides tools for data processing , data extraction and data manipulation.

It is designed on the NumPy library, hence this increased its rapid spread of Pandas. This makes the library compatible with the other modules and it also takes advantage of the high quality performance in the calculations of the NumPy module. Some of the key features of Pandas include the following:

- It processes a variety of data sets in different formats such as time series, tabular, heterogeneous, and matrix data
- Facilitates the loading/importing of data from varied sources such as CSV and DB/SQL
- It handles a myriad of operations on data sets such as sub-setting, slicing, filtering, merging, groupBy, re-ordering and re-shaping
- It deals with missing data as per the rules defined by the user/developer
- It is used for parsing and munging (conversion) of data as well as modeling and statistical analysis
- It integrates with other Python modules such as statsmodels, SciPy, and scikit-learn
- It provides fast performance and the speed can be improved by making use of Cython (C extensions to Python)

Variable identification

In this recipe, we will see how to identify predictor (input) and target (output) variables for data at scale in Spark. Then the next step is to identify the category of the variables.

Getting ready

To step through this recipe, you will need Ubuntu 14.04 (Linux flavor) installed on the machine. Also, you need to have Apache Hadoop 2.6 and Apache Spark 1.6.0 installed.

How to do it...

1. Let's take an example of student's data, using which we want to predict whether a student will play cricket or not. Here is what the sample data looks like:

Student_ID	Gender	Prev_Exam_Marks	Height	Weight	Play_Cricket
S001	M	65	178	61	1
S002	F	75	174	56	0
S003	M	45	163	62	1
S004	M	57	175	70	0
S005	F	59	162	67	0

2. The preceding data resides in HDFS and load the data into Spark as follows:

```scala
import org.apache.spark._
import org.apache.spark.sql._
  object tricky_Stats {
    def main(args:Array[String]): Unit = {
      val conf = new SparkConf()
            .setMaster("spark://master:7077")
            .setAppName("Variable_Identification")
      val sc = new SparkContext(conf)
      val sqlContext = new SQLContext(sc)
import sqlContext.implicits._
      val students_data = sqlContext.read.format
      ("com.databricks.spark.csv")
      .option("header","true")
      .option("inferSchema", "true")
      .load("hdfs://namenode:9000/students.csv")
      students_data.show(5)    }
  }
```

The following is the output:

```
+---------+------+---------------+------+------+-----------+
|Sudent_ID|Gender|Prev_Exam_Marks|Height|Weight|Play_Cricket|
+---------+------+---------------+------+------+-----------+
|     S001|    M|             65|   178|    61|          1|
|     S002|    F|             75|   174|    56|          0|
|     S003|    M|             45|   163|    62|          1|
|     S004|    M|             57|   175|    70|          0|
|     S005|    F|             59|   162|    67|          0|
+---------+------+---------------+------+------+-----------+
```

3. From the preceding result, the variables have been defined in different categories as follows:

Type of Variable	Data Type of Variables	Variable Category
Predictor	**Character**	**Categorical**
Gender	StudentID	Gender
Prev_Exam_Marks	Gender	Play_Cricket
Height	**Numeric**	**Continuous**
Weight	Play_Cricket	Prev_Exam_Marks
Target Variable	Prev_Exam_Marks	Height
Play_Cricket	Height	Weight
	Weight	

How it works...

In the preceding code snippet, since the file is of CSV format, we imported the data initially into Spark using the CSV package. Once the DataFrame is loaded, it internally has the schema, and the line `students_data.show(5)` displays the first five records. From this sample data, the independent and dependent variables are identified. Also, the data type of the variables and category of the variables is known.

There's more...

The data can be in multiple formats, such as JSON, Parquet, ORC, Avro, Hive tables, and so on. For loading the semi-structured files, the related packages are available. In the case of unstructured files, the data can be loaded in RDD format. After bringing the data into structured format, it can be converted into a DataFrame and then it can proceed with the analysis on the variables.

See also

Please refer to `Chapter 1`, *Big Data Analytics with Spark* to get familiar with Spark and refresh your knowledge of basic statistics and distributions.

Sampling data

In this recipe, we will see how to generate sample data from the entire population.

Getting ready

To step through this recipe, you need Ubuntu 14.04 (Linux flavor) installed on the machine. Also, have Apache Hadoop 2.6 and Apache Spark 1.6.0 installed. Readers are expected to have knowledge of sampling techniques.

How to do it...

Let's take an example of load prediction data. Here is what the sample data looks like:

Loan_ID	Gender	Married	Dependents	Education	Self_Employed	ApplicantIncome	CoapplicantIncome	LoanAmount	Loan_Amount_Term	Credit_History	Property_Area	Loan_Status
LP001002	Male	No	0	Graduate	No	5849	0		360	1	Urban	Y
LP001003	Male	Yes	1	Graduate	No	4583	1508	128	360	1	Rural	N
LP001005	Male	Yes	0	Graduate	Yes	3000	0	66	360	1	Urban	Y

 Download the data from the following location `https://github.com/ChitturiPadma/datasets/blob/master/Loan_Prediction_Data.csv`.

1. Here is the code for sampling data from a DataFrame:

```
import org.apache.spark._
import org.apache.spark.sql.SQLContext
import org.apache.spark.sql.types.{StructType,
StringType,DoubleType, StructField}
object Sampling_Demo {
  def main(args:Array[String]): Unit = {
    val conf = new SparkConf()
      .setMaster("spark://master:7077")
        .setAppName("Sampling")
    val sc = new SparkContext(conf)
    val sqlContext = new SQLContext(sc)
```

```
    import sqlContext.implicits._
    val schemaString =
      "Loan_ID,Gender,Married,Dependents,Education,
        Self_Employed,ApplicantIncome,
  CoapplicantIncome,LoanAmount,Loan_Amount_Term,
  Credit_History,Property_Area, Loan_Status"
   val schema = schemaString.split(",").map {
     field =>
       if (field == "ApplicantIncome" || field ==
  "CoapplicantIncome" || field ==   "LoanAmount" || field ==
  "Loan_Amount_Term" || field == "Credit_History")
           StructField(field, DoubleType)
         else
           StructField(field, StringType)
   }
   val schema_Applied = StructType(schema)
   val loan_Data =
sqlContext.read.format("com.databricks.spark.csv")
     .option("header", "true")
     .schema(schema_Applied).load("hdfs://namenode:9000/
     loan_prediction_data.csv")
// Generating Sample data (10%) without replacement
   val sampled_Data1 = loan_Data.sample(false, 0.1)
   println("Sample Data Row Count (without Replacement):
   "+sampled_Data1.count)
// Generating Sample data (10%) with replacement
   val sampled_Data2 = loan_Data.sample(true, 0.2)
   println("Sample Data Row Count (with Replacement):
   "+sampled_Data2.count)
  }
}
```

The following is the output:

```
Sample Data Row Count (without Replacement): 60
Sample Data Row Count (with Replacement): 135
```

2. Spark MLlib provides other sampling methods (stratified sampling) that can be performed on RDDs of key-value pairs:

Please download the KDD99 dataset, which contains network traffic details, from
http://kdd.ics.uci.edu/databases/kddcup99/kddcup99.html.

3. Here is what the data looks as follows:

```
0,tcp,http,SF,181,5450,0,0,0,0,0,1,0,0,0,0,0,0,0,0,0,0,0,8,8,0.00,
0.00,0.00,0.00,1.00,0.00,0.00,9,9,1.00,0.00,0.11,0.00,0.00,0.00,
0.00,0.00,normal.
0,tcp,http,SF,239,486,0,0,0,0,0,1,0,0,0,0,0,0,0,0,0,0,0,8,8,0.00,
0.00,0.00,0.00,1.00,0.00,0.00,19,19,1.00,0.00,0.05,0.00,0.00,0.00,
0.00,0.00,normal.
0,icmp,ecr_i,SF,1032,0,0,0,0,0,0,0,0,0,0,0,0,0,0,0,0,0,511,511,
0.00,0.00,0.00,0.00,1.00,0.00,0.00,255,255,1.00,0.00,1.00,0.00,
0.00,0.00,0.00,0.00,smurf.
0,tcp,telnet,S0,0,0,0,0,0,0,0,0,0,0,0,0,0,0,0,0,0,0,16,15,0.94,
1.00,0.00,0.00,0.94,0.12,0.00,15,16,1.00,0.00,0.07,0.12,1.00,0.94,
0.00,0.00,neptune.
1,tcp,private,RSTR,0,0,0,0,0,0,0,0,0,0,0,0,0,0,0,0,0,0,8,2,0.00,
0.00,1.00,1.00,0.25,0.50,0.00,178,2,0.01,0.04,0.04,0.00,0.01,0.00,
0.32,1.00,portsweep.
```

4. Each observation contains various features such as `duration`, `protocol`, `service`, `src_bytes`, `dst_bytes`, and so on. The last feature is the label which indicates the type of attack. From the entire dataset, the percentage of attacks in the sample should represent the same percentage in the population as well. Here is the way to generate sample data with the same ratio as in the population:

```scala
import org.apache.spark._
import org.apache.spark.mllib.linalg.{Vector, Vectors}
import org.apache.spark.mllib._
object StratifiedSampling {
  def main(args:Array[String]): Unit =
  {
    val conf = new SparkConf
    conf.setMaster("spark://master:7077").setAppName
    ("StratifiedSampling")
    val sc = new SparkContext(conf)
    val fractions: Map[String, Double] =
    Map("loadmodule." -> 0.000018, "nmap." -> 0.004728,
    "guess_passwd." -> 0.000108, "rootkit.-> 0.000020,
    "satan." ->   0.032443, "perl." -> 0.000006,
    "imap." -> 0.000024, "multihop." -> 0.000014,
    "neptune." -> 2.188490, "normal." -> 1.985903,
    "pod." -> 0.000539, "warezmaster." -> 0.000040,
    "back." -> 0.004497, "ipsweep." -> 0.025480,
    "buffer_overflow." -> 0.000061,   "warezclient." ->
     0.002082,   "phf." -> 0.000008, "spy." -> 0.000004,
    "ftp_write." -> 0.000016,"portsweep." -> 0.021258,
    "land." -> 0.000042, "teardrop." -> 0.001999,
    "smurf." -> 5.732214)
```

```
      val fractionsBroadcasted = sc.broadcast(fractions)
      val inputRdd =
      sc.textFile("hdfs://namenode:9000//data/kddcup.data.
      corrected.csv")
      val labelsAndVectors = inputRdd.map{
      record => val parts = record.split(",").toBuffer
      parts.remove(1,3)
      val label = parts.remove(parts.length-1)
      val vector = Vectors.dense(parts.map(_.toDouble).toArray)
      (label, vector)
   }
  val approxSample = labelsAndVectors.sampleByKey
  (withReplacement = false, fractions)
  val exactSample = labelsAndVectors.sampleByKeyExact(false,
  fractions)
  approxSample.saveAsTextFile("hdfs://namenode:9000/data/
  Approx_Sample/")
  exactSample.saveAsTextFile("hdfs://namenode:9000/data/
  Exact_Sample/")
   }
 }
```

How it works...

Initially, we imported the data into Spark using the csv package. Once the DataFrame was loaded, we generated sample data (10% of the population) without replacement using the line `loan_Data.sample(false, 0.1)`. The next line `loan_Data.sample(true, 0.2)` generates 20% of the population as sample data with replacement. (When `withReplacement = true`, there could exist the same observation multiple times in the sample.)

In the preceding code of stratified sampling, initially a map of key-value pair fractions is constructed, where `key` represents the key in the data and value represents the fraction of observations that need to be extracted from each key. The line `labelsAndVectors.sampleByKey(withReplacement = false, fractions)` generates an approximate sample and the line `labelsAndVectors.sampleByKeyExact(false, fractions)` generates an exact sample.

There's more…

In the stratified sampling technique, the sample should represent the exact ratio of the observations as in the population pertaining to a particular key. Spark supports applying stratified sampling on pair RDDs. There are two ways of applying this sampling technique: `sampleByKey` requires one pass over the data and generates the expected sample size, whereas `sampleByKeyExact` generates the exact sample size.

In many situations, we are presented only with a sample and then must decide if this sample represents the entire population so that we can use statistical inference to draw conclusions about the entire population by studying the elements of the sample.

See also

Please refer `Chapter 1`, *Big Data Analytics with Spark* to get familiar with Spark and revise your knowledge of basic statistics and distributions.

Summary and descriptive statistics

In this recipe, we will see how to get the summary statistics for data at scale in Spark. The descriptive summary statistics helps in understanding the distribution of data.

Getting ready

To step through this recipe, you need Ubuntu 14.04 (Linux flavor) installed on the machine. Also, have Apache Hadoop 2.6 and Apache Spark 1.6.0 installed.

How to do it…

Let's take an example of load prediction data. Here is what the sample data looks like:

Loan_ID	Gender	Married	Dependents	Education	Self_Employed	ApplicantIncome	CoapplicantIncome	LoanAmount	Loan_Amount_Term	Credit_History	Property_Area	Loan_Status
LP001002	Male	No	0	Graduate	No	5849	0		360	1	Urban	Y
LP001003	Male	Yes	1	Graduate	No	4583	1508	128	360	1	Rural	N
LP001005	Male	Yes	0	Graduate	Yes	3000	0	66	360	1	Urban	Y

Download the data from the following location: `https://github.com/Chi` `tturiPadma/datasets/blob/master/Loan_Prediction_Data.csv`.

1. The preceding data contains numerical as well as categorical fields. We can get the summary of numerical fields as follows:

```scala
import org.apache.spark._
import org.apache.spark.sql._
object Summary_Statistics {
   def main(args:Array[String]): Unit = {
      val conf = new SparkConf()
        .setMaster("spark://master:7077")
        .setAppName("Summary_Statistics")
      val sc = new SparkContext(conf)
      val sqlContext = new SQLContext(sc)
      import sqlContext.implicits._
        val loan_Data =
   sqlContext.read.format("com.databricks.spark.csv")
      .option("header","true")
      .option("inferSchema", "true")
      .load("hdfs://namenode:9000/loan_prediction_data.csv")
     // Gets summary of all numeric fields
     val summary = loan_Data.describe()
      summary.show()
     // Get Summary on subset of columns
     val summary_subsetColumns =
     loan_Data.describe("ApplicantIncome", "Loan_Amount_Term")
     summary_subsetColumns.show()
 // Get subset of statistics
 val subset_summary = loan_Data.select(mean("ApplicantIncome"),
 min("ApplicantIncome"), max("ApplicantIncome"))
 subset_summary.show() } }
```

The summary for all columns is as follows:

```
+-------+-----------------+------------------+-----------------+
|summary|   ApplicantIncome| CoapplicantIncome|       LoanAmount|
+-------+-----------------+------------------+-----------------+
|  count|              614|               614|              592|
|   mean|5403.459283387622|1621.2457980271008|146.41216216216216|
| stddev|6109.041673387179|2926.2483692241885| 85.58732523570544|
|    min|              150|               0.0|                9|
|    max|            81000|           41667.0|              700|
+-------+-----------------+------------------+-----------------+
```

```
-------------------+------------------+
| Loan_Amount_Term | Credit_History   |
+------------------+------------------+
|  600             | 564              |
|342.0             | 0.8421985815602837|
|65.12040985461256 | 0.3648783192364048|
|12                | 0                |
|480               | 1                |
+------------------+------------------+
```

The summary for the subset of columns is as follows:

```
+-------+-----------------+-----------------+
|summary|   ApplicantIncome| Loan_Amount_Term|
+-------+-----------------+-----------------+
|  count|              614|              600|
|   mean|5403.459283387622|            342.0|
| stddev|6109.041673387179|65.12040985461256|
|    min|              150|               12|
|    max|            81000|              480|
+-------+-----------------+-----------------+
```

The subset of descriptive stats on a column is as follows:

```
+-------------------+-------------------+--------------------+
|avg(ApplicantIncome)|min(ApplicantIncome)|max(ApplicantIncome)|
+-------------------+-------------------+--------------------+
| 5403.459283387622| 150| 81000|
+-------------------+-------------------+--------------------+
```

2. There is also an API-based on RDDs in the `org.apache.spark.mllib.stat` package which generates summary statistics on a few columns as follows:

```
val selected_Df =
loan_Data.select("ApplicantIncome","CoapplicantIncome",
"LoanAmount")
```

```
val observations = selected_Df.rdd.map{
row =>
val applicantIncome = row.getDouble(0)
val co_applicantIncome = row.getDouble(1)
val loan_Amount = if(row.isNullAt(2)) 0.0 else row.getDouble(2)
Vect  ors.dense(applicantIncome, co_applicantIncome,loan_Amount) }
val summary = Statistics.colStats(observations)
println("Mean: "+summary.mean)
println("Variance: "+summary.variance)
println("Num of Non-zeros: "+summary.numNonzeros)
```

The following is the output:

```
Mean: [5403.459283387623,1621.2457980271017,141.16612377850163]
Variance: [3.732039016718122E7,8562929.518387223,7804.066974509938]
Num of Non-zeros: [614.0,341.0,592.0]
```

How it works...

Initially, we imported the data into Spark using the CSV package. Once the DataFrame is loaded, the line `loan_Data.describe()` gives the summary statistics of all the numeric fields. Next, the line `loan_Data.describe("ApplicantIncome",` `"Loan_Amount_Term")` gives summary statistics for the subset of columns. Also, a subset of stats could be obtained for one or more columns as `loan_Data.select(mean("ApplicantIncome"), min("ApplicantIncome"), max("ApplicantIncome"))`.

Later, we used an API based on RDDs which is available in `org.apache.spark.mllib.stat`. From the DataFrames, the numeric columns `ApplicantIncome`, `CoapplicantIncome`, and `LoanAmount` are selected and `RDD[Vector]` is generated out of these fields. The line `Statistics.colStats(observations)` generates the `MultiVariateStatisticalSummary` object, using which the stats such as `mean`, `variance` and `numNonZeros` are displayed.

There's more...

Apart from the summary and descriptive stats that can be obtained, there are also other statistical measures available, such as correlation, covariance, generating the frequency distribution of a set of variables, identifying the items that are frequent in each column can be very useful to understand a dataset. Mathematical functions such as `cos`, `sin`, `floor`, `ceil`, `exp`, `round`, `sqrt`, and so on are also available with DataFrames.

See also

Please refer `Chapter 1`, *Big Data Analytics with Spark* to get familiar with Spark and revise your knowledge of basic statistics and distributions. Also visit the previous *Variable identification* recipe, which is the primary step in data preparation.

Generating frequency tables

In this recipe, we will see how to analyze the distribution of various variables in the data. Generally, we can take a histogram/boxplot of the variables to understand the distribution and also identify the outliers. But currently, Spark has no support for plotting the data. Let's see how we can perform analysis by generating frequency tables.

Getting ready

To step through this recipe, you need Ubuntu 14.04 (Linux flavor) installed on the machine. Also, have Apache Hadoop 2.6 and Apache Spark 1.6.0 installed.

How to do it...

Let's take an example of load prediction data. Here is what the sample data looks like:

Loan_ID	Gender	Married	Dependents	Education	Self_Employed	ApplicantIncome	CoapplicantIncome	LoanAmount	Loan_Amount_Term	Credit_History	Property_Area	Loan_Status
LP001002	Male	No	0	Graduate	No	5849	0		360	1	Urban	Y
LP001003	Male	Yes	1	Graduate	No	4583	1508	128	360	1	Rural	N
LP001005	Male	Yes	0	Graduate	Yes	3000	0	66	360	1	Urban	Y

Download the data from the following location: `https://github.com/ChitturiPadma/datasets/blob/master/Loan_Prediction_Data.csv`.

The total record count is 614.

1. Let us look at the chances of getting a loan-based on `Credit_History`. Here is the code to generate the frequency distribution of set of variables such as `Loan_Status` and `Credit_History`:

```
import org.apache.spark._
import org.apache.spark.sql.SQLContext
import org.apache.spark.sql.types.{StructType, StringType,
    DoubleType, StructField}
object Frequency_Tables {
  def main(args:Array[String]): Unit = {
    val conf = new SparkConf()
      .setMaster("spark://master:7077")
      .setAppName("Frequency_Tables")
    val sc = new SparkContext(conf)
    val sqlContext = new SQLContext(sc)
    import sqlContext.implicits._
    val schemaString =
    "Loan_ID,Gender,Married,Dependents,Education,Self_Employed,
     ApplicantIncome, CoapplicantIncome,LoanAmount,
     Loan_Amount_Term,Credit_History,Property_Area,Loan_Status"
    val schema = schemaString.split(",").map {
      field =>
        if (field == "ApplicantIncome" || field ==
    "CoapplicantIncome" || field == "LoanAmount" || field ==
    "Loan_Amount_Term" || field == "Credit_History")
        StructField(field, DoubleType)
      else
        StructField(field, StringType)
    }
    val schema_Applied = StructType(schema)
    val loan_Data =
    sqlContext.read.format("com.databricks.spark.csv")
      .option("header", "true")
      .schema(schema_Applied).load("hdfs://namenode:9000/
      loan_prediction_data.csv")
    val crossTab_Df= loan_Data.stat.crosstab("Credit_History",
    "Loan_Status")
    crossTab_Df.show()
    }
}
```

The following is the output:

```
+--------------------------+---+---+
|Credit_History_Loan_Status|  N|  Y|
+--------------------------+---+---+
|                       1.0| 97|378|
|                      null| 13| 37|
|                       0.0| 82|  7|
+--------------------------+---+---+
```

2. Suppose we want to understand the average `ApplicantIncome` for a particular `Loan_Staus` and `Credit_History`. We can generate a pivot table which helps in understanding the distribution as follows:

```
val pivot_Df =
        loan_Data.groupBy("Loan_Status").pivot("Credit_History").avg
          ("ApplicantIncome")
pivot_Df.show()
```

The following is the output:

```
+-----------+----+----------------+----------------+
|Loan_Status|null|             0.0|             1.0|
+-----------+----+----------------+----------------+
|          N|null|5382.841463414634|5613.927835051546|
|          Y|null|9153.857142857143|5378.436507936508|
+-----------+----+----------------+----------------+
```

How it works...

In the preceding code snippet, we have seen how we could analyze the distribution of a set of variables using cross tables and pivot tables. The `crosstab` and `pivot` functions are available in the `stat` library of DataFrame. The line `loan_Data.stat.crosstab("Credit_History", "Loan_Status")` generates a table which contains the frequency distribution of `Credit_History` and `Loan_Status`. For `Credit_History` =1, the number of observations with `Loan_Status` = "N" is 97 and with `Loan_Status` = "Y" is 378. Similarly for `Credit_History` =0, the number of observations with `Loan_Status` = "N" is 82 and with `Loan_Status` = "Y" is 7.

Next, we generated a pivot table. Pivot is an aggregation where one of the grouping columns having distinct values are transposed into columns. These tables are essential for data analysis and reporting. Most of the popular data manipulation tools, such as Excel, MS SQL, Oracle, Pandas, and so on, have the ability to pivot data. The line `loan_Data.groupBy("Loan_Status").pivot("Credit_History").avg("Applicant Income")` groups the observations based on `Loan_Status`, and calculates the mean of the `ApplicantIncome` for distinct `fordistinct`, and `Credit_History` values.

There's more...

Apart from the cross table and Pivot tables used for data analysis, there are other statistical functions available which generate frequent items in each column in a dataset. Data analysis would also involves identifying outliers and extracting relationships between the variables, which requires plotting the data. As Spark is a distributed computing framework, it doesn't support plots. Although this seems to be a limitation when compared with R and Pandas, plotting data at scale is not a feasible methodology with any framework.

See also

Please refer `Chapter 1`, *Big Data Analytics with Spark* to get familiar with Spark and refresh your knowledge of basic statistics and distributions. Also visit the previous *Variable identification* recipe, which is the primary step in data preparation.

Installing Pandas on Linux

In this recipe, we will see how to install Pandas on Linux. Before proceeding with the installation, let's consider the version of Python we're going to use. There are two versions or flavors of Python, namely Python 2.7.x and Python 3.x. Although the latest version, Python 3.x, appears to be the better choice, for scientific, numeric, or data analysis work, Python 2.7 is recommended.

Getting ready

To step through this recipe, you need Ubuntu 14.04 (Linux flavor) installed on the machine. Python comes pre-installed. The `python --version` command gives the version of Python installed. If the version seems to be 2.6.x, upgrade it to Python 2.7 as follows:

```
sudo apt-get install python2.7
```

How to do it...

1. Once Python version is available, make sure that the Python `.dev` files are installed. If not, install them as follows:

   ```
   sudo apt-get install python-dev
   ```

2. Installing through `pip`:

   ```
   sudo apt-get install python-pip
   sudo pip install numpy
   sudo pip install pandas
   ```

3. Sometimes, pip-installed NumPy might be slower and the installation might require dependencies such as `python-setuptools`. Hence, instead of pip, `easy-install` can be used as follows:

   ```
   sudo apt-get install python-setuptools
   sudo easy_install pandas
   ```

4. Instead of `easy_install`, `sudo apt-getinstall python-pandas` also installs the Pandas library.

How it works...

The preceding commands install NumPy, the Pandas library, and the related dependencies. If the installation fails with missing dependencies, please install the required ones and continue with the installation.

There's more...

The easiest and most general way to install the Pandas library is to use a pre-packaged solution, that is, installing it through the distribution Anaconda or Enthought distributions. Also, when installing other Linux flavors such as Centos and OpenSuse, we use the following code:

```
sudo yum install <package> and sudo zypper install <package>
```

See also

For installing Pandas from the Anaconda distribution, please refer to http://docs.continu um.io/anaconda/install and http://pandas.pydata.org/pandas-docs/stable/install .html.

Installing Pandas from source

In this recipe, we will see how to install Pandas from Source on Linux. Before proceeding with the installation, let's consider the version of Python we're going to use. There are two versions or flavors of Python, namely Python 2.7.x and Python 3.x. Although the latest version, Python 3.x, appears to be the better choice, for scientific, numeric, or data analysis work, Python 2.7 is recommended.

Getting ready

To step through this recipe, you need Ubuntu 14.04 (Linux flavor) installed on the machine. Python comes pre-installed. The `python --version` command gives the version of Python installed. If the version seems to be 2.6.x, upgrade it to Python 2.7 as follows:

```
sudo apt-get install python2.7
```

How to do it...

1. Install the `easy_install` program:

```
wget http://python-distribute.org/distribute_setup.pysudo python
distribute_setup.py
```

2. Install Cython:

```
sudo easy_install -U Cython
```

3. Install from the source code as follows:

```
git clone git://github.com/pydata/pandas.git
cd pandas
sudo python setup.py install
```

How it works...

The preceding commands install the Pandas library and the related dependencies. The source code could be found on `http://github.com/pydata/pandas`. It has to be ensured that Cython is installed at compile time.

There's more...

The easiest and most general way to install the Pandas library is to use a pre-packaged solution, that is, installing it through the distribution Anaconda or Enthought. Also, when installing other Linux flavors such as Centos and OpenSuse, we use:

```
sudo yum install <package> and sudo zypper install <package>
```

See also

For installing Pandas from the Anaconda distribution, please refer to `http://docs.continuum.io/anaconda/install` and `http://pandas.pydata.org/pandas-docs/stable/install.html`. Visit the earlier *Installation on Linux* recipe for details on installing Pandas.

Using IPython with PySpark

As Python is the most preferred choice for data scientists due to its high-level syntax and extensive library of packages, Spark developers have considered it for data analysis. The PySpark API has been developed for working with RDDs in Python. IPython Notebook is an essential tool for data scientists to present the scientific and theoretical work in an interactive fashion, integrating both text and Python code.

This recipe shows how to configure IPython with PySpark and also focuses on connecting the IPython shell to PySpark.

Getting ready

To step through this recipe, you need Ubuntu 14.04 (Linux flavor) installed on the machine. Python comes pre-installed. The `python --version` command gives the version of the Python installed. If the version seems to be 2.6.x, upgrade it to Python 2.7 as follows:

```
sudo apt-get install python2.7
```

How to do it...

1. Install IPython as follows:

   ```
   sudo pip install ipython
   ```

2. Create an IPython profile for use with PySpark as follows:

   ```
   ipython profile create pyspark
   ```

3. Create a profile startup script as follows:

   ```
   vim ~/.ipython/profile_pyspark/startup/00-pyspark-setup.py
   ```

4. Put the following code inside the file:

```
import os
import sys
spark_home = os.environ.get('SPARK_HOME', None)
if not spark_home:
raise ValueError('SPARK_HOME environment variable is not set')
sys.path.insert(0, os.path.join(spark_home, 'python'))
sys.path.insert(0, os.path.join(spark_home, 'python/lib/py4j-0.9-
  src.zip'))
execfile(os.path.join(spark_home, 'python/pyspark/shell.py'))
```

5. Edit the `~/.ipython/profile_pyspark/ipython_config.py` file and put the following inside the file:

```
c = get_config()
c.NotebookApp.ip = '*'
c.NotebookApp.open_browser = False
c.NotebookApp.port = 8880
```

6. Install `py4j` as follows:

```
sudo pip install py4j
```

7. Place the following environment variables inside `~/.bashrc`:

```
export PYTHONPATH=
$SPARK_HOME/python/:$SPARK_HOME/python/lib/py4j-0.9-src.zip
export PYTHONSTARTUP=$SPARK_HOME/python/pyspark/shell.py
export PYSPARK_SUBMIT_ARGS="--master
spark://master: pyspark-shell"
```

8. If you are using Jupyter, create a kernel that uses this profile as touch `~/.ipython/kernels/pyspark/kernel.json` and place the following content in the kernel file:

```
{
  "display_name": "pySpark (Spark 1.6.0)",
  "language": "python",
  "argv": [
  "/usr/bin/python2",
  "-m",
  "IPython.kernel",
  "-f",
  "{connection_file}"
  ]
}
```

9. Invoke the IPython console as follows:

```
ipython console –profile=pyspark
```

10. Invoke IPython Notebook as follows:

```
ipython notebook --profile=pyspark
```

How it work...

The preceding commands install the IPython console and IPython notebook, which are used to develop code by importing the PySpark API.

There's more...

From Spark 1.4,'the Pandas DataFrame computation can be moved to the Apache Spark parallel computation framework using Spark SQL's DataFrame. A few operations in Pandas don't translate to Spark as DataFrames are immutable data sets. Spark is trying to bridge the gap that data analysis performed using Pandas, that is, from Spark 1.4, port any Pandas computation in a distributed environment using the very similar DataFrame API.

See also

Please refer the earlier *Installing Pandas on Linux* and *Installing Pandas from Source* recipes to understand how to proceed with Pandas installation.

Creating Pandas DataFrames over Spark

A DataFrame is a distributed collection of data organized into named columns. It is equivalent to a table in a relational database or a DataFrame in R/Python Python with rich optimizations. These can be constructed from a wide variety of sources, such as structured data files (JSON and parquet files), Hive tables, external databases, or from existing RDDs.

PySpark is the Python API for Apache Spark which is designed to scale to huge amounts of data. This recipe shows how to make use of Pandas over Spark.

Getting ready

To step through this recipe, you will need a running Spark cluster either in pseudo distributed mode or in one of the distributed modes, that is, standalone, YARN, or Mesos. Also, have Python and IPython installed on the Linux machine, that is, Ubuntu 14.04.

How to do it...

1. Invoke `ipython console –profile=pyspark` as follows:

   ```
   In [4]: from pyspark import SparkConf, SparkContext, SQLContext
   In [5]: import pandas as pd
   ```

2. Creating a Pandas DataFrame as follows:

   ```
   In [6]: pdf = pd.DataFrame({'Name':['Padma','Major','Priya'],
   'Age':  [23,45,30]})
   ```

3. Creating a Spark DataFrame from a Pandas DataFrame as follows:

   ```
   In [7]: sqlc=SQLContext(sc)
   In [8]: spark_df = sqlc.createDataFrame(pdf)
   ```

4. Referring a column in Pandas as follows:

   ```
   In [9]: pdf.Name
   Out[9]:
   0     Padma
   1     Major
   2     Priya
   Name: Name, dtype: object
   In [10]: pdf['Name']
   Out[10]:
   0     Padma
   1     Major
   2     Priya
   Name: Name, dtype: object
   ```

5. Referring a column in a Spark DataFrame as follows:

```
In [11]: spark_df.Name
Out[11]: Column<Name>
In [12]: spark_df['Name']
Out[12]: Column<Name>
```

6. Adding a column to a Pandas DataFrame as follows:

```
In [13]: pdf['C']=0
In [14]: pdf
Out[14]:
    Age    Name   C
0    23   Padma   0
1    45   Major   0
2    30   Priya   0
```

7. Adding a column to a Spark DataFrame as follows:

```
In [15]: from pyspark.sql import functions
In [16]: spark_df.withColumn('C',functions.lit(0))
Out[16]: DataFrame[Age: bigint, Name: string, C: int]
In [17]: spark_df.show()
+---+-----+
|Age| Name|
+---+-----+
| 23|Padma|
| 45|Major|
| 30|Priya|
+---+-----+
In [18]: spark_df.withColumn('C',functions.lit(0)).show()
+---+-----+---+
|Age| Name|  C|
+---+-----+---+
| 23|Padma|  0|
| 45|Major|  0|
| 30|Priya|  0|
+---+-----+---+
```

8. Manipulating column C to take values twice the value of column `Age`:

```
In [19]:spark_df.withColumn('C',spark_df.Age  *2).show()
+---+-----+---+
|Age| Name|  C|
+---+-----+---+
| 23|Padma| 46|
| 45|Major| 90|
| 30|Priya| 60|
```

```
+---+-----+---+
In [20]: pdf['C']=pdf.Age*2
In [21]: pdf
Out[21]:
   Age   Name   C
0   23  Padma  46
1   45  Major  90
2   30  Priya  60
```

9. Selecting a column in a Spark DataFrame:

```
In [22]: spark_df.select(spark_df.Age > 0).show()

+---------+
|(Age > 0)|
+---------+
|     true|
|     true|
|     true|
+---------+
```

10. Selecting a column in a Pandas DataFrame:

```
In [23]: pdf['Age']>0
Out[23]:
0     True
1     True
2     True
Name: Age, dtype: bool
```

11. Converting a Spark DataFrame back to Pandas:

```
In [47]: spark_df.toPandas
```

How it works...

In the preceding code snippets, we have seen that `pdf = pd.DataFrame` creates a Pandas DataFrame and `sqlcontext.createDataFrame(pdf)` converts a Pandas DataFrame to a Spark DataFrame. We have seen various ways to add a column in Pandas and the same which could be done in Spark. The only difference is that in Pandas, it is a mutable data structure whereas in Spark, it is immutable. Also, the columns can be manipulated using an expression such as `spark_df.withColumn('C', spark_df.Age *2)`. The Spark DataFrame can be converted to a Pandas DataFrame as `spark_df.toPandas`.

There's more...

Spark and Pandas DataFrames are very similar. Although the Pandas API remains more convenient and powerful, the gap is shrinking quickly. Spark is well known for its features such as immutability, distributed computation, lazy evaluation, and so on. Spark wants to mimic Pandas. With `Spark.ml` available, it becomes the perfect one-stop-shop for industrialized data science.

See also

Please refer to the earlier *Installing Pandas on Linux, Installing Pandas from Source* and *Using IPython with PySpark* recipes to understand how to proceed with Pandas and IPython installation.

Splitting, slicing, sorting, filtering, and grouping DataFrames over Spark

This recipe shows how to filter, slice, sort, index, and group Pandas DataFrames as well as Spark DataFrames.

Getting ready

To step through this recipe, you will need a running Spark cluster either in pseudo distributed mode or in one of the distributed modes, that is, standalone, YARN, or Mesos. Also, have Python and IPython installed on the Linux machine, that is, Ubuntu 14.04.

How to do it...

1. Invoke `ipython console -profile=pyspark` as follows:

```
In [4]: from pyspark import SparkConf, SparkContext, SQLContext
In [5]: import pandas as pd
```

2. Creating a Pandas DataFrame as follows:

```
In [6]: pdf = pd.DataFrame({'Name':['Padma','Major','Priya'],
                            'Age':  [23,45,30]})
```

3. Creating a Spark DataFrame from a Pandas DataFrame as follows:

```
In [7]: sqlc=SQLContext(sc)
In [8]: spark_df = sqlc.createDataFrame(pdf)
```

4. Splitting a Pandas DataFrame into two based on column `Age`:

```
In [9]: pdf1 = pdf[pdf['Age'] >=30]
In [10]: pdf1
Out[10]:
    Age    Name    C
1    45   Major   90
2    30   Priya   60
In [11]: pdf2 = pdf[pdf['Age'] <30]
In [12]: pdf2
Out[12]:
    Age    Name    C
0    23   Padma   46
```

5. Splitting a Spark DataFrame into two based on column `Age`:

```
In [13]: spark_df2 = spark_df[spark_df['Age'] >=30]
In [14]: spark_df2.show()
+---+-----+
|Age| Name|
+---+-----+
| 45|Major|
| 30|Priya|
+---+-----+
```

6. Slicing a Pandas DataFrame as follows:

```
In [15]: pdf[0:1]
Out[15]:
     Age    Name    C
 0    23   Padma   46
In [16]: pdf[1:2]
Out[16]:
    Age    Name    C
1    45   Major   90
```

7. Slicing a Spark DataFrame as follows:

```
In [17]: spark_df['Age','Name'].show()
+---+-----+
|Age| Name|
+---+-----+
| 23|Padma|
| 45|Major|
| 30|Priya|
+---+-----+
```

8. Sorting a Pandas DataFrame as follows:

```
In [18]: pdf.sort('Name')
Out[18]:
Age    Name    C
1    45   Major   90
0    23   Padma   46
2    30   Priya   60
In [19]: pdf.sort(['Name','Age'], ascending=False)
Out[19]:
    Age    Name    C
2    30   Priya   60
0    23   Padma   46
1    45   Major   90
```

9. Sorting a Spark DataFrame as follows:

```
In [20]: spark_df.sort(spark_df['Name']).show()
+---+-----+
|Age| Name|
+---+-----+
| 45|Major|
| 23|Padma|
| 30|Priya|
+---+-----+
```

10. Filtering pandas and Spark DataFrames as follows:

```
pdf = pd.DataFrame.from_items([('A', [1, 2, 3]), ('B', [4, 5,
                                 6])])
df = sqlcontext.createDataFrame([(1, 4), (2, 5), (3, 6)], ["A",
                                 "B"])
In [21]: pdf[(pdf.B > 0) & (pdf.A < 2)]
Out[21]:
   A  B
0  1  4
In [22]:  df.filter((df.B > 0) & (df.A < 2)).show()
```

```
+---+---+
|  A|  B|
+---+---+
|  1|  4|
+---+---+
```

11. The `GroupBy` operation on Pandas and Spark DataFrames as follows:

```
In [23]: pdf.groupby(['A']).mean()
Out[23]:
     B
A
1    4
2    5
3    6
In [117]: df.groupBy("A").avg("B").show()
+---+------+
|  A|avg(B)|
+---+------+
|  1|   4.0|
|  2|   5.0|
|  3|   6.0|
+---+------+
```

How it works...

In the preceding code snippets, we have seen splitting Pandas as well as Spark DataFrames as `pdf[pdf['Age'] <30]` and `spark_df[spark_df['Age'] >=30]`. Also, we have seen how to slice, sort, and group the data in Pandas and Spark DataFrames. The syntax of the operations seem to be almost the same in both.

There's more...

There are numerous other operations available in Pandas, such as indexing, merging, joining, concatenating, reshaping, dealing with time-series data and so on. Spark and Pandas DataFrames are very similar. Although the Pandas API remains more convenient and powerful, the gap is shrinking quickly. Spark is well known for its features, such as immutability, distributed computation, lazy evaluation, and so on. Spark wants to mimic Pandas. With `Spark.ml` available, it becomes the perfect one-stop-shop for industrialized data science.

See also

Please refer to earlier *Creating Pandas DataFrames over Spark* recipe to get familiar with working on Pandas with Spark.

Implementing co-variance and correlation using Pandas

This recipe shows how to implement co-variance using Pandas DataFrames over Spark.

Getting ready

To step through this recipe, you will need a running Spark cluster either in pseudo distributed mode or in one of the distributed modes, that is, standalone, YARN, or Mesos. Also, have Python and IPython installed on the Linux machine, that is, Ubuntu 14.04.

How to do it...

1. Invoke `ipython console –profile=pyspark`.
2. Computing correlation and co-variance using Pandas in PySpark:

```
In [1]: from pyspark import SparkConf, SparkContext, SQLContext
In [2]: import pandas as pd
In [3]: seq=pd.Series([1,2,3,4,4,3,2,1],
['2006','2007','2008','2009','2010','2011','2012','2013'])
In [4]: seq2 = pd.Series([3,4,3,4,5,4,3,2],
['2006','2007','2008','2009','2010','2011','2012','2013'])
In [5]: seq.corr(seq2)
Out[5]: 0.77459666924148329
In [6]: seq.cov(seq2)
Out[6]: 0.8571428571428571
```

3. Computing correlation and co-variance using Spark DataFrames:

```
In [186]: seq=pd.DataFrame.from_items([('A', [1,2,3,4,4,3,2,1]),
 ('B',[1,4,2,3,4,2,3,2]) ])
In [187]: df = sqlc.createDataFrame(seq)
In [189]: df.stat.cov('A','B')
Out[189]: 0.6428571428571429
In [190]: df.stat.corr('A','B')
Out[190]: 0.50709255283711
```

How it works...

In the preceding code snippets, we have seen how covariance and correlation can be calculated using Pandas over PySpark as well as using Spark. DataFrames.

 For more detail on correlation and co-variance, please refer to https://en .wikipedia.org/wiki/Covariance and https://en.wikipedia.org/wik i/Pearson_product-moment_correlation_coefficient.

There's more...

Apart from correlation and co-variance, there are other statistical functions such as random data generation, cross tabulation, frequent item set generation, mathematical functions, and so on. For details, please refer to https://databricks.com/blog/2015/06/02/statistical-and-mathematical-functions-w ith-dataframes-in-spark.html.

See also

Please refer to the earlier *Creating Pandas DataFrames over Spark* recipe to get familiar with working on Pandas with Spark and splitting, slicing, sorting, filtering, and grouping DataFrames over Spark to get hands-on with Pandas on different functionalities.

Concatenating and merging operations over DataFrames

This recipe shows how to concatenate, merge/join, and perform complex operations over Pandas DataFrames as well as Spark DataFrames.

Getting ready

To step through this recipe, you will need a running Spark cluster either in pseudo distributed mode or in one of the distributed modes, that is, standalone, YARN, or Mesos. Also, have Python and IPython installed on the Linux machine, that is, Ubuntu 14.04.

How to do it...

1. Invoke `ipython console –profile=pyspark`:

```
In [1]: from pyspark import SparkConf, SparkContext, SQLContext
In [2]: import pandas as pd
In [3]: sqlcontext = SQLContext(sc)
In [4]: pdf1 = pd.DataFrame({'A':['A0','A1','A2','A3'], 'B':
['B0','B1','B2','B3'], 'C':['C0','C1','C2','C3'],'D':
['D0','D1','D2','D3']},index=[0,1,2,3])
In [5]: pdf2 = pd.DataFrame({'A':['A4','A5','A6','A7'], 'B':
['B4','B5','B6','B7'], 'C':['C4','C5','C6','C7'],'D':
['D4','D5','D6','D7']},index=[4,5,6,7])
In [6]: frames = [pdf1,pdf2]
```

2. Concatenating Pandas DataFrames:

```
In [7]: result = pd.concat(frames)
In [8]: df1 = sqlcontext.createDataFrame(pdf1)
In [9]: df2 = sqlcontext.createDataFrame(pdf2)
In [10]: df1.unionAll(df2).show()
+---+---+---+---+
|  A|  B|  C|  D|
+---+---+---+---+
| A0| B0| C0| D0|
| A1| B1| C1| D1|
| A2| B2| C2| D2|
| A3| B3| C3| D3|
| A4| B4| C4| D4|
```

```
| A5|  B5|  C5|  D5|
| A6|  B6|  C6|  D6|
| A7|  B7|  C7|  D7|
+---+---+---+---+
```

3. Displaying concatenated Pandas DataFrame result:

```
In [11]: result
Out[11]:
     A    B    C    D
0   A0   B0   C0   D0
1   A1   B1   C1   D1
2   A2   B2   C2   D2
3   A3   B3   C3   D3
4   A4   B4   C4   D4
5   A5   B5   C5   D5
6   A6   B6   C6   D6
7   A7   B7   C7   D7
```

4. Here is an example of a many-to-many join case in Pandas:

```
In [12]: left = pd.DataFrame({'key': ['K0', 'K1', 'K2', 'K3'],
'A': ['A0', 'A1', 'A2', 'A3'],
'B': ['B0', 'B1', 'B2', 'B3']})
In [13]: right = pd.DataFrame({'key': ['K0', 'K1', 'K2', 'K3'],
'C': ['C0', 'C1', 'C2', 'C3'],
'D': ['D0', 'D1', 'D2', 'D3']})
In [14]: result = pd.merge(left, right, on='key')
In [15]: result
Out[25]:
     A    B key    C    D
0   A0
B0   K0   C0   D0
 1   A1   B1   K1   C1   D1
 2   A2   B2   K2   C2   D2
 3   A3   B3   K3   C3   D3
```

5. Merging the preceding DataFrames in Spark:

```
In [26]: left_df = sqlContext.createDataFrame(left)
In [27]: right_df = sqlContext.createDataFrame(right)
In [28]: result_df = left_df1.join(right_df, left_df1.key ==
right_df.key, "leftOuter")
In [29]: result_df.show()
+---+---+---+---+---+---+
|  A|  B|key|  C|  D|key|
+---+---+---+---+---+---+
| A0| B0| K0| C0| D0| K0|
```

```
| A1| B1| K1| C1| D1| K1|
| A2| B2| K2| C2| D2| K2|
| A3| B3| K3| C3| D3| K3|
+---+---+---+---+---+---+
```

How it works...

In the preceding code snippets, the Pandas DataFrames are concatenated using `pd.concat`. There are also joins similar to SQL. We have shown an example of a many-to-many join case which generates the Cartesian product of the associated data on a key that appears in both the tables. `pd.merge(left, right, on='key')` joins DataFrames on the column `key`. The Spark DataFrames are joined using `left_df1.join(right_df, left_df1.key == right_df.key, "leftOuter")`. In both the `left_df1` and `right_df`, the common column is `key` on which join is imposed.

There's more...

In Pandas, there are other advanced functionalities, such as multi-indexing, concatenating objects (using append, with mixed ndims, with group keys), a variety of joins (joining on index, joining key columns on an index, joining single index to a multi-index), merging ordered data, time series data, reshaping using pivot tables, visualization, a variety of data structures, a number of I/O tools (text, CSV, HDFS, and so on), and so on. The Spark community is slowly incorporating all the operations doable with Pandas into Spark. However, it takes little time to have DataFrame API in Spark fully evolved and this will ultimately be a one-stop solution for data scientists and data engineers.

See also

Please refer to the earlier *Creating Pandas DataFrames over Spark* recipe to get familiar with working on Pandas with Spark and splitting, slicing, sorting, filtering, and grouping DataFrames over Spark to get hands-on with Pandas on different functionalities.

 For more on the advanced functionalities of Pandas, please refer to
`http://pandas.pydata.org/pandas-docs/stable/`.

Complex operations over DataFrames

This recipe shows how to perform complex operations such as computing difference on a column in Pandas DataFrames as well as Spark DataFrames.

Getting ready

To step through this recipe, you will need a running Spark cluster either in pseudo distributed mode or in one of the distributed modes, that is, standalone, YARN, or Mesos. Also, have Python and IPython installed on the Linux machine, that is, Ubuntu 14.04.

How to do it...

1. Invoke `ipython console -profile=pyspark`:

```
In [1]: from pyspark import SparkConf, SparkContext, SQLContext
   In [2]: import pandas as pd
   In [3]: sqlcontext = SQLContext(sc)
```

2. Computing `diff` on a column in Pandas:

```
In [4]: df = sqlCtx.createDataFrame([(1, 4), (1, 5), (2, 6),
(2,    6), (3, 0)], ["A", "B"])
In [5]: pdf = df.toPandas()
In [6]: pdf
Out[6]:
A    B
0    1    4
1    1    5
2    2    6
3    2    6
4    3    0
In [7]: pdf['diff'] = pdf.B.diff()
In [8]: pdf
Out[8]:
     A    B    diff
0    1    4    NaN
1    1    5      1
2    2    6      1
3    2    6      0
4    3    0     -6
```

3. Computing `diff` on a column given a specific key using the Window operation:

```
In [9]: from pyspark.sql.window import Window
In [10]: window_over_A = Window.partitionBy("A").orderBy("B")
In [11]: df.withColumn("diff", F.lead("B").over(window_over_A) -
    df.B).show()
+---+---+-----+
|  A|  B|diff |
+---+---+-----+
| 1 | 4 | 1   |
| 1 | 5 | null|
| 2 | 6 | 0   |
| 2 | 6 | null|
| 3 | 0 | null|
+---+---+-----+
```

How it works...

The above code snippets show how to perform complex operations. In Pandas, we can compute diff on a column by comparing the values of one line to the last one and computing the difference between them. `pdf['diff'] = pdf.B.diff()` computes the difference. But the same feature is tough to implement in a distributed environment because each line is supposed to be treated independently. In Spark 1.4, there is support for window operations that is, Window is defined over a column on which Spark will execute some aggregation functions but relative to a specific line. The `df.withColumn("diff",` `F.lead("B").over(window_over_A) - df.B)` line computes the difference line-by-line ordered or not given a specific key.

With Window operations, the results are copied as additional columns without any explicit join.

There's more...

The Spark community is slowly incorporating all the operations doable with Pandas in to. However, it takes a little time to have DataFrame API fully evolved in Spark and this will ultimately be one-stop solution for data scientists and data engineers.

See also

Please refer to the earlier *Creating Pandas DataFrames over Spark* recipe to get familiar with working on Pandas with Spark and splitting, slicing, sorting, filtering, and grouping DataFrames over Spark to get hands-on with Pandas on different functionalities.

 For more on the advanced functionalities of Pandas, please refer to http://pandas.pydata.org/pandas-docs/stable/.

Sparkling Pandas

Sparkling Pandas aims to make use of the distributed computing power of PySpark to scale the data analysis with Pandas. This is built on Spark's DataFrame and provides API similar to Pandas. This recipe shows how to use Sparkling Pandas.

Getting ready

To step through this recipe, you will need a running Spark Cluster either in pseudo distributed mode or in one of the distributed modes, that is, standalone, YARN, or Mesos. Also, have Python and IPython installed on the Linux machine, that is, Ubuntu 14.04.

How to do it...

1. Install `blas`, `scipy`, and `sparklingpandas` as follows:

```
apt-get install libblas-dev liblapack-dev libatlas-base-dev
gfortran
pip install scipy
pip install sparklingpandas
```

2. Now import the package as follows:

```
import sparklingpandas
ipython console -profile=pyspark
In [1]: from pyspark import SparkConf, SparkContext, SQLContext
In [2]: import pandas as pd
In [3]: sqlcontext = SQLContext(sc)
In [4]: import sparklingpandas
```

3. Creating a distributed collection of DataFrames in Spark:

```
In [5]: input = [1,2,3,4]
In [6]: rdd = sc.parallelize(zip(range(len(input)), input))
In [7]: frames_rdd = rdd.map(lambda x:pd.DataFrame(data=
        [x[1]],index=[x[0]]))
```

4. Distributed operations:

```
In [8]: sqF = (frames_rdd.map(lambda f:f.applymap(lambda x:x*x)))
In [9]: sqDFs = sqF.collect()
In [10]: sqDF = reduce(lambda x,y:x.append(y),sqDFs)
```

5. Creating distributed DataFrames using `sparklingpandas`:

```
In [11]: from sparklingpandas.pcontext import PsparkContext
In [12]: ddf = psc.read_csv()
In [13]: schema_rdd = sqlContext.sql("SELECT panda_id, num_babies,
         city FROM panda_info")
         ddf = psc.from_schema_rdd(schema_rdd) //creating from
         schema rdd of spark SQL
```

6. Simple analysis with the data:

```
pandas_with_kids = ddf.dropna(subset=['num_babies'])
sqDDF = ddf.applymap(lambda x:x*x)
ddfFour = ddf.query("b==4")
sqDF = sqDDF.collect()
```

How it works...

In the preceding code snippets, we have seen how to use distributed DataFrame operations that could be done using Sparkling Pandas. The normal DataFrames on Spark as are created in such a way that each partition contains many DataFrames instead of one DataFrame containing many rows in each partition which is slightly less efficient.

This works in a way that we started with the data in-memory on single node, distributed across the operations, and finally retrieved the results back to the single node. If the data doesn't fit into the memory of a single node initially, the approach doesn't work. Hence `sparklingpandas` distributes the data on multiple nodes in the initial stage itself. `ddf` is the distributed DataFrame which can be created either directly or from the schema `rdd` of Spark SQL.

There's more...

Sparkling Pandas is a new library that brings together the best features of Pandas and PySpark: expressiveness, speed, and scalability. This is comparatively faster than PySpark. However, with the latest improvements in Spark's DataFrame API, the gap between Spark DataFrames and Pandas is slowly being minimized and the project `sparklingpandas` is no longer active.

See also

Please refer to the earlier *Creating Pandas DataFrames over Spark* recipe to get familiar with working on Pandas with Spark and splitting, slicing, sorting, filtering, and grouping DataFrames over Spark to get hands-on with Pandas on different functionalities.

 For details on `sparklingpandas`, please visit `https://github.com/spar klingpandas/sparklingpandas`and `http://sparklingpandas.com/`.

3
Data Analysis with Spark

In this chapter, we will cover the following recipes on performing data analysis with Spark:

- Univariate analysis
- Bivariate analysis
- Missing value treatment
- Outlier detection
- Use case – analyzing the MovieLens dataset
- Use case – analyzing the Uber dataset

Introduction

The techniques for data exploration and preparation are typically applied before applying models on the data and this also helps in developing complex statistical models. These techniques are also important for eliminating or sharpening a potential hypothesis which can be addressed by the data. The amount of time spent in preprocessing and data exploration provides the quality input which decides the quality of the output. Once the business hypothesis is ready, a series of steps in data exploration and preparation decides the accuracy of the model and reliable results.

In this chapter, we are going to look at the following common data analysis techniques such as univariate analysis, bivariate analysis, missing values treatment, identifying the outliers, and techniques for variable transformation.

Univariate analysis

Once the data is available, we have to spend lot of time and effort in data exploration, cleaning and preparation because the quality of the high input data decides the quality of calculating the output. Hence, once we identify the business questions, the first step of data exploration/analysis is univariate analysis, which explores the variables one by one. The methods of univariate analysis depend on whether the variable type is categorical or continuous.

Getting ready

To step through this recipe, you will need a running Spark cluster in any one of the modes, that is, local, standalone, YARN, or Mesos. For installing Spark on a standalone cluster, please refer to http://spark.apache.org/docs/latest/spark-standalone.html. Also, include the Spark MLlib package in the build.sbt file so that it downloads the related libraries and the API can be used. Install Hadoop (optionally), Scala, and Java.

How to do it...

1. Let's take the example of Titanic dataset. On April 15, 1912, the titanic sank after colliding with an iceberg, killing 1,502 out of 2,224 passengers. Some groups of people were more likely to survive than others, such as women, children, and the upper class. Let's try to do some data exploration on each variable and come up with inferences about the data.

    Please download the data from https://github.com/ChitturiPadma/dat asets/blob/master/titanic_data.csv and the description about the variables from https://github.com/ChitturiPadma/datasets/blob/ma ster/titanic_data_description.

2. The data resides in HDFS. Here is the code which loads the data. Let's have a look at a few records of the data:

```
import org.apache.spark._
import org.apache.spark.sql._
import org.apache.spark.sql.functions._
import org.apache.spark.sql.DataFrameNaFunctions
import org.apache.spark.sql.types._
object Univariate_Analysis {
  def main(args:Array[String]): Unit = {
```

```
val conf = new SparkConf()
  .setMaster("spark://master:7077")
  .setAppName("Univariate_Analysis")
val sc = new SparkContext(conf)
val sqlContext = new SQLContext(sc)
import sqlContext.implicits._
//Loading data
val titanic_data =
sqlContext.read.format("com.databricks.spark.csv")
  .option("header", "true")
  .option("inferSchema","true")
.load("hdfs://namenode:9000/titanic_data.csv")
titanic_data.show(10) } }
```

The following is the output:

```
+-----------+--------+------+--------------------+------+
|PassengerId|Survived|Pclass|                Name|   Sex|
+-----------+--------+------+--------------------+------+
|          1|       0|     3|Braund, Mr. Owen ...|  male|
|          2|       1|     1|Cumings, Mrs. Joh...|female|
|          3|       1|     3|Heikkinen, Miss. ...|female|
|          4|       1|     1|Futrelle, Mrs. Ja...|female|
|          5|       0|     3|Allen, Mr. Willia...|  male|
|          6|       0|     3|   Moran, Mr. James|  male|
|          7|       0|     1|McCarthy, Mr. Tim...|  male|
|          8|       0|     3|Palsson, Master. ...|  male|
|          9|       1|     3|Johnson, Mrs. Osc...|female|
|         10|       1|     2|Nasser, Mrs. Nich...|female|
+-----------+--------+------+--------------------+------+

+-----+------+-----+----------------+-------+-----+---------+
|Age  |SibSp |Parch|          Ticket|   Fare |Cabin|Embarked |
+-----+------+-----+----------------+-------+-----+---------+
|22.0 |1     |0    | A/5 21171      |7.25   |     |S        |
|38.0 |1     |0    | PC 17599       |71.2833|C85  |C        |
|26.0 |0     |0    | STON/O2. 3101282|7.925  |     |S        |
|35.0 |1     |0    |113803          |53.1   |C123 |S        |
|35.0 |0     |0    |373450          |8.05   |     |S        |
|null |0     |0    |330877          |8.4583 |     |Q        |
|54.0 |0     |0    |17463           |51.8625|E46  |S        |
|2.0  |3     |1    |349909          |21.075 |     |S        |
|27.0 |0     |2    |347742          |11.1333|     |S        |
|14.0 |1     |0    |237736          |30.0708|     |C        |
+-----+------+-----+----------------+-------+-----+---------+
```

3. For the continuous variables, let's try to understand the central tendency and spread of the variables:

```
/* Mean value of Fare charged to board Titanic Ship using
MultiVariateStatisticalSummary */
 val fare_Details_Df = titanic_data.select("Fare")
 val fareObservations = fare_Details_Df.map{row =>
   Vectors.dense(row.getDouble(0))}
 val summary_Fare:MultivariateStatisticalSummary =
    Statistics.colStats(fareObservations)
println("Mean of Fare: "+summary_Fare.mean)

// Other way of finding the mean
 val fare_DetailsRdd = fare_Details_Df.map{row =>
                       row.getDouble(0)}
 val meanValue = fare_DetailsRdd.mean()
 println("Mean Value of Fare From RDD: "+meanValue)

// Median of the variable Fare
 val countOfFare = fare_DetailsRdd.count()
 val sortedFare_Rdd = fare_DetailsRdd.sortBy(fareVal => fareVal )
 val sortedFareRdd_WithIndex = sortedFare_Rdd.zipWithIndex()
 val median_Fare = if(countOfFare%2 ==1)
 sortedFareRdd_WithIndex.filter{case(fareVal:Double, index:Long) =>
index == (countOfFare-1)/2}.first._1
   else{
   val elementAtFirstIndex =
      sortedFareRdd_WithIndex.filter{case(fareVal:Double,
      index:Long) => index == (countOfFare/2)-1}.first._1
   val elementAtSecondIndex =
   sortedFareRdd_WithIndex.filter{case(fareVal:Double,index:Long)
   => index == (countOfFare/2)}.first._1
   (elementAtFirstIndex+elementAtSecondIndex)/2.0
 }
   println("Median of Fare variable is: "+median_Fare)

// Mode of the variable Fare
 val fareDetails_WithCount =
 fare_Details_Df.groupBy("Fare").count()
 val maxOccurrence_CountsDf =
 fareDetails_WithCount.select(max("count")).alias("MaxCount")
 val maxOccurrence = maxOccurrence_CountsDf.first().getLong(0)
 val fares_AtMaxOccurrence =
 fareDetails_WithCount.filter(fareDetails_WithCount("count") ===
maxOccurrence)
  if(fares_AtMaxOccurrence.count() == 1)
  println ("Mode of Fare variable is:
  "+fares_AtMaxOccurrence.first().getDouble(0))
```

```
  else {
    val modeValues = fares_AtMaxOccurrence.collect().map{row =>
                        row.getDouble(0)}
    println("Fare variable has more 1 mode: ")
    modeValues.foreach(println)
  }
//Spread of the variable
println("Variance is: "+summary_Fare.variance)
```

The following is the output:

```
Mean of Fare: [32.20420796857466]
Mean Value of Fare From RDD: 32.20420796857464
Median of Fare variable is: 14.4542
Mode of Fare variable is: 8.05
Variance is: [2469.436845743116]
```

4. For the nominal variables, let's try to understand the frequency distribution of each category. Here is the code for the same:

```
// Univariate analysis for Categorical data
val class_Details_Df = titanic_data.select("Pclass")
val count_OfRows = class_Details_Df.count()
println("Count of Pclass rows: "+count_OfRows)
val classDetails_GroupedCount =
class_Details_Df.groupBy("Pclass").count()
val classDetails_PercentageDist =
classDetails_GroupedCount.withColumn("PercentDistribution",
classDetails_GroupedCount("count")/count_OfRows)
classDetails_PercentageDist.show()
```

The following is the output:

```
Count of Pclass rows: 891
+------+-----+-------------------+
|Pclass|count|PercentDistribution|
+------+-----+-------------------+
|     1|  216|0.24242424242424243|
|     2|  184|0.20650953984287318|
|     3|  491| 0.5510662177328844|
+------+-----+-------------------+
```

How it works...

Initially, the dataset is loaded as a CSV file with
the `sqlContext.read.format("com.databricks.spark.csv").option("header",`
`"true").option("inferSchema","true").load("hdfs://namenode:9000/titanic`
`_data.csv")` statement. The schema is inferred and the statement
`titanic_data.show(10)` displays the first 10 rows of all the available fields. We
identified that the variable `Fare` is continuous and performed analysis on it.

Next, as part of the data analysis, the `Fare` details are selected using the
`titanic_data.select("Fare")` statement. The `fare_Details_Df` statement is
converted to an RDD of vectors, that is, `fareObservations`. The
`Statistics.colStats(fareObservations)` statement generates a statistical summary
of the `Fare` variable. Now, the mean is obtained using `summary_Fare.mean`. The mean is
also calculated using an alternative way by converting `fare_Details_Df` to `rdd` and
invoking the `mean` function on the `rdd` as `fare_DetailsRdd.mean()`.

Now, to calculate the median, there is no built-in function available with DataFrames or
RDDs. The `fare_DetailsRdd` variable is sorted using the
`fare_DetailsRdd.sortBy(fareVal => fareVal )` statement. Next, for the sorted `rdd`,
indices are generated as `sortedFare_Rdd.zipWithIndex()`. If the number of rows,
`countOfFare`, is odd, then the value at the index `(countOfFare-1)/2` is the median. If
the `countOfFare` value is `even`, then the mean of the values at indices
`(countOfFare/2)-1` and `countOfFare/2` becomes the median.

For calculating the mode, first the `Fare` values are grouped and `count` is calculated using
the `fare_Details_Df.groupBy("Fare").count()` statement. Next, from
the `fareDetails_WithCount` DataFrame, the maximum count is obtained as
`fareDetails_WithCount.select(max("count"))`. Once the maximum count is known,
the fare values with maximum count are obtained using the
`fareDetails_WithCount.filter(fareDetails_WithCount("count") ===`
`maxOccurrence)` statement. The `fares_AtMaxOccurrence` DataFrame contains mode
values for the variable `Fare`, which can be 1 or > 1. The calculated `summary_Fare`, which is
of type `MultivariateStatisticalSummary`, also contains the measure `variance`, which
is directly displayed as `summary_Fare.variance`.

Finally, for the `nominal` variable `Pclass`, the frequency distribution is calculated by
aggregating the `Pclass` categories and obtaining the `Count` and `Count%` against each
category.

There's more...

In the preceding recipe, we saw how to perform univariate analysis on the continuous variables. Statistics such as `min`, `max`, `count`, `man`, and `stddev` can also be obtained using `describe`. Apart from variance and standard deviation, there are also other measures, such as range and interquartile range which explain the spread of the variable. The distribution of the variable and outliers can be identified using box plot and histograms. Since Spark doesn't have support for visualization, sample data from RDDs can be collected on the driver and the plots can be visualized in PySpark.

See also

Please refer to `Chapter 1`, *Big Data Analytics with Spark* to get familiar with Spark and refresh your knowledge of basic statistics and distributions. Also refer to `Chapter 2`, *Tricky Statistics with Spark* to understand how to apply statistical functions of DataFrames/RDDs in Spark.

Bivariate analysis

Bivariate analysis finds out the relationship between two variables. In this, we always look for association and disassociation between variables at a predefined significance level. This analysis could be performed for any combination of categorical and continuous variables. The various combinations can be: both the variables categorical, categorical and continuous, and continuous and continuous.

Getting ready

To step through this recipe, you will need a running Spark cluster in any one of the modes, that is, local, standalone, YARN, or Mesos. For installing Spark on a standalone cluster, please refer to `http://spark.apache.org/docs/latest/spark-standalone.html`. Also, include the Spark MLlib package in the `build.sbt` file so that it downloads the related libraries and the API can be used. Install Hadoop (optionally), Scala, and Java.

How to do it...

1. After univariate analysis, let's try to perform bivariate analysis on various combinations of continuous and categorical variables. Here is the code:

```
import org.apache.spark._
import org.apache.spark.sql._
import org.apache.spark.sql.functions._
import org.apache.spark.sql.DataFrameNaFunctions
import org.apache.spark.sql.types._
import org.apache.spark.mllib.linalg.Vectors
import org.apache.spark.mllib.stat.
{MultivariateStatisticalSummary, Statistics}
object Bivariate_Analysis {
  def main(args:Array[String]): Unit = {
    val conf = new SparkConf()
      .setMaster("spark://master:7077")
      .setAppName("Bivariate_Analysis")
    val sc = new SparkContext(conf)
    val sqlContext = new SQLContext(sc)
    import sqlContext.implicits._
//Loading data
    val titanic_data =
sqlContext.read.format("com.databricks.spark.csv")
      .option("header", "true")
      .option("inferSchema", "true")
.load("hdfs://namenode:9000/titanic_data.csv")

//Correlation and Covariance between Age and Fare
val correlated_value_AgeFare = titanic_data.stat.corr("Age",
"Fare")
val covariance_AgeFare = titanic_data.stat.cov("Age","Fare")
println("Correlation Value For Age and Fare:
"+correlated_value_AgeFare)
println("Covariance For Age and Fare: "+ covariance_AgeFare)

//Correlation and Covariance between Pclass and Fare
val correlated_value_PclassFare =
titanic_data.stat.corr("Pclass", "Fare")
val covariance_PclassFare =
titanic_data.stat.cov("Pclass","Fare")
println("Correlation Value For Pclass and Fare:
"+correlated_value_PclassFare)
println("Covariance For Pclass and Fare: "+
covariance_PclassFare)
  }
}
```

The following is the output:

```
Correlation Value For Age and Fare: 0.135515853527051
Covariance For Age and Fare: 118.49631587080917

Correlation Value For Pclass and Fare: -0.5494996199439078
Covariance For Pclass and Fare: -22.8301961700652
```

2. The relationship between two categorical variables can be determined using a two-way table. This table is created by calculating `count` and `count%`. The row represents the category of one variable and the columns represent the categories of the other variable. Here is the code:

```
// Creating two-way table between Pclass and Sex variables
println("Frequency distribution of Pclass against variable Sex:")
val twoWayTable_PclassSex = titanic_data.stat.crosstab("Pclass", "Sex")
twoWayTable_PclassSex.show()
// Creating two-way table between Sex and Embarked variables
println("Frequency distribution of Sex variable against Embarked:")
titanic_data.stat.crosstab("Sex","Embarked").show()
```

The following is the output:

```
Frequency distribution of Pclass against variable Sex:
+----------+------+----+
|Pclass_Sex|female|male|
+----------+------+----+
|         2|    76| 108|
|         1|    94| 122|
|         3|   144| 347|
+----------+------+----+

Frequency distribution of Sex variable against Embarked:
+------------+---+---+---+---+
|Sex_Embarked|  C|  Q|  S|   |
+------------+---+---+---+---+
|        male| 95| 41|441|  0|
|      female| 73| 36|203|  2|
+------------+---+---+---+---+
```

3. Let's try to test the statistical significance of the relationship between the variables in the above two-way table generated for `Pclass` and `Sex` as follows:

```
val PclassSex_Array = twoWayTable_PclassSex
 .drop("Pclass_Sex")
 .collect()
 .map{row => val female = row.getLong(0).toDouble
    val male = row.getLong(1).toDouble
  (female,male)}
val femaleValues = PclassSex_Array.map{case(female, male) =>
                   female}
val maleValues = PclassSex_Array.map{case(female, male) => male}
val goodnessOfFitTestResult =
Statistics.chiSqTest(Matrices.dense(
twoWayTable_PclassSex.count().toInt,
twoWayTable_PclassSex.columns.length-1,
femaleValues ++ maleValues ))
println("Chi Square Test Value: "+goodnessOfFitTestResult)
```

The following is the output:

```
Chi Square Test Value: Chi squared test summary:
method: pearson
degrees of freedom = 2
statistic = 16.971499095517114
pValue = 2.0638864348232477E-4
Very strong presumption against null hypothesis: the occurrence of
the outcomes is statistically independent..
```

4. Now, let's try to perform analysis between the `Pclass` and `Fare` variables where `Pclass` is nominal and `Fare` is continuous:

```
// Analysis between categorical and continuous variables
titanic_data.groupBy("Pclass").agg(sum("Fare"), count("Fare"),
max("Fare"), min("Fare"), stddev("Fare") ).show()
```

The following is the output:

```
Summary Of Fare value per each Pclass category:
```

Pclass	sum(Fare)	count(Fare)	max(Fare)	min(Fare)
1	18177.412500000006	216	512.3292	0.0
2	3801.8417	184	73.5	0.0
3	6714.695100000002	491	69.55	0.0

```
+------------------+
|stddev_samp       |
+------------------+
|78.38037264672882 |
|13.41739875614934 |
|11.778141704387306|
+------------------+
```

How it works...

Initially, the dataset is loaded as a CSV file with the
`sqlContext.read.format("com.databricks.spark.csv").option("header",`
`"true").option("inferSchema","true").load("hdfs://namenode:9000/titanic`
`_data.csv")` statement and the schema is also inferred. Next, for continuous `Age` and
`Fare` variables, correlation is obtained using the `val correlated_value_AgeFare =`
`titanic_data.stat.corr("Age", "Fare")` statement. Also, the co-variance is obtained
as `val covariance_AgeFare = titanic_data.stat.cov("Age","Fare")`.
Correlation takes values between −1 and +1. −1 indicates perfect negative linear correlation,
+1 indicates perfect positive linear correlation and 0 indicates no correlation. The
correlation value of `0.136` specifies weak positive correlation between the `Age` and `Fare`
variables.

Next, the correlation value of `-0.55` between `Pclass` and `Fare` variables indicates that
they are negatively correlated. However, from the description of the dataset, `Pclass` of 1
indicates upper class, 2 indicates middle class, and 3 indicates lower class, which means
when `Pclass` value is higher, that is, 3, `fare` is low and this satisfies the hypothesis that for
lower class, the ticket fare should be low. Covariance also indicates how two variables
change or vary with respect to each other, that is, it explains the dependency between two
variables. In fact, it is difficult to compare co-variances among datasets that have different
scales. Correlation addresses this by normalizing the co-variance to the product of the
standard deviations of the variables.

Next, the relationship between the categorical variables `Pclass` and `Sex` is analyzed by
creating a two-way table which represents the count of males and females for each `Pclass`
category using the `titanic_data.stat.crosstab("Pclass", "Sex").show()`
statement. The first row indicates that there are 76 females and 108 males under `Pclass2`.
Similarly, for the variables `Sex` and `Embarked` the
`titanic_data.stat.crosstab("Sex","Embarked").show()` table is created. The first
row indicates that under males, there are 95 embarked as `C`, 41 embarked as `Q`, and 441
embarked as `S`.

A chi-square test assesses whether the evidence in the sample is strong enough to generalize a relationship for a large population. From the frequency distribution table created for `Pclass` and `Sex`, the column `Pclass_Sex` is dropped and the DataFrame is converted to `Array[(Double,Double)]` represented by `PclassSex_Array`. The female values and male values are generated into two separate arrays as `val femaleValues = PclassSex_Array.map{case(female, male) => female}` and `val maleValues = PclassSex_Array.map{case(female, male) => male}`. The chi-square test is invoked by constructing `DenseMatrix` from the `femaleValues` and `maleValues` lists with the `val goodnessOfFitTestResult = Statistics.chiSqTest(Matrices.dense( twoWayTable_PclassSex.count().toInt, twoWayTable_PclassSex.columns.length-1, femaleValues ++ maleValues))` statement.

Finally, between the `Pclass` and `Fare` variables which are categorical and continuous, statistical measures such as `min`, `max`, `sum`, `count`, and `stddev` are determined for each `Pclass` category using the `titanic_data.groupBy("Pclass").agg(sum("Fare"), count("Fare"), max("Fare"), min("Fare"), stddev("Fare")).show()` statement.

There's more...

In the preceding recipe, we saw how to perform bivariate analysis on different combination of variables such as continuous and continuous, categorical and categorical, and, finally, categorical and continuous. The relationship between continuous variables can be determined using a scatter plot. Since Spark doesn't have support for visualization, sample data from RDDs can be collected on the driver and the plots can be visualized in PySpark.

Between the categorical variables, the statistical significance is derived by a chi-square test, which is based on the difference between the expected and observed frequencies in one or more categories in the two-way table. There are also other statistical measures which analyze the power of relationships, such as Cramer's V for nominal categorical variables and Mantel-Haenszel Chi-Square for ordinal categorical variables.

Also, for categorical and continuous variables, the statistical significance is known by performing a Z-test, T-test, or ANOVA. A Z-test/T-test determines whether the means of two groups are statistically different from each other or not. ANOVA indicates whether the averages of more than two groups are statistically different. As of now, Spark doesn't have support for performing the above-mentioned tests natively; either one can write code for the same or sample data from rdds can be taken and the measures can be applied at the Spark driver using Python.

See also

Please refer to `Chapter 2`, *Tricky Statistics with Spark* to understand how to apply statistical functions of DataFrames/rdds in Spark. Also refer to the earlier *Univariate analysis* recipe to understand the types of analysis on single variables.

Missing value treatment

Missing data in the training dataset can reduce the fitness of a model or can lead to a biased model because we have not analyzed the behavior and relationship with other variables correctly. This could also lead to wrong predictions or classifications. The reasons for the occurrence of the missing values could be that while extracting data from multiple sources, there is a possible chance to have missing data. Hence, using some hashing procedure ensures that the data extraction is correct. The errors that occur at the time of data collection are tougher to correct as the values might miss at random and the missing values might also depend on the unobserved predictors.

Getting ready

To step through this recipe, you will need a running Spark cluster in any one of the modes, that is, local, standalone, YARN, or Mesos. For installing Spark on a standalone cluster, please refer `http://spark.apache.org/docs/latest/spark-standalone.html`. Also, include the Spark MLlib package in the `build.sbt` file so that it downloads the related libraries and the API can be used. Install Hadoop (optionally), Scala, and Java.

How to do it...

1. Let's take an example of load prediction data. Here is what the sample data looks like:

Loan_ID	Gender	Married	Dependents	Education	Self_Employed	ApplicantIncome	CoapplicantIncome	LoanAmount	Loan_Amount_Term	Credit_History	Property_Area	Loan_Status
LP001002	Male	No	0	Graduate	No	5849	0		360	1	Urban	Y
LP001003	Male	Yes	1	Graduate	No	4583	1508	128	360	1	Rural	N
LP001005	Male	Yes	0	Graduate	Yes	3000	0	66	360	1	Urban	Y

Please download the data from the following location: `https://github.c om/ChitturiPadma/datasets/blob/master/Loan_Prediction_Data.csv` .

The total record count is `614`.

2. The preceding data contains numeric as well as categorical data. The data resides in HDFS. Here is the code which loads the data and obtains a summary on the numeric fields:

```
import org.apache.spark._
import org.apache.spark.sql._
import org.apache.spark.sql.functions._
import org.apache.spark.sql.DataFrameNaFunctions
import org.apache.spark.sql.types._
import org.apache.spark.mllib.linalg.Vectors
import org.apache.spark.mllib.stat.
{MultivariateStatisticalSummary, Statistics}

object MissingValue_Treatment {
def main(args:Array[String]): Unit = {
    val conf = new SparkConf()
      .setMaster("spark://master:7077")
      .setAppName("MissingValue_Treatment")
    val sc = new SparkContext(conf)
    val sqlContext = new SQLContext(sc)
    import sqlContext.implicits._
    //Loading data
    val loan_Data = sqlContext.read.format
("com.databricks.spark.csv")
      .option("header", "true")
      .option("inferSchema", "true")
.load("hdfs://namenode:9000/Loan_Prediction_Data.csv")
   val summary = loan_Data.describe()
   summary.show() }}
```

The following is the output:

```
+-------+-----------------+------------------+------------------+
|summary|  ApplicantIncome| CoapplicantIncome|        LoanAmount|
+-------+-----------------+------------------+------------------+
|  count|              614|               614|               592|
|   mean|5403.459283387622|1621.2457980271008|146.41216216216216|
| stddev|6109.041673387179|2926.2483692241885| 85.58732523570544|
|    min|              150|               0.0|                 9|
|    max|            81000|           41667.0|               700|
```

```
+-------+----------------+-------------------+------------------+-
+----------------+-------------------+
| Loan_Amount_Term| Credit_History   |
+----------------+-------------------+
|      600       |       564         |
|342.0           |0.8421985815602837 |
|65.12040985461256|0.3648783192364048 |
|12              |0                  |
|480             |1                  |
+----------------+-------------------+
```

3. From the preceding results, here are the few inferences:

```
LoanAmount has (614-592) = 22 missing values
Loan_Amount_Term has (614-600) = 14 missing values
Credit_History has (614 - 564) 50 missing values.
```

The ApplicantIncome and CoapplicantIncome distribution seems to be as per the expectation.

4. The rows containing missing values in the specified columns can be deleted as follows:

```
val newDf_afterDroppedRows =
loan_Data.na.drop(Seq("LoanAmount",
"Loan_Amount_Term", "Credit_History"))
println("Total Rows Count after Deleting null value records:
"+newDf_afterDroppedRows.count())
```

The following is the output:

```
Total Rows Count after Deleting null value records: 529
```

5. The missing values in columns can be replaced with a specified value as follows:

```
val schemaString =
  "Loan_ID,Gender,Married,Dependents,Education,
    Self_Employed,ApplicantIncome,
CoapplicantIncome,LoanAmount,Loan_Amount_Term,
   Credit_History,Property_Area,Loan_Status"
val schema = schemaString.split(",").map{
  field =>
if(field == "ApplicantIncome" || field == "CoapplicantIncome" ||
field == "LoanAmount" || field == "Loan_Amount_Term" || field ==
"Credit_History")
   StructField(field, DoubleType)
```

```
    else
     StructField(field, StringType)
   }
val schema_Applied = StructType(schema)
val  loan_Data =
sqlContext.read.format("com.databricks.spark.csv")
      .option("header","true")

   .schema(schema_Applied).load("hdfs://namenode:9000/
   loan_prediction_data.csv")
 /* Fill missing values (null or NaN) with a
   specific value for  all columns */
  val filledWith_half = loan_Data.na.fill(0.5)
/* Fill missing values (null or NaN) with a specific
 value for certain columns */
 val filledWith_halfFewColumns = loan_Data.na.fill(0.5,
 Seq("Credit_History"))
/* Fill missing values of each column with specified value */
   val fill_FewColumns = loan_Data.na.fill(
     Map(
       "ApplicantIncome" -> 1000.0,
       "LoanAmount" -> 500.0,
           "Credit_History" -> 0.5
     ) ) } }
```

6. The missing values can also be imputed with the measures of central tendency. Here is the code which inputs the mean into the missing values:

```
val df_CreditHistoryNull =
    loan_Data.filter(loan_Data("Credit_History").isNull)
 println("Missing rows for Credit_History:
   "+df_CreditHistoryNull.count)
val mean_CreditHist = loan_Data.select(mean("Credit_History"))
   .first()(0).asInstanceOf[Double]
val fill_MissingValues_CrediHist =
   loan_Data.na.fill(mean_CreditHist,Seq("Credit_History"))

println("After replacing the mean for Credit History..."+
fill_MissingValues_CrediHist.filter(fill_MissingValues_CrediHist
("Credit_History").isNull).count)
```

   The following is the output:

```
 Missing rows for Credit_History: 50
 After replacing the mean for Credit History...0
```

How it works...

Initially, we imported the data into Spark and the summary on the data reveals that the field `LoanAmount` has 22 missing values, `Loan_Amount_Term` has 14 missing values, and `Credit_History` has 50 missing values. The `loan_Data.na.fill(0.5)` line replaces the null or NaN values in all columns with `0.5`. The next line `loan_Data.na.fill(0.5, Seq("Credit_History"))` replaces null or NaN values in the `Credit_History` column with `0.5`. Similarly, the `loan_Data.na.fill(Map("ApplicantIncome" -> 1000.0,"LoanAmount" -> 500.0,"Credit_History" -> 0.5))` line takes a map of key-value pairs where the key is the column name and the value contains either `int`, `float`, `string`, or `double` type data that needs to replace the null or NaN entries.

Next, the missing values for `Credit_History` are replaced with the mean of the remaining values. The `loan_Data.select(mean("Credit_History")).first()(0).asInstanceOf[Double]` line generates the mean of the `Credit_History` column. The `loan_Data.na.fill(mean_CreditHist,Seq("Credit_History"))` line replaces the missing values with the calculated mean.

The missing values can be treated in several ways. The first approach is to delete observations where any of the variables is missing. This we term it as listwise deletion. The second approach is pairwise deletion, where we perform analysis with all cases in which the variables of interest are present. This approach keeps as many cases available for analysis but uses a different sample size for different variables.

There's more...

In the preceding discussion of treating missing values, if we remove the observations where any of the variables is missing with the likewise deletion approach, it reduces the power of the model because it reduces the sample size. Similarly, the pairwise deletion approach uses a different sample size for different variables, which also affects the model output. The observations are deleted when the nature of the missing data is *missing completely at random*.

The other way of dealing with missing values is imputation, which is a method to fill in the missing values with estimated ones. Mean/mode/median imputation is one of the most frequently used methods, which replaces the missing data for a given attribute by the mean or median (quantitative attribute) or mode (qualitative attribute) of all known values of that variable.

See also

Please refer `Chapter 1`, *Big Data Analytics with Spark* to get familiar with Spark. Also visit the earlier *Univariate analysis* and *Bivariate analysis* recipes to understand the types of analysis on a single variable and two variables.

Outlier detection

Outliers are infrequent observations, that is, the data points that do not appear to follow the characteristic distribution of the rest of the data. They appear far away and diverge from the overall pattern of the data. These might occur due to measurement errors or other anomalies which result in wrong estimations. Outliers can be univariate and multivariate. Univariate outliers can be determined by looking at the distribution of a single variable whereas multivariate outliers are present in an *n*-dimensional space which can be found by looking at the distributions in multi-dimensions.

Getting ready

To step through this recipe, you will need a running Spark cluster in any one of the modes, that is, local, standalone, YARN, or Mesos. For installing Spark on a standalone cluster, please refer `http://spark.apache.org/docs/latest/spark-standalone.html`. Also, include the Spark MLlib package in the `build.sbt` file so that it downloads the related libraries and the API can be used. Install Hadoop (optionally), Scala, and Java.

How to do it...

We'll see how to detect outliers using the following code snippets:

1. Let's take the `titanic` dataset. Please download the data from the following location:

   `https://github.com/ChitturiPadma/datasets/blob/master/titanic_data.csv`
   .

   The data contains numeric and categorical fields. Let's try to load the dataset and see the summary statistics on the dataset. Here is the code for the same:

```
import org.apache.spark._
import org.apache.spark.sql._
import org.apache.spark.sql.functions._
import org.apache.spark.sql.DataFrameNaFunctions
import org.apache.spark.sql.types._
object Outlier_Detection {
  def main(args:Array[String]): Unit = {
    val conf = new SparkConf()
      .setMaster("spark://master:7077")
      .setAppName("Outlier_Detection")
     val sc = new SparkContext(conf)
     val sqlContext = new SQLContext(sc)
     import sqlContext.implicits._
 //Loading data
val titanic_data =
sqlContext.read.format("com.databricks.spark.csv")
    .option("header", "true")
    .option("inferSchema","true")
    .load("hdfs://namenode:9000/titanic_data.csv")
  val summary = titanic_data.describe()
  summary.show() } }
```

The following is the output:

```
+-------+-----------------+-------------------+------------------
|summary|      PassengerId|           Survived|            Pclass|
+-------+-----------------+-------------------+------------------
|  count|              891|                891|               891|
|   mean|            446.0| 0.3838383838383838| 2.308641975308642|
| stddev|257.3538420152301|0.48659245426485737|0.8360712409770491|
|    min|                1|                  0|                 1|
|    max|              891|                  1|                 3|
+-------+-----------------+-------------------+------------------+
+-----------------+-------------------+------------------+
```

```
|SibSp              |       Parch        |        Fare       |
+------------------+-------------------+-------------------+
|891               |891                |891                |
|0.5230078563411896|0.38159371492704824|32.204207968574615|
|1.102743432293432 |0.8060572211299486 |49.6934285971809   |
|0                 |0                  |0.0                |
|8                 |6                  |512.3292           |
+------------------+-------------------+-------------------+
+------------------+
|Age               |
+------------------+
|714               |
|29.69911764705882 |
|14.526497332334039|
|0.42              |
|80.0              |
+------------------+
```

2. From the preceding values of the variable `Fare`, we observe that the mean of `891` values is `32.204`, whereas the maximum value is `512.3292`, which has huge variation from the mean and it potentially looks like an outlier. The minimum value is 0 and maximum value is `512.292`, which indicates that the range is `512.292`. Now, let's try to analyze the distribution of `Fare` values across multiple intervals:

```scala
val fareVaues_AtDiffr_Itervals =
scala.collection.mutable.ListBuffer[Long]()
val  minValue = 0.0
val maxValue = 513
val bins = 5
val range = (maxValue - minValue)/5.0
var minCounter = minValue
var maxCounter = range
while(minCounter < maxValue)
  {
    val valuesBetweenRange =
      titanic_data.filter(titanic_data("Fare").between
      (minCounter,maxCounter))
     fareVaues_AtDiffr_Itervals.+=(valuesBetweenRange.count())
    minCounter = maxCounter
    maxCounter = maxCounter+range
  }
println("Fare Values at Different Ranges:")
fareVaues_AtDiffr_Itervals.foreach(println)
```

The following is the output:

```
Fare Values at Different Ranges:
838
33
17
0
3
```

3. The preceding output shows that out of 891, 838 values, that is, 94% of the `Fare` values, are in the range of `[0 - 102.6]` and only three values, that is, 0.3% of them, are in the range of `[410.4 - 513]`. By assuming that the observations obey normal distribution, the data points which fall above `mean+2(stddev)` and below `mean - 2(stddev)` are considered as outliers. The constant can be either 2 or 3 depending on the extent to which values are distributed. Here is the code to detect outliers:

```
val meanFare = titanic_data.select(mean("Fare"))
    .first()(0).asInstanceOf[Double]
val stddevFare = titanic_data.select(stddev("Fare"))
    .first()(0).asInstanceOf[Double]
val upper_threshold = meanFare + 2*stddevFare
val lower_threshold = meanFare - 2*stddevFare
val fareValues_MoreThanUpperthrshold =
    titanic_data.select("Fare").filter(titanic_data("Fare")
        > upper_threshold)
 val fareValues_LessThanLowerthrshold =
    titanic_data.select("Fare").filter(titanic_data("Fare") <
        lower_threshold)
 val summary_FareValuesMoreThanUppr =
    fareValues_MoreThanUpperthrshold.describe()
println("Summary Of Fare Values Greater Than Upper
        Threshold:")
summary_FareValuesMoreThanUppr.show()
val summary_FareValuesLessThanLowr =
    fareValues_LessThanLowerthrshold.describe()
println("Summary Of Fare Values Less Than Lower Threshold:")
summary_FareValuesLessThanLowr.show()
```

The following is the output:

```
Summary Of Fare Values Greater Than Upper Threshold:
+-------+------------------+
|summary|              Fare|
+-------+------------------+
|  count|                38|
|   mean|216.28245526315789|
| stddev| 99.81881725000063|
|    min|            133.65|
|    max|          512.3292|
+-------+------------------+

Summary Of Fare Values Less Than Lower Threshold:
+-------+----+
|summary|Fare|
+-------+----+
|  count|   0|
|   mean|null|
| stddev|null|
|    min|null|
|    max|null|
+-------+----+
```

4. Let's take the upper threshold and lower threshold as mean+3 (stddev) and mean-3(stddev) and see the how the outliers are detected:

```
val upper_threshold1 = meanFare + 3*stddevFare
val lower_threshold1 = meanFare - 3*stddevFare
val fareValues_MoreThanUpperthrshold1 =
    titanic_data.select("Fare").filter(titanic_data("Fare") >
    upper_threshold1)
val fareValues_LessThanLowerthrshold1 =
    titanic_data.select("Fare").filter(titanic_data("Fare") <
            lower_threshold1)
val summary_FareValuesMoreThanUppr1 =
    fareValues_MoreThanUpperthrshold1.describe()
 println("Summary Of Fare Values Greater Than Upper
        Threshold:")
summary_FareValuesMoreThanUppr1.show()

 val summary_FareValuesLessThanLowr1 =
 fareValues_LessThanLowerthrshold1.describe()
 println("Summary Of Fare Values Less Than Lower Threshold:")
 summary_FareValuesLessThanLowr1.show()
```

The following is the output:

```
Summary Of Fare Values Greater Than Upper Threshold:
+-------+------------------+
|summary|              Fare|
+-------+------------------+
|  count|                20|
|   mean|         279.308545|
| stddev|102.35339148065432|
|    min|          211.3375|
|    max|          512.3292|
+-------+------------------+

Summary Of Fare Values Less Than Lower Threshold:
+-------+----+
|summary|Fare|
+-------+----+
|  count|   0|
|   mean|null|
| stddev|null|
|    min|null|
|    max|null|
+-------+----+
```

5. We can also standardize the values by calculating z-scores as `(x-mean)/stddev` which force fits standard normal distribution and can apply the same technique. Here is the code:

```
val titanic_Data_StdFareValues =
  titanic_data.withColumn("StdFareValue", (titanic_data("Fare")-
  meanFare)/stddevFare)
val mean_FareStdvalue =
  titanic_Data_StdFareValues.select(mean("StdFareValue"))
  .first()(0).asInstanceOf[Double]
val stddev_FareStdvalue =
  titanic_Data_StdFareValues.select(stddev("StdFareValue")
  ).first()(0).asInstanceOf[Double]
val upper_threshold_std = mean_FareStdvalue +
  3*stddev_FareStdvalue
val lower_threshold_std = mean_FareStdvalue -
  3*stddev_FareStdvalue
val fareValues_MoreThanUpperthrshold_std =
  titanic_Data_StdFareValues.select("StdFareValue")
  .filter(titanic_Data_StdFareValues("StdFareValue") >
  upper_threshold_std)
val fareValues_LessThanLowerthrshold_std =
  titanic_Data_StdFareValues.select("StdFareValue")
  .filter(titanic_Data_StdFareValues("StdFareValue") <
```

```
          lower_threshold_std)

     val summary_FareValuesMoreThanUppr_Std =
        fareValues_MoreThanUpperthrshold_std.describe()
        println("Summary Of Standardized Fare Values Greater Than
        Upper Threshold")
     summary_FareValuesMoreThanUppr_Std.show()
     val summary_FareValuesLessThanLowr_Std =
        fareValues_LessThanLowerthrshold_std.describe()
     println("Summary Of Standardized Fare Values Less Than Lower
        Threshold")
     summary_FareValuesLessThanLowr_Std.show()
```

The following is the output:

```
Summary Of Fare Values Greater Than Upper Threshold:
+-------+------------------+
|summary|      StdFareValue|
+-------+------------------+
|  count|                20|
|   mean| 4.972575730977911|
| stddev|2.0596967118195746|
|    min| 3.604768217614745|
|    max| 9.661740104981664|
+-------+------------------+

Summary Of Fare Values Less Than Lower Threshold:
+-------+------------+
|summary|StdFareValue|
+-------+------------+
|  count|           0|
|   mean|        null|
| stddev|        null|
|    min|        null|
|    max|        null|
+-------+------------+
```

6. Here is another statistical technique, **median absolute deviation** (**MAD**), which is a robust measure of variability. We use the median calculated for the variable `Fare` in the *Univariate analysis* recipe, which is `14.4542`. Here is the code for MAD:

```
     def main(args:Array[String]): Unit = {

     val sqlFunc = udf(coder)
     val fare_Details_WithAbsDeviations =
        fare_Details_Df.withColumn("AbsDev_FromMedian",
```

```
    sqlFunc(col("Fare"), lit(median_Fare)))
val fare_AbsDevs_Rdd = fare_Details_WithAbsDeviations.map{row =>
    row.getDouble(1)}
val count = fare_AbsDevs_Rdd.count()
val sortedFareAbsDev_Rdd = fare_AbsDevs_Rdd.sortBy(fareAbsVal =>
    fareAbsVal )
val sortedFare_AbsDevRdd_WithIndex =
    sortedFareAbsDev_Rdd.zipWithIndex()
val median_AbsFareDevs = if(count%2 ==1)
    sortedFare_AbsDevRdd_WithIndex.filter{case(fareAbsVal:Double,
    index:Long) =>    index == (count-1)/2}.first._1
else{
val elementAtFirstIndex =
    sortedFare_AbsDevRdd_WithIndex.filter{case(fareAbsVal:Double,
    index:Long) =>    index == (count/2)-1}.first._1
val elementAtSecondIndex =
    sortedFare_AbsDevRdd_WithIndex.filter{case(fareAbsVal:Double,
    index:Long) =>    index == (count/2)}.first._1
    (elementAtFirstIndex+elementAtSecondIndex)/2.0
}
val mad = 1.4826*median_AbsFareDevs
println("Median Absolute Deviation is:"+mad)}
 //UDF Code
val coder= (fareValue:Double, medianValue:Double) =>
if((fareValue-medianValue)    < 0) -1*(fareValue-medianValue)
else (fareValue-medianValue)
```

The following is the output:

```
Median Absolute Deviation is:10.23616692
```

7. As seen in the earlier case, the outliers lie preceding `median+3(mad)` and following `median-3(mad)`. Here is the code for the same:

```
val upper_mad = median_Fare + 3 * mad
val lower_mad = median_Fare - 3 * mad
val fareValues_MoreThanUpperthrshold_mad=
    titanic_data.select("Fare").filter(titanic_data("Fare") >
    upper_mad)
val fareValues_LessThanLowerthrshold_mad =
    titanic_data.select("Fare").filter(titanic_data("Fare") <
    lower_mad)

val summary_FareValuesMoreThanUppr_MAD =
    fareValues_MoreThanUpperthrshold_mad.describe()
    println("Summary Of Fare Values Greater Than Upper Threshold
    In MAD Approach:")
```

```
summary_FareValuesMoreThanUppr_MAD.show()
val summary_FareValuesLessThanLowr_MAD =
fareValues_LessThanLowerthrshold_mad.describe()
println("Summary Of Fare Values Less Than Lower Threshold In MAD
   Approach:")
summary_FareValuesLessThanLowr_MAD.show()
```

The following is the output:

```
Summary Of Fare Values Greater Than Upper Threshold In MAD Approach:
+-------+------------------+
|summary|              Fare|
+-------+------------------+
|  count|               171|
|   mean|104.41825029239766|
| stddev| 77.85677558392068|
|    min|              46.9|
|    max|          512.3292|
+-------+------------------+

Summary Of Fare Values Less Than Lower Threshold In MAD Approach:
+-------+----+
|summary|Fare|
+-------+----+
|  count|   0|
|   mean|null|
| stddev|null|
|    min|null|
|    max|null|
+-------+----+
```

How it works...

Initially, we imported the `titanic` dataset into Spark and the summary of the data for the variable `Fare` reveals that there are no missing values. Also, we notice that the mean of the values is `32.204`, whereas the maximum value is `512.3292`, indicating the existence of potential outliers. Next, from the minimum value of `0.0` to the maximum value of `512.3292`, we divided the data into five bins and analyzed the frequency of `Fare` values across five intervals, that is, `[0-102.6]`, `[102.6-205.2]`, `[205.2-307.8]`, `[307.8-410.4]`, and `[410.4-513]`.

This is done by running the loop as long as the condition `minCounter < maxValue` is satisfied and values between `minCounter` and `maxCounter` are picked with the statement `titanic_data.filter(titanic_data("Fare").between(minCounter,maxCounter))`. The output indicates that 94% of the values are in the range `[0-102.6]` and 3% of the values in the interval `[410.4-513]`, which increases the confidence for the existence of outliers in the extreme interval, that is, `[410.4 - 513]`.

If a random variable X obeys normal distribution then 68% of the values lie within mean plus or minus `stddev`, 95% of the values lie within mean plus or minus two times `stddev`, and 99% lie within mean plus or minus three times `stddev`. Hence the approach mean plus or minus three or two times `stddev` will detect the outliers. The `titanic_data.select(mean("Fare")).first()(0).asInstanceOf[Double]` statement calculates the mean of the `Fare` variable. The `titanic_data.select(stddev("Fare")).first()(0).asInstanceOf[Double]` line calculates the standard deviation of `Fare`. The upper threshold is calculated as `meanFare + 2*stddevFare` and the lower threshold as `meanFare - 2*stddevFare`. The values above the upper threshold and below the lower threshold are identified with the statements `titanic_data.select("Fare").filter(titanic_data("Fare") > upper_threshold)` and `titanic_data.select("Fare").filter(titanic_data("Fare") < lower_threshold)`. The output of values above the upper threshold specifies that there are a total of 38 values above the 95th percentile and the maximum value among them is `512.3292`. With the same approach, values above `meanFare + 3*stddevFare` and values below `meanFare-3*stddevFare` are identified. The other variation of the approach is to standardize the values, which is done with the `titanic_data.withColumn("StdFareValue", (titanic_data("Fare")-meanFare)/stddevFare)` statement and then the mean plus or minus three times `stddev` approach is applied on the standardized values.

Finally, the MAD technique is applied, which is based on median central tendency. The median of `Fare` values is `14.4542` (please refer the *Univariate analysis* recipe for the calculation). The `fare_Details_Df.withColumn("AbsDev_FromMedian", sqlFunc(col("Fare"),lit(median_Fare)))` statement calculates absolute values for the observations deviating from the median. Next, the median of the absolute deviations is calculated with similar approach of calculating the median as seen in the *Univariate analysis* recipe. Next, the MAD is calculated as `1.4836*(median of absolute deviations)`. The thresholds, median plus or minus three times MAD, are calculated to identify the outliers.

There's more...

In the preceding recipe, we saw statistical techniques for detecting outliers. Outliers can be well identified by visualizing the data, that is, looking at the scatter plot for a single variable or from the box plots. As Spark doesn't have native support for visualization, sample data can be taken and it can be visualized using Python or R.

Although both the statistical approaches, mean plus or minus three times `stddev` and median plus or minus three times MAD, determine the outliers, the MAD is robust and is not affected by the outliers. The central tendency mean and the measure of spread, that is, standard deviation, are strongly impacted by the outliers. In the case of the mean, if one of the observations is infinite, the mean of all values becomes infinite, whereas the median value remains unchanged. The median becomes absurd only when more than 50% of the observations are infinite. Also, MAD is totally immune to the sample size. MAD is multiplied by the content `1.4826`, if the distribution of the data is assumed to be normal. If another distribution is measured then the content is calculated as `1/Q(0.75)` where `Q(0.75)` is the `0.75` quantile of that underlying distribution.

The ways to deal with outliers are similar to the methods of missing values, such as deleting observations, transforming them, binning them, treating them as a separate group, imputing values, and other statistical methods. We can delete outlier values if they occur due to data entry error or data processing error, or outlier observations are very small in number. Transforming variables can also eliminate outliers. The natural log of a value reduces the variation caused by extreme values. Binning is also a form of variable transformation. Similar to the missing value treatment, we can also impute outliers. The measures of central tendency, mean, median, and mode, can be applied. Before imputing values, we should analyze whether it is a natural or artificial outlier. If it is artificial, we can go with imputing values. We can also use a statistical model to predict the values of outlier observation and after that we can impute it with predicted values.

See also

Please refer the *Univariate analysis, Bivariate analysis* and *Missing value treatment* recipes to understand the types of analysis that can be performed on a single variable and two variables and also various ways of imputing missing values.

Use case – analyzing the MovieLens dataset

In the previous recipes, we saw various steps of performing data analysis. In this recipe, let's download the commonly used dataset for movie recommendations. The dataset is known as the MovieLens dataset. The dataset is quite applicable for recommender systems as well as potentially for other machine learning tasks.

Getting ready

To step through this recipe, you will need a running Spark cluster in any one of the modes, that is, local, standalone, YARN, or Mesos. For installing Spark on a standalone cluster, please refer to http://spark.apache.org/docs/latest/spark-standalone.html. Also, include the Spark MLlib package in the build.sbt file so that it downloads the related libraries and the API can be used. Install Hadoop (optionally), Scala, and Java.

How to do it...

Let's see how to analyse the MovieLens dataset.

1. Let's download the MovieLens dataset from the following location: https://drive.google.com/file/d/0Bxr27gVaXO5sRUZnMjBQR0lqNDA/view?usp=sharing.

   The dataset contains 100,000 data points related to ratings given by a set of users to a set of movies. It also contains movie metadata and user profiles.

2. Once you have downloaded the data, unzip it using your terminal as follows:

   ```
   >unzip ml-100k.zip
   inflating: ml-100k/allbut.pl
   inflating: ml-100k/mku.sh
   inflating: ml-100k/README
   ...
   inflating: ml-100k/ub.base
   inflating: ml-100k/ub.test
   ```

3. This will create a directory called ml-100k. Change into this directory and examine the contents. The important files are u.user (user profiles), u.item (movie metadata), and u.data (the ratings given by users to movies).

4. The README file contains more information on the dataset, including the variables present in each data file. We can use the head command to examine the contents of the various files. For example, we can see that the u.user file contains the user ID, age , gender , occupation , and ZIP code fields, separated by a pipe (| character) as follows:

```
>head -5 u.user
  1|24|M|technician|85711
  2|53|F|other|94043
  3|23|M|writer|32067
  4|24|M|technician|43537
  5|33|F|other|15213
```

5. The u.item file contains the movie ID, title, release data, and IMDB link fields and a set of fields related to movie category data. It is also separated by a character as follows:

```
>head -5 u.item
1|Toy Story (1995)|01-Jan-1995||http://us.imdb.com/M/title-exact?
Toy%20
Story%20(1995)|0|0|0|1|1|1|0|0|0|0|0|0|0|0|0|0|0|0|0
2|GoldenEye (1995)|01-Jan-1995||http://us.imdb.com/M/title-
exact?GoldenEye%20(1995)|0|1|1|0|0|0|0|0|0|0|0|0|0|0|0|0|0|1|0|0
3|Four Rooms (1995)|01-Jan-1995||http://us.imdb.com/M/title-
exact?Four%20Rooms%20(1995)|0|0|0|0|0|0|0|0|0|0|0|0|0|0|0|0|0|1|0|0
4|Get Shorty (1995)|01-Jan-1995||http://us.imdb.com/M/title-
exact?Get%20Shorty%20(1995)|0|1|0|0|0|1|0|0|1|0|0|0|0|0|0|0|0|0|0
5|Copycat (1995)|01-Jan-1995||http://us.imdb.com/M/title-
exact?Copycat%20(1995)|0|0|0|0|0|0|1|0|1|0|0|0|0|0|0|0|1|0|0
```

6. Finally, the u.data file contains the user ID , movie ID , rating (1-5 scale) , and timestamp fields is separated by a tab (the \t character) as follows:

```
>head -5 u.data
    196   242   3     881250949
    186   302   3     891717742
    22    377   1     878887116
    244   51    2     880606923
    166   346   1     886397596
```

7. Let's try to load the `u.data` file. Here is the code for the same:

```
import org.apache.spark._
import org.apache.spark.sql._
import org.apache.spark.sql.functions._
import org.apache.spark.sql.DataFrameNaFunctions
import org.apache.spark.sql.types._

object MovieLens_DataAnalysis {
case class MovieLens(userId:String, movieId:String, rating:Int,
timestamp:Long)
def main(args:Array[String]): Unit = {
  val conf = new SparkConf()
    .setMaster("spark://master:7077")
    .setAppName("MovieLens_DataAnalysis")
  val sc = new SparkContext(conf)
  val sqlContext = new SQLContext(sc)
  import sqlContext.implicits._
 //Loading data
  val movieLens_data = sc.textFile("hdfs://namenode:9000/ml-
  100k/u.data")
  val movieLens_DataStructured = movieLens_data.map{record => val
fields = record.split("\t")
      val userId = fields(0)
      val movieId = fields(1)
      val rating = fields(2).toInt
      val timestamp = fields(3).toLong
      MovieLens(userId, movieId, rating, timestamp)
    }
  val movieLens_Df=
 sqlContext.createDataFrame(movieLens_DataStructured)
 pspspps
 println("Movie Lens data:")
  movieLens_Df.show(10)
  }
 }
```

The following is the output:

```
Movie Lens data:
+------+-------+------+---------+
|userId|movieId|rating|timestamp|
+------+-------+------+---------+
|   196|    242|     3|881250949|
|   186|    302|     3|891717742|
|    22|    377|     1|878887116|
|   244|     51|     2|880606923|
|   166|    346|     1|886397596|
|   298|    474|     4|884182806|
|   115|    265|     2|881171488|
|   253|    465|     5|891628467|
|   305|    451|     3|886324817|
|     6|     86|     3|883603013|
+------+-------+------+---------+
```

8. Now let's try to calculate the number of movies that are rated on a scale of 1 to 5. Here is the code:

```
val ratings_Count = movieLens_Df.groupBy("rating").count()
  println("Ratings Count:")
ratings_Count.show()
```

The following is the output:

```
Ratings Count:
+------+-----+
|rating|count|
+------+-----+
|     1| 6110|
|     2|11370|
|     3|27145|
|     4|34174|
|     5|21201|
+------+-----+
```

How it works...

Initially, the dataset is downloaded and all the files are extracted. The files such as u.user, u.item and u.data are identified in the dataset. The u.user file contains user details, u.item contains movie details, and u.data contains ratings information for movies from different users. Since the data is not in structured format, it is loaded into the RDD using the sc.textFile("hdfs://namenode:9000/ml-100k/u.data") statement. After loading the data, each record is split on the tab space \t as val fields = record.split("\t"). The individual fields are extracted as val userId = fields(0), val movieId = fields(1) and so on, and movieLens_DataStructured, which is of type RDD[MovieLens], is created. Now, the movieLens_Df DataFrame is created from the RDD with the sqlContext.createDataFrame (movieLens_DataStructured) statement. The DataFrame is aggregated on the field rating and count is extracted as val ratings_Count = movieLens_Df.groupBy("rating").count().

There's more...

Similar to the above problem, in the subsequent recipes, we'll address some more problems on various datasets.

See also

Please refer to the *Univariate analysis, Bivariate analysis, Missing value treatment,* and *Outlier detection* recipes to understand the types of analysis that can be performed on a single variable and two variables, various ways of imputing missing values and statistical techniques in detecting outliers.

Use case – analyzing the Uber dataset

In the previous recipes, we saw various steps of performing data analysis. In this recipe, let's download the Uber dataset and try to solve some of the analytical questions that arise on such data.

Getting ready

To step through this recipe, you will need a running Spark cluster in any one of the modes, that is, local, standalone, YARN, or Mesos. For installing Spark on a standalone cluster, please refer http://spark.apache.org/docs/latest/spark-standalone.html. Also, include the Spark MLlib package in the build.sbt file so that it downloads the related libraries and the API can be used. Install Hadoop (optionally), Scala, and Java.

How to do it...

In this section, let's see how to analyse the Uber dataset.

1. Let's download the Uber dataset from the following location: https://github.com/ChitturiPadma/datasets/blob/master/uber.csv.

2. The dataset contains four columns: dispatching_base_number, date, active_vehicles, and trips. Let's load the data and see what the records look like with the following code:

```
import org.apache.spark._
import org.apache.spark.sql._
import org.apache.spark.sql.functions._
import org.apache.spark.sql.DataFrameNaFunctions
import org.apache.spark.sql.types._
import org.apache.spark.mllib.linalg.Vectors
import org.apache.spark.mllib.stat.
{MultivariateStatisticalSummary, Statistics}

object Ubser_Dataset_Analysis {
  def main(args:Array[String]): Unit = {
    val conf = new SparkConf()
      .setMaster("spark://master:7077")
      .setAppName("Uber_Dataset_Analysis")
    val sc = new SparkContext(conf)
    val sqlContext = new SQLContext(sc)
    import sqlContext.implicits._
val uber_data = sqlContext.read.format("com.databricks.spark.csv")
      .option("header", "true")
      .option("inferSchema","true").load
        ("hdfs://namenode:9000/uber.csv")
    println("Uber Data:")
    uber_data.show(5) } }
```

The following is the output:

```
Uber Data:
+---------------------+--------+---------------+-----+
|dispatching_base_number|    date|active_vehicles|trips|
+---------------------+--------+---------------+-----+
|               B02512|1/1/2015|            190| 1132|
|               B02765|1/1/2015|            225| 1765|
|               B02764|1/1/2015|           3427|29421|
|               B02682|1/1/2015|            945| 7679|
|               B02617|1/1/2015|           1228| 9537|
+---------------------+--------+---------------+-----+
```

3. Let's try to find the days on which each base has more trips. Here is the code:

```
val uberData_new = uber_data.withColumn("BaseNo_Date",
concat($"dispatching_base_number", lit(":"), $"date"))

val maxTrips_PerBaseAndDate =
uberData_new.groupBy("BaseNo_Date").max("trips")
maxTrips_PerBaseAndDate.show(10)
```

The following is the output:

```
+---------------+----------+
|    BaseNo_Date|max(trips)|
+---------------+----------+
| B02617:1/9/2015|     13165|
|B02512:1/15/2015|      1636|
| B02512:1/5/2015|       984|
|B02598:2/23/2015|      8943|
|B02617:2/23/2015|     11720|
|B02764:1/10/2015|     38864|
|B02512:1/19/2015|      1025|
| B02512:1/9/2015|      1560|
|B02682:1/23/2015|     11767|
|B02682:2/12/2015|     13786|
+---------------+----------+
```

4. Now let's try to find the month on which each basement has more trips. Here is the code:

```
 def main(args:Array[String]): Unit = {
 // Loading data
  .
  .
 // Find the month on which basement has more trips
 val sqlFunc1 = udf(coder1)
 val sqlFunc2 = udf(coder2)
 val uberdata_newMonthCol = uber_data.withColumn("month",
 sqlFunc1(col("date")))
 val uberData_ConcatBaseNo_Month =
 uberdata_newMonthCol.withColumn("BaseNo_Month",
 concat($"dispatching_base_number", lit(":"), $"month"))
 val sumTrips_PerBaseAndMonth =
 uberData_ConcatBaseNo_Month.groupBy("BaseNo_Month").sum("trips")
 val sumTrips_PerBaseMonth_new =
 sumTrips_PerBaseAndMonth.withColumn("BaseNo",
 sqlFunc2(col("BaseNo_Month")))
 val maxTrips_PerBaseMonth =
 sumTrips_PerBaseMonth_new.groupBy("BaseNo").max("sum(trips)")
  .withColumnRenamed("max(sum(trips))","MaxTrips_PerMonth")
 val maxTrips_Final =
 maxTrips_PerBaseMonth.join(sumTrips_PerBaseMonth_new,
 sumTrips_PerBaseMonth_new("BaseNo") ===
 maxTrips_PerBaseMonth("BaseNo") &&
 sumTrips_PerBaseMonth_new("sum(trips)") ===
 maxTrips_PerBaseMonth("MaxTrips_PerMonth")).select
 ("BaseNo_Month","MaxTrips_PerMonth")

 println("Maximum Trips per basement per month:")
 maxTrips_Final.show() }
val coder1 = (dateValue:String) => {
val format =   new java.text.SimpleDateFormat("MM/dd/yyyy")
val formated_Date = format.parse(dateValue)
formated_Date.getMonth()+1
}
val coder2 =(baseMonthConcat:String) => baseMonthConcat.split(":")
(0)
```

The following is the output:

```
Maximum Trips per basement per month

+----------------+----------+
|     baseNo_Date|max(trips)|
```

```
+----------------+----------+
|  B02617:1/9/2015|     13165|
|B02512:1/15/2015|      1636|
|  B02512:1/5/2015|       984|
|B02598:2/23/2015|      8943|
|B02617:2/23/2015|     11720|
|B02764:1/10/2015|     38864|
|B02512:1/19/2015|      1025|
|  B02512:1/9/2015|      1560|
|B02682:1/23/2015|     11767|
|B02682:2/12/2015|     13786|
+----------------+----------+
```

How it works...

Initially, the dataset is loaded in CSV format and the schema is inferred using the `sqlContext.read.format("com.databricks.spark.csv").option("header", "true").option("inferSchema", "true").load("hdfs://namenode:9000/uber.csv")` statement. A new column, `BaseNo_Date`, is created by concatenating the columns `dispatching_base_number` and `date`. The `uberData_new` DataFrame is aggregated on the field `BaseNo_Date` and the maximum of trips is determined using the `uberData_new.groupBy("BaseNo_Date").max("trips")` statement.

Next, to find the month on which each basement has more trips, a new column month is created with the `uber_data.withColumn("month", sqlFunc1(col("date")))` statement. The `uberdata_newMonthCol.withColumn("BaseNo_Month", concat($"dispatching_base_number", lit(":"), $"month"))` statement creates a new column `BaseNo_Month` by concatenating `dispatching_base_number` and `month`. Next, the `uberData_ConcatBaseNo_Month` DataFrame is aggregated on `BaseNo_Month` and sum of trips is calculated. The `sumTrips_PerBaseAndMonth` DataFrame contains aggregated trips across `dispatching_base_number` and `month`. The maximum trips for a particular `dispatching_base_number` and `month` is obtained with the `sumTrips_PerBaseMonth_new.groupBy("BaseNo").max("sum(trips)").withColumnRenamed("max(sum(trips))","MaxTrips_PerMonth")` statement. The `maxTrips_PerBaseMonth.join(sumTrips_PerBaseMonth_new, sumTrips_PerBaseMonth_new("BaseNo") === maxTrips_PerBaseMonth("BaseNo") && sumTrips_PerBaseMonth_new("sum(trips)") === maxTrips_PerBaseMonth("MaxTrips_PerMonth")).select("BaseNo_Month", "MaxTrips_PerMonth")` final statement displays the `dispatching_base_number`, month and maximum trips.

There's more...

In the preceding recipe, we addressed two problem statements using the Spark DataFrame API. When we deal with real-world problems, there is a need for building model on the analyzed data, which is seen in the next chapter.

See also

Please refer the *Univariate analysis*, *Bivariate analysis*, *Missing value treatment*, and *Outlier detection* recipes to understand the types of analysis that can be performed on a single variable and two variables, various ways of imputing missing values and statistical techniques in detecting outliers.

4
Clustering, Classification, and Regression

In this chapter, we will cover the following recipes:

- Introduction
- Applying regression analysis for sales data
    - Variable identification
    - Data exploration
    - Feature engineering
    - Applying linear regression
- Applying logistic regression on bank marketing data
    - Variable identification
    - Data exploration
    - Feature engineering
    - Applying logistic regression
- Real-time intrusion detection using streaming k-means
    - Variable identification
    - Producer code generating real-time data
    - Applying streaming k-means

Introduction

Machine learning is a field of study that gives computers the ability to learn without being explicitly programmed. Many successful applications of machine learning exist already, including systems that analyse past sales data to predict customer behavior, optimizing robot behavior so that a task can be completed using minimum resources and extracting knowledge from bio-informatics data. With the advent of big data, maintaining large collections of data is one thing, but extracting useful information from these collections is even more challenging. The ML system should be able to scale on high volumes of data, the accuracy of the models built would also have to be quite high as the training takes place on large data.

Big data and machine learning take place in three steps—collecting, analyzing, and predicting. For this purpose, the Spark ecosystem supports a wide range of workloads including batch applications, iterative algorithms, interactive queries, and stream processing. The Spark MLlib component offers a variety of scalable ML algorithms.

Supervised learning

Supervised learning deals with training algorithms with labeled data, inputs for which the outcome or target variables are known. It then predicts the outcome/target with the trained model for unseen future data. For example, historical e-mail data will have individual e-mails marked as ham or spam; this data is then used for training a model that can predict future e-mails as ham or spam. Supervised learning problems can be broadly divided into two major areas; classification and regression. Classification deals with predicting categorical variables or classes; for example, whether an e-mail is ham or spam or whether a customer is going to renew a subscription or not in a post-paid telecom subscription. This target variable is discrete and has a predefined set of values.

Regression deals with a target variable, which is continuous. For example, when we need to predict house prices, the target variable price is continuous and doesn't have a predefined set of values. In order to solve a given problem of supervised learning, one has to perform the following steps:

- Determine the objective
- Decide the training data
- Cleaning the training dataset

- Feature extraction
- Training the models
- Validation
- Evaluation of trained model

Unsupervised learning

Unsupervised learning deals with unlabeled data. The objective is to observe the structure of data and find patterns. Tasks like cluster analysis, association rule mining, outlier detection, dimensionality reduction and so on can be modeled as unsupervised learning problems. As the tasks involved in unsupervised learning vary vastly, there is no single process outline that we can follow.

Cluster analysis is a subset of unsupervised learning that aims to create groups of similar items from a set of items. This analysis helps us identify interesting groups of objects that we are interested in. It could be items we encounter in day-to-day life such as movies or songs according to taste, or interests of users in terms of their demography or purchasing patterns.

Applying regression analysis for sales data

Regression analysis is a type of predictive modeling technique which investigates the relationship between variables. This is widely used for forecasting, time series modeling and finding the effect of relationships between the variables. In this, we try to fit a curve/line for the data points such that the differences between the distances of data points from the curve or line is minimized. Linear regression is the mostly frequently used technique. In this technique, the dependent variable is continuous, independent variables can be continuous or discrete, and the nature of the regression line is linear. The equation which is used to predict the value of the target variable is based on the following predictor variables:

```
y = aX +E
y = target variable
X = input variable
a = regression coefficient
E = the error term
```

Regression techniques are driven by three metrics–the number of independent variables, the type of dependent variables, and the shape of the regression line. We can also evaluate the model performance using the metric R-square. In this recipe, we'll see how to apply regression analysis on sales data at scale.

Variable identification

In this recipe, we'll see how to identify the required variables for analysis and understand their description.

Getting ready

To step through this recipe, you will need a running Spark cluster in any one of the modes, that is, local, standalone, YARN, or Mesos. For installing Spark on a standalone cluster, please refer to `http://spark.apache.org/docs/latest/spark-standalone.html`. Also, include the Spark MLlib package in the `build.sbt` file so that it downloads the related libraries and the API can be used. Install Hadoop (optionally), Scala, and Java.

How to do it...

Let's look at an example of sales data. It contains 2013 sales data for nearly 1600 products across 10 stores in different cities. The data contains product and store attributes. We'll look at the properties of the different variables.

Please download the data from the following locations:
`https://github.com/ChitturiPadma/datasets/blob/master/Sales_Train.csvhttps://github.com/ChitturiPadma/datasets/blob/master/Sales_Test.csv`

We have train and test datasets available. The data contains the following variables:

Variable	Description
Item_Identifier	Unique product ID
Item_Weight	Weight of the product
Item_Fat_Content	Whether the product has low fat or not
Item_Visibility	Percentage of total display area of all products in a store allocated to the particular product

Item_Type	Category to which the product belongs
Item_MRP	Maximum Retail Price of the product
Outlet_Identifier	Unique store ID
Outlet_Establishement_Year	Year in which store was established
Outlet_Size	Size of the store in terms of ground area covered
Outlet_Location_Type	Type of the city in which store is located.
Outlet_Type	If the outlet is grocery or pharmacy
Item_Outlet_Sales	Sales of the product in a particular store. This is the outcome to be predicted.

The data resides in HDFS. Let's load the data into Spark and see the values corresponding to different variables:

```
import org.apache.spark._
import org.apache.spark.mllib.linalg.Vectors
import org.apache.spark.sql._
import org.apache.spark.sql.functions._
import org.apache.spark.sql.DataFrameNaFunctions
import org.apache.spark.sql.types._
importorg.apache.spark.mllib.stat
.{MultivariateStatisticalSummary, Statistics}

 object Sales_Prediction {
  def main(args:Array[String]): Unit ={
    val conf = new SparkConf()
      .setMaster("spark://master:7077")
      .setAppName("Sales_Prediction")
    val sc = new SparkContext(conf)
    val sqlContext = new SQLContext(sc)
    import sqlContext.implicits._
          //Loading data
    val sales_data_train =
    sqlContext.read.format("com.databricks.spark.csv")
    .option("header", "true")
    .option("inferSchema","true")
    .load("hdfs://namenode:9000/Sales_Train.csv")
    val sales_data_test =
    sqlContext.read.format("com.databricks.spark.csv")
    .option("header", "true")
    .option("inferSchema","true")
    .load("hdfs://namenode:9000/Sales_Test.csv")
```

```
val sales_data_union = sales_data_train.unionAll(sales_data_test)
val sales_data = sales_data_union.withColumn("Item_Outlet_Sales",
sales_data_union.col("Item_Outlet_Sales").cast(DoubleType))
sales_data.show(5) } }
```

The following is the output:

Item_Identifier	Item_Weight	Item_Fat_Content	Item	Item_Visibility
FDA15	9.3	Low Fat		0.016047301
DRC01	5.92	Regular		0.019278216
FDN15	17.5	Low Fat		0.016760075
FDX07	19.2	Regular		0.0
NCD19	8.93	Low Fat		0.0

Item_Type	Item_Outlet_Sales	Outlet_Identifier
Dairy	249.8092	OUT049
Soft Drinks	48.2692	OUT018
Meat	141.618	OUT049
Fruits and	182.095	OUT010
Household	53.8614	OUT013

Outlet_Establishment_Year	Outlet_Size	Outlet_Location_Type
1999	Medium	Tier 1
2009	Medium	Tier 3
1999	Medium	Tier 1
1998		Tier 3
1987	High	Tier 3

Outlet_Type	Item_Outlet_Sales
Supermarket Type1	3735.138
Supermarket Type2	443.4228
Supermarket Type1	2097.27
Grocery Store	732.38
Supermarket Type1	994.7052

How it works...

In the previous code snippet, since the file is of CSV format, we imported the data initially into Spark using the CSV package. The schema is inferred and variables are identified. Next, the `sales_data_train.unionAll(sales_data_test)` statement merges the training and testing datasets. The `val sales_data = sales_data_union.withColumn("Item_Outlet_Sales",sales_data_union.col("Item_Outlet_Sales").cast(DoubleType))` statement converts the `Item_Outlet_Sales` to double attribute. The `sales_data.show(5)` line displays the first five records. From this sample data, the independent and dependent variables are identified.

There's more...

In the subsequent recipes, let's see how to explore data and apply feature engineering.

See also

Please refer to the *Data exploration* and *Feature engineering* recipes for the subsequent steps.

Data exploration

In this recipe, we'll see how to explore data.

Getting ready

To step through this recipe, you will need a running Spark cluster in any one of the modes, that is, local, standalone, YARN, or Mesos. For installing Spark on a standalone cluster, please refer to `http://spark.apache.org/docs/latest/spark-standalone.html`. Also, include the Spark MLlib package in the `build.sbt` file so that it downloads the related libraries and the API can be used. Install Hadoop (optionally), Scala, and Java.

How to do it…

1. After variable identification, let's try to do some data exploration and come up with inferences about the data. Here is the code which does data exploration:

```
// Basic Statistics for numerical variables
val summary_stats = sales_data.describe()
println("Summary Statistics")
summary_stats.show()
// Unique values in each field
val columnNames = sales_data.columns
val uniqueValues_PerField = columnNames.map{
fieldName => fieldName + ":" +
sales_data.select(fieldName).distinct().count.toString
 }
uniqueValues_PerField.foreach(println)

 //Frequency of Categories for categorical variables
 val frequency_Variables  = columnNames.map{
 fieldName =>
 if(fieldName == "Item_Fat_Content" || fieldName ==
 "Item_Type" || fieldName ==
 "Outlet_Size" || fieldName == "Outlet_Location_Type" ||
 fieldName == "Outlet_Type")
 Option(fieldName,sales_data.groupBy(fieldName).count())
 else  None
 }
 val seq_Df_WithFrequencyCount =
 frequency_Variables.filter(optionalDf =>
 optionalDf!=None).map{optionalDf => optionalDf.get}
 seq_Df_WithFrequencyCount.foreach{case(fieldName, df) =>
 println("Frequency Count of "+fieldName)
 df.show()
```

The following is the output:

```
Summary statistics:
+-------+------------------+-------------------+------------------+
|summary| Item_Weight      | Item_Visibility   |Item_MRP          |
+-------+------------------+-------------------+------------------+
|count  |11765             |14204              |14204             |
|mean   |12.792854228644092|0.0659527800739932 |141.00497725992673|
|stddev |4.65250228641284  |0.05145859524842308|62.086938014764094|
|min    |4.555             |0.0                |31.29             |
|max    |21.35             |0.328390948        |266.8884          |
+-------+------------------+-------------------+------------------+
```

```
+-----------------+-------------------+
| Outlet_Est_Year |Item_Outlet_Sales  |
+-----------------+-------------------+
|14204            |8523               |
|1997.8306814981695|2181.2889135750343|
|8.37166387089612 |1706.4996157338342 |
|1985             |33.29              |
|2009             |13086.9648         |
+-----------------+-------------------+
```

```
Unique values of each field
Item_Identifier:1559
Item_Weight:416
Item_Fat_Content:5
Item_Visibility:13006
Item_Type:16
Item_MRP:8052
Outlet_Identifier:10
Outlet_Establishment_Year:9
Outlet_Size:4
Outlet_Location_Type:3
Outlet_Type:4
Item_Outlet_Sales:3494
```

```
Frequency Count of Item_Fat_Content:
+----------------+-----+
|Item_Fat_Content|count|
+----------------+-----+
| low fat        | 178 |
| Low Fat        | 8485|
| reg            | 195 |
| LF             | 522 |
| Regular        | 4824|
+----------------+-----+
Frequency Count of Item_Type:
+-------------------+-----+
| Item_Type         |count|
+-------------------+-----+
| Frozen Foods      | 1426|
| Breakfast         | 186 |
| Dairy             | 1136|
|Fruits and Vegeta...| 2013|
| Breads            | 416 |
| Starchy Foods     | 269 |
| Others            | 280 |
| Soft Drinks       | 726 |
| Household         | 1548|
| Health and Hygiene| 858 |
```

```
| Baking Goods        | 1086|
| Canned              | 1084|
| Snack Foods         | 1989|
| Meat                | 736 |
| Seafood             | 89  |
| Hard Drinks         | 362 |
+--------------------+-----+
```

Frequency Count of Outlet_Size:
```
+-----------+-----+
|Outlet_Size|count|
+-----------+-----+
| High      | 1553|
| Small     | 3980|
| Medium    | 4655|
|           | 4016|
+-----------+-----+
```

Frequency Count of Outlet_Location_Type:
```
+--------------------+-----+
|Outlet_Location_Type|count|
+--------------------+-----+
| Tier 1             | 3980|
| Tier 2             | 4641|
| Tier 3             | 5583|
+--------------------+-----+
```

Frequency Count of Outlet_Type:
```
+-----------------+-----+
| Outlet_Type     |count|
+-----------------+-----+
| Grocery Store   | 1805|
|Supermarket Type1| 9294|
|Supermarket Type2| 1546|
|Supermarket Type3| 1559|
+-----------------+-----+
```

2. The next step in data exploration is to deal with missing values. Here is the code which involves imputing missing values:

```scala
// Replace Missing values for Item_Weight
val df_Item_WeightNull =
  sales_data.filter(sales_data("Item_Weight").isNull)
println("Missing rows for Item_Weight: "+df_Item_WeightNull.count)
val mean_ItemWeight = sales_data.select(mean("Item_Weight"))
.first()(0).asInstanceOf[Double]
val fill_MissingValues_ItemWeight =
    sales_data.na.fill(mean_ItemWeight,Seq("Item_Weight"))
    println("After replacing the mean for Item_Weight..."+
fill_MissingValues_ItemWeight.filter(fill_MissingValues_ItemWeight
("Item_Weight").isNull).count)


//Replace missing values for Outlet_Size with the mode of
Outlet_Size
val df_OutletSizeNull =
fill_MissingValues_ItemWeight.filter(fill_MissingValues_ItemWeight
("Outlet_Size").like("") )
println("Missing Outlet Size Rows: "+df_OutletSizeNull .count)
val new_Df =
fill_MissingValues_ItemWeight.withColumn("Outlet_Type_Size",
concat($"Outlet_Type", lit(":"), $"Outlet_Size"))
val aggregated_Df  = new_Df.groupBy("Outlet_Type_Size").count()
val modified_Df = new_Df.na.replace("Outlet_Size", Map("" -> "NA"))
modified_Df.show()
val df_SuperMarketType1 =
modified_Df.filter(new_Df("Outlet_Type").contains
("SupermarketType1"))
val df_SuperMarketType2 =
modified_Df.filter(new_Df("Outlet_Type").contains
("Supermarket Type2"))
val df_SuperMarketType3 =
modified_Df.filter(new_Df("Outlet_Type").contains
("SupermarketType3"))
val df_GroceryStore =
modified_Df.filter(new_Df("Outlet_Type").contains
("Grocery Store"))
val replacedMissingValues_ForOutletSize_With_SuperMarketType1 =
df_SuperMarketType1.na.replace("Outlet_Size", Map("NA" -> "Small"))
val replacedMissingValues_ForOutletSize_With_SuperMarketType2 =
df_SuperMarketType2.na.replace("Outlet_Size", Map("NA" ->
"Medium"))
val replacedMissingValues_ForOutletSize_With_SuperMarketType3 =
df_SuperMarketType3.na.replace("Outlet_Size", Map("NA" ->
"Medium"))
val replacedMissingValues_ForOutletSize_With_GroceryStore =
```

```
df_GroceryStore.na.replace("Outlet_Size", Map("NA" -> "Small"))

val replaced_MissingValues_ForOutletSize =
replacedMissingValues_ForOutletSize_With_SuperMarketType1
.unionAll(replacedMissingValues_ForOutletSize_With_SuperMarketType2)
.unionAll(replacedMissingValues_ForOutletSize_With_SuperMarketType3)
.unionAll(replacedMissingValues_ForOutletSize_With_GroceryStore)

val missing_Rows =  replaced_MissingValues_ForOutletSize.filter
(replaced_MissingValues_ForOutletSize("Outlet_Size").like(""))
println("After replacing the mode for missing values of Outlet Size:
"+missing_Rows.count)
```

The following is the output:

```
Missing rows for Item_Weight: 2439
After replacing the mean for Item_Weight ...0
Missing Outlet Size Rows: 4016
After replacing the mode for missing values of Outlet Size: 0
```

How it works...

As a part of data exploration, the `sales_data.describe()` line gives the summary statistics of all the numeric fields. A few observations that we could figure out are:

- `Item_Visibility` has a minimum value of zero and this doesn't make practical sense since when a product is sold in a store, visibility cannot be zero.
- `Outlet_Establishment_Years` varies from 1985 to 2009. If we convert the values to how old a particular store is, it will have better impact on the sales.

Next, for each field, we had a number of unique values. The line `val columnNames = sales_data.columns` generates all column names. Next we iterate through all the columns and generate unique values as `sales_data.select(fieldName).distinct().count.toString`

From this, we can understand that there are 1559 products and 10 outlet/stores. Also, `Item_Type` has 16 unique values. We also explored the frequency of different categories for each nominal attribute as `sales_data.groupBy(fieldName).count()`. The output provides the following observations:

- For `Item_Fat_Content` field, some of the low-fat values are miscoded as `low fat` and `LF`. Also, regular is mentioned as `regular` and `reg`.
- All categories for the attribute `Item_Type` doesn't have significant numbers. It looks like combining them would give better results.

Next, in the data cleaning stage, missing values for `Item_Weight` are replaced with the mean of the remaining values. The `sales_data.select(mean("Item_Weight")).first()(0).asInstanceOf[Double]` line, generates the mean of the `Item_Weight` column. The line, `sales_data.na.fill(mean_ItemWeight,Seq("Item_Weight"))` replaces the missing values with the calculated mean. Also, for treating missing values of `Outlet_Size`, mode is the statistic to be used. Since spark doesn't have support for mode, for each `Outlet_Type`, whichever `Outlet_Size` combination gives the maximum number of rows, the corresponding `Outlet_Size` is replaced with the missing value for the respective `Outlet_Type`.

The `new_Df.na.replace("Outlet_Size", Map("" -> "NA"))` line, replaces the blank values of `Outlet_Size` with "NA". Next, the entire data frame is split into four parts, each containing records with a unique `Outlet_Type` using the statement `modified_Df.filter(new_Df("Outlet_Type").contains("Supermarket Type1"))`.

Now, the `SupermarketType1` outlet type has the maximum number of rows with the outlet size 'Small'. Hence the line, `df_SuperMarketType1.na.replace("Outlet_Size", Map("NA" -> "Small"))` replaces all the missing values (represented as NA) with `Small`. This is done for other data frames containing records of other outlet types.

There's more...

In the preceding recipe, we saw how to explore data. The missing value treatment for the variables could be done in various ways as replacing it with the mean value, removing the rows if the majority of the fields also have a value missing for a particular row, and so on. In the next recipe, let's see how to apply feature engineering.

See also

Please refer to the *Variable identification* recipe to understand the initial steps.

Feature engineering

In this recipe, we'll see how to apply feature engineering on the explored data.

Getting ready

To step through this recipe, you will need a running Spark cluster in any one of the modes, that is, local, standalone, YARN, or Mesos. For installing Spark on a standalone cluster, please refer to http://spark.apache.org/docs/latest/spark-standalone.html. Also, include the Spark MLlib package in the build.sbt file so that it downloads the related libraries and the API can be used. Install Hadoop (optionally), Scala, and Java.

How to do it...

1. After data exploration, the next step is to perform feature engineering. Let's try to apply feature engineering and make the data ready for analysis.
2. From the available attributes, we can see that the minimum value of Item_Visibility is 0. We can consider this missing information and replace with mean values as follows:

```
// Replace Missing values for Item_Visibility
val df_Item_VisibilityNull =
replaced_MissingValues_ForOutletSize
.filter(sales_Data_Refined("Item_Visibility") === 0)
println("Missing rows for Item_Visibility:
"+df_Item_VisibilityNull.count)
val mean_ItemVisibility = replaced_MissingValues_ForOutletSize
.select(mean("Item_Visibility")).first()(0).asInstanceOf[Double]
val df_ForFeatureEngg  =
replaced_MissingValues_ForOutletSize
.na.replace("Item_Visibility", Map(0.0 -> mean_ItemVisibility))
println("After replacing the mean for Item_Visibility ..."
+df_ForFeatureEngg
.filter(df_ForFeatureEngg("Item_Visibility") === 0).count)
```

The following is the output:

```
Missing rows for Item_Visibility: 879
After replacing the mean for Item_Visibility ...0
```

3. From the data exploration step, the `Frequency Count for Outlet_Type` output reflects that for the variables supermarket type2 and type3, the count of variables is the same. Let's try to analyze the mean sales per `Outlet_Type` and see if we can combine the supermarket type2 and type3 variables:

```
val df_MeanSales_PerOutletType =
        df_ForFeatureEngg.groupBy("Outlet_Type").mean
      ("Item_Outlet_Sales")
println("Mean Sales Per Outlet_Type")
df_MeanSales_PerOutletType.show()
```

The following is the output:

```
+-----------------+----------------------+
| Outlet_Type     |avg(Item_Outlet_Sales) |
+-----------------+----------------------+
| Grocery Store   | 339.82850046168045    |
|Supermarket Type1| 2316.1811481082987    |
|Supermarket Type2| 1995.498739224137     |
|Supermarket Type3| 3694.038557647059     |
+-----------------+----------------------+
```

4. We also see that the `Item_Type` variable has 16 categories. The categories seem to be `Food`, `Drinks`, `Non-Consumables`, and the `Item_Identifier` starts with `FD`, `DR` or `NC`. Using the `Item_Identifier`, we can create a broader item type column as:

```
val sqlFunc = udf(coder)
val new_Df_WithItemTypeCombined = df_ForFeatureEngg
.withColumn("Item_Type_Combined",sqlFunc(col("Item_Identifier")
))
 new_Df_WithItemTypeCombined.groupBy
 ("Item_Type_Combined").count().
show()
val coder = (id:String) => id.substring(0,2) match{
case "FD" => "Food"
case "NC" => "Non-Consumable"
case "DR" => "Drinks"
 }
```

The following is the output:

```
+----------------------------+-------+
|Item_Type_Combined          |count  |
+----------------------------+-------+
| Drinks                     | 1317  |
| Food                       |10201  |
| Non-Consumable             | 2686  |
+----------------------------+-------+
```

5. We can also make a new column showing the years of operation of a store. This could be done in the following way:

```
val sqlFunc2 = udf(coder2)
val revised_Df
=new_Df_WithItemTypeCombined.withColumn("Outlet_Years",
sqlFunc2(col("Outlet_Establishment_Year")) )
revised_Df.select("Outlet_Years").describe().show()
val coder2 = (value:Int) => 2013 - value
```

The following is the output:

```
+----------+------------------+
|summary   | Outlet_Years     |
+----------+------------------+
| count    | 14204            |
| mean     |15.169318501830471|
| stddev   | 8.371663870896116|
| min      | 4                |
| max      | 28               |
+----------+------------------+
```

6. Also, create a broader category for `Item_Fat_Content` as follows:

```
val sqlFunc3 = udf(coder3)
val new_Df_WithItem_Fat_Content_Combined =  revised_Df
.withColumn("Item_Fat_Content_Combined",sqlFunc(col
("Item_Fat_Content")))
new_Df_WithItem_Fat_Content_Combined
.groupBy("Item_Fat_Content_Combined").count().show()

val coder3 = (id:String) => id match{
case "LF" | "Low Fat"  => "Low Fat"
case "reg" | "Regular" => "Regular"
case "low fat" => "Low Fat" }
```

The following is the output:

```
+------------------------+-----+
|Item_Fat_Content_Combined|count|
+------------------------+-----+
|                 Low Fat| 9185|
|                 Regular| 5019|
+------------------------+-----+
```

7. Remove the ID variable and unused column as follows:

```
// Exclude ID variable
val sales_Data_new = new_Df_WithItem_Fat_Content_Combined
.drop("Item_Identifier").drop("Outlet_Identifier")
// Removing unused Columns
val sales_Data_Final = sales_Data_new
.drop("Item_Fat_Content").drop("Item_Type").drop
("Outlet_Type_Size")
.drop("Outlet_Establishment_Year")
```

8. Finally, as linear regression accepts only numerical variables, we need to convert categories of nominal variables into numeric types as follows:

```
/* Applying One Hot encoding of Categorical Variables */
val sqlFunc_CreateDummyVariables = udf(udf_returnDummyValues)
// One Hot Encoding for Outlet_Type
val new_Df_WithDummy_OutletType =
create_DummyVariables(sales_Data_Final,
sqlFunc_CreateDummyVariables, "Outlet_Type", 0)
// One Hot Encoding for  Outlet_Size
val new_Df_WithDummy_OutletSize =
create_DummyVariables(new_Df_WithDummy_OutletType,
sqlFunc_CreateDummyVariables, "Outlet_Size", 0)
// One Hot Encoding for  Outlet_Location_Type
val new_Df_WithDummy_OutletLocationType =
create_DummyVariables(new_Df_WithDummy_OutletSize,
sqlFunc_CreateDummyVariables, "Outlet_Location_Type", 0)
// One Hot Encoding for  Item_Type_Combined
val new_Df_WithDummy_ItemTypeCombined =
create_DummyVariables(new_Df_WithDummy_OutletLocationType,
sqlFunc_CreateDummyVariables, "Item_Type_Combined", 0)
// One Hot Encoding for  Item_Fat_Content_Combined
val new_Df_WithDummy_ItemFatContentCombined =
create_DummyVariables(new_Df_WithDummy_ItemTypeCombined,
sqlFunc_CreateDummyVariables, "Item_Fat_Content_Combined", 0)
```

9. Here is the function which creates *n* columns for all the categorical variables having *n* distinct categories:

```
def create_DummyVariables(df:DataFrame,
udf_Func:UserDefinedFunction,
variableType:String, i:Int ): DataFrame = {
variableType match {
case "Outlet_Type" => if (i == 4) df
else {
  val df_new = df.withColumn (variableType + "_" + i.toString,
  udf_Func(lit(variableType),col ("Outlet_Type"), lit (i) ) )
  create_DummyVariables (df_new, udf_Func, variableType, i + 1)
}
case "Outlet_Size" => if(i == 3)   df
else {
 val df_new = df.withColumn (variableType + "_" + i.toString,
 udf_Func(lit(variableType), col ("Outlet_Size"), lit (i) ) )
 create_DummyVariables (df_new, udf_Func, variableType, i + 1)
}
case "Outlet_Location_Type" =>  if(i == 3)   df
else {
 val df_new = df.withColumn (variableType + "_" + i.toString,
 udf_Func(lit(variableType), col ("Outlet_Location_Type"),
 lit (i) ) )
 create_DummyVariables (df_new, udf_Func, variableType, i + 1)
}
case "Item_Type_Combined" =>  if(i == 3)   df
else {
 val df_new = df.withColumn (variableType + "_" + i.toString,
 udf_Func(lit(variableType), col ("Item_Type_Combined"),
 lit (i) ) )
 create_DummyVariables (df_new, udf_Func, variableType, i + 1)
}
case "Item_Fat_Content_Combined" =>  if(i == 2)   df
else {
 val df_new = df.withColumn (variableType + "_" + i.toString,
 udf_Func(lit(variableType), col("Item_Fat_Content_Combined"),
 lit (i) ) )
 create_DummyVariables (df_new, udf_Func, variableType, i + 1)
} } }
```

10. Here is the definition for UDF `udf_returnDummyValues` which returns values 0/1 for every distinct category:

```
val udf_returnDummyValues  = (variableType:String,
columnValue:String,   jobNo:Int) => variableType match{
case "Outlet_Type" => columnValue match {
case "Grocery Store" => if (jobNo == 0) 1.0 else 0.0
case "Supermarket Type1" => if (jobNo == 1) 1.0    else 0.0
case "Supermarket Type2" => if (jobNo == 2) 1.0
else 0.0
case "Supermarket Type3" => if (jobNo == 3) 1.0
else 0.0
}
case "Outlet_Size" => columnValue match {
case "High" => if(jobNo == 0) 1.0 else 0.0
case "Small" => if(jobNo == 1) 1.0 else 0.0
case "Medium" => if(jobNo == 2) 1.0 else 0.0
}
case "Outlet_Location_Type" => columnValue match {
case "Tier 1" => if(jobNo == 0) 1.0 else 0.0
case "Tier 2" => if(jobNo == 1) 1.0 else 0.0
case "Tier 3" => if(jobNo == 2) 1.0 else 0.0
}
case "Item_Type_Combined" => columnValue match {
case "Drinks" => if(jobNo == 0) 1.0 else 0.0
case "Food" => if(jobNo == 1) 1.0 else 0.0
case "Non-Consumable" => if(jobNo == 2) 1.0 else 0.0
}
case "Item_Fat_Content_Combined" => columnValue match {
case "Low Fat" => if(jobNo == 0) 1.0 else 0.0
case "Regular" => if(jobNo == 1) 1.0 else 0.0
} }
```

11. Now, as the dummy variables are created, let's remove the original categorical variables from the final data frame to fit into a linear regression model:

```
//Remove categorical columns
val final_Df = new_Df_WithDummy_ItemFatContentCombined
        .drop("Outlet_Size")
        .drop("Outlet_Location_Type")
        .drop("Outlet_Type")
        .drop("Item_Type_Combined")
        .drop("Item_Fat_Content_Combined")
    final_Df.show(5)
```

The following is the output:

Item_Weight	Item_Visibility	Item_MRP	Item_Outlet_Sales
9.3	0.016047301	249.8092	3735.138
17.5	0.016760075	141.618	2097.27
8.93	0.06595278007399324	53.8614	994.7052
13.65	0.012741089	57.6588	343.5528
16.2	0.016687114	96.9726	1076.5986

Outlet_Years	Outlet_Type_0	Outlet_Type_1	Outlet_Type_2
14	0.0	1.0	0.0
14	0.0	1.0	0.0
26	0.0	1.0	0.0
26	0.0	1.0	0.0
11	0.0	1.0	0.0

Outlet_Type_3	Outlet_Size_0
0.0	0.0
0.0	0.0
0.0	1.0
0.0	1.0
0.0	0.0

How it works...

The final step is performing feature engineering and as a part of this, the missing values for `Item_Visibility` are replaced with its mean as `val df_ForFeatureEngg replaced_MissingValues_ForOutletSize.na.replace("Item_Visibility", Map(0.0 -> mean_ItemVisibility))`. We also noticed from the data exploration step, the frequency count of `Outlet_Type` shows that for the variables supermarket type2 and type3, the count of variables is almost the same. When we took mean sales by `Outlet_Type` as `df_ForFeatureEngg.groupBy("Outlet_Type").mean("Item_Outlet_Sales")`, it clearly shows significant differences, hence we leave it as it is.

Also, `Item_Type` has 16 unique categories. The first two characters of `Item_Identifier` are either FD, DR or NC. We created a broader category as `Item_Type_Combined from the column Item_Identifier using the lines val sqlFunc = udf(coder)` and `val new_Df_WithItemTypeCombined = df_ForFeatureEngg.withColumn("Item_Type_Combined sqlFunc(col("Item_Identifier")))`. The variable coder takes the initial two characters of `Item_Identifier` and a broader category is generated. Similarly, for `Item_Fat_Content`, a broader category is generated as `Item_Fat_Content_Combined`. A new `Outlet_Years` column depicting the years of operation of a store is created as `new_Df_WithItemTypeCombined.withColumn("Outlet_Years",sqlFunc2(col("Out let_Establishment_Year")))`. The ID variables and unused columns are dropped as `val sales_Data_new = new_Df_WithItem_Fat_Content_Combined.drop("Item_Identifier")`.

```
.drop("Outlet_Identifier") and val sales_Data_Final =
sales_Data_new.drop("Item_Fat_Content").drop("Item_Type").drop("Outlet_Type
_Size")
.drop("Outlet_Establishment_Year").
```

Next, all the categorical variables need to be converted to numeric types. For this, a `create_DummyVariables(df:DataFrame, udf_Func:UserDefinedFunction, variableType:String, i:Int ): DataFrame` function is created which takes the data frame, user defined function, categorical variable and iteration count as input. For each categorical variable; `Outlet_Type`, `Outlet_Size`, `Outlet_Location_Type`, `Item_Type_Combined`, `Item_Fat_Content_Combined`, the dummy variables such as `Outlet_Type_0`, `Outlet_Type_1`, `Outlet_Type_2`, `Outlet_Type_3` are created in an iterative fashion as `val df_new = df.withColumn (variableType + "_" + i.toString, udf_Func (lit(variableType),col ("Outlet_Type"), lit (i)))` and `create_DummyVariables (df_new, udf_Func, variableType, i + 1)`. This is done for all five categorical variables. The user defined `udf_returnDummyValues` function generates values for the dummy variables using a match clause. For example, the `Outlet_Size` variable has three unique categories; High, Small, and Medium. These three variables, `Outlet_Size_0` (represents High), `Outlet_Size_1` (represents Small), and `Outlet_Size_2` (represents Medium) are created, where `Outlet_Size_0` represents High created as part of the recursive `create_DummyVariables` function.

After this, the categorical variables are dropped using the `val final_Df = new_Df_WithDummy_ItemFatContentCombined.drop("Outlet_Size").drop("Outle t_Location_Type").drop("Outlet_Type").drop("Item_Type_Combined").drop(" Item_Fat_Content_Combined")` statement.

There's more...

In the preceding recipe, we saw how to apply feature engineering. In the next recipe, let's see how to apply the algorithm on the final dataset.

See also

Please refer to the earlier *Variable identification* and *Data exploration* recipes.

Applying linear regression

In this recipe, we'll see how to apply linear regression.

Getting ready

To step through this recipe, you will need a running Spark cluster in any one of the modes, for instance, local, standalone, YARN, or Mesos. For installing Spark on a standalone cluster, please refer to http://spark.apache.org/docs/latest/spark-standalone.html. Also, include the Spark MLlib package in the build.sbt file so that it downloads the related libraries and the API can be used. Install Hadoop (optionally), Scala, and Java.

How to do it...

1. The final step is to convert data into train and test datasets and apply the regression model on the training data:

```
//Split the data frame into train and test sets
val train_Df =
final_Df.filter(final_Df("Item_Outlet_Sales").isNotNull)
val test_Df =
final_Df.filter(final_Df("Item_Outlet_Sales").isNull)
val train_Rdd = train_Df.rdd.map {
row => val item_weight = row.getAs[Double]("Item_Weight")
val item_Visibility = row.getAs[Double]("Item_Visibility")
val item_mrp = row.getAs[Double]("Item_MRP")
val item_outlet_sales = row.getAs[Double]("Item_Outlet_Sales")
val otlet_years = row.getAs[Int]("Outlet_Years").toDouble
val outlet_type_0 = row.getAs[Double]("Outlet_Type_0")
val outlet_type_1 = row.getAs[Double]("Outlet_Type_1")
```

```
val outlet_type_2 = row.getAs[Double]("Outlet_Type_2")
val outlet_type_3 = row.getAs[Double]("Outlet_Type_3")
val outlet_size_0 = row.getAs[Double]("Outlet_Size_0")
val outlet_size_1 = row.getAs[Double]("Outlet_Size_1")
val outlet_size_2 = row.getAs[Double]("Outlet_Size_2")
val outlet_Location_Type_0 = row.getAs[Double]
("Outlet_Location_Type_0")
val outlet_Location_Type_1 = row.getAs[Double]
("Outlet_Location_Type_1")
val outlet_Location_Type_2 = row.getAs[Double]
("Outlet_Location_Type_2")
val item_type_0 =  row.getAs[Double]("Item_Type_Combined_0")
val item_type_1 =  row.getAs[Double]("Item_Type_Combined_1")
val item_type_2 =  row.getAs[Double]("Item_Type_Combined_2")
val item_fat_content_0 = row.getAs[Double]
("Item_Fat_Content_Combined_0")
val item_fat_content_1 = row.getAs[Double]
("Item_Fat_Content_Combined_1")
val featurecVec = Vectors.dense(Array(item_weight,
item_Visibility,item_mrp,otlet_years,outlet_type_0,
outlet_type_1,outlet_type_2,outlet_type_3,outlet_size_0,
outlet_size_1,outlet_size_2,outlet_Location_Type_0,
outlet_Location_Type_1,outlet_Location_Type_2,
item_type_0,item_type_1,item_type_2,item_fat_content_0,
item_fat_content_1))
LabeledPoint(item_outlet_sales, featurecVec)
}.cache()
val numIters = 500
val stepSize =0.0001
// Applying the linear Regression Model
val lm = new LinearRegressionWithSGD().setIntercept(true)
lm.optimizer.setStepSize(stepSize)
lm.optimizer.setNumIterations(numIters)
lm.optimizer.setMiniBatchFraction(0.2)
lm.optimizer.setConvergenceTol(0.0001)
lm.optimizer.setRegParam(0.1)
val model = lm.run(train_Rdd)
val predictedData = train_Rdd.map{
labeledPoint =>
val featureVec = labeledPoint.features
val originalValue = labeledPoint.label
val predictedValue = model.predict(featureVec)
(originalValue, predictedValue)
 }
val mse = predictedData.map{case(original, predicted) =>
(original-predicted)*(original-predicted)
 }.mean()
val metricsObject = new RegressionMetrics(predictedData )
```

```
println("R2 Value: "+metricsObject.r2)
println("Mean Squared Error: "+mse)
```

The following is the output:

```
R2 Value: 0.8346890
Mean Squared Error:7573.1746617937
```

How it works...

The final steps of applying the algorithm are the DataFrame is split into train and test sets as `final_Df.filter(final_Df("Item_Outlet_Sales").isNotNull)` and `final_Df.filter(final_Df("Item_Outlet_Sales").isNull)`. Now, the `train_Df` varaible is converted to RDD. The output variable `Item_Outlet_Sales` is the label and from the remaining variables, a dense vector is created. Once the `RDD[LabeledPoint]` is generated, the `val lm = new LinearRegressionWithSGD().setIntercept(true)` line creates the object `LinearRegressionWithSGD`. The necessary parameters such as step-size are set as `lm.optimizer.setStepSize(stepSize)`. The other parameters such as `NumIterations`, `MiniBatchFraction`, `ConvergenceTol`, `RegParam` are also set. Now the algorithm runs on the training dataset with the `val model = lm.run(train_Rdd)` statement. Once the model is ready, mean squared error and `r2` value are seen. The algorithm is made to fit on the data by changing the parameters such as step-size, number of iterations, regularization parameter, convergence tolerance, setIntercept and so on.

There's more...

Once the model is built, the initially-created hypothesis would be tested and the data needs to be sufficient to test all the scenarios. In the above case study, we applied the linear regression model from MLlib, Spark has support for `ml` pipelines as well which means we can apply algorithms directly on the data frame. There are other flavors of regression such as ridge regression, stepwise regression, **Ordinary Least Squares Regression** (OLSR), multivariate regression, and so on. Spark MLlib offers several regression algorithms with different estimation techniques.

See also

Please refer to this textbook for better understanding of regression algorithms and implementation of the different techniques using Spark MLlib: http://www.statsoft.com/Textbook/Multiple-Regression.

Applying logistic regression on bank marketing data

Logistic regression is a classification algorithm. It is used to predict a binary outcome (0/1, Yes/No, True/False) from the set of independent variables. It is a special case of linear regression where the outcome variable is categorical. The log of odds is the dependent variables, that is, it predicts the probability of occurrence of an event by fitting data to a logit function. Logistic regression is also termed as **linear classification model**. The link function used in the logistic regression is the logic link $1/(1+exp(-wTx))$. The related loss function for logistic regression is the logistic loss, that is, $log(1+exp(-ywTx))$. Here y is the actual target variable (either 1 for the positive class or -1 for the negative class).

This recipe shows how to apply the logistic regression algorithm available in the Spark MLlib package on Bank Marketing Data. The code is written in Scala.

Variable identification

In this recipe, we'll see how to identify the required variables for analysis and understand their description.

Getting ready

To step through this recipe, you will need a running Spark cluster in any one of the modes, that is, local, standalone, YARN, or Mesos. For installing Spark on a standalone cluster, please refer to http://spark.apache.org/docs/latest/spark-standalone.html. Also, include the Spark MLlib package in the build.sbt file so that it downloads the related libraries and the API can be used. Install Hadoop (optionally), Scala, and Java.

How to do it...

Let's take *Bank Marketing* data which contains information related to a direct marketing campaign of a Portuguese bank institute and its attempts to make their clients subscribe for a term deposit. The data originally contains 41,188 rows and 21 columns. For our analysis, we'll use 10 variables. Let's see the properties of the variables.

Please download the dataset from the following location:
`https://github.com/ChitturiPadma/datasets/blob/master/bank_marke`
`ting_data.csv`.

1. Here is the description of the variables that we are going to use in our analysis:

Variable	Description
age	Age of the customer
job	Customer's occupation
marital	Marital status
default	Indicates whether the customer has credit in default.
housing	Indicates if the customer has a housing loan
loan	Indicates if the customer has a personal loan
duration	Duration of last contact in seconds
previous	Number of contacts performed before the campaign for the customer
poutcome	Outcome of the previous marketing campaign
empvarrate	Employment variation rate
y	Response variable which indicates if the customer has subscribed for deposit

2. The data resides in HDFS. Let's load the data into Spark and see the values corresponding to different variables:

```
import org.apache.spark._
import org.apache.spark.ml.feature.StringIndexer
import org.apache.spark.mllib.evaluation.RegressionMetrics
import org.apache.spark.mllib.linalg.Vectors
import org.apache.spark.mllib.regression.
{LinearRegressionWithSGD, LabeledPoint}
```

```
import org.apache.spark.sql._
import org.apache.spark.sql.functions._
import org.apache.spark.sql.DataFrameNaFunctions
import org.apache.spark.sql.types._
import org.apache.spark.mllib.stat.
{MultivariateStatisticalSummary, Statistics}
import org.apache.spark.ml.regression.LinearRegression

object Logistic_Regression_Demo {
def main(args: Array[String]): Unit = {
val conf = new SparkConf().setMaster("spark://master:7077")
.setAppName("Logistic_Prediction")
 val sc = new SparkContext(conf)
 val sqlContext = new SQLContext(sc)
 import sqlContext.implicits._
 //Loading data
 val bank_Marketing_Data =
sqlContext.read.format("com.databricks.spark.csv")
        .option("header", "true")
        .option("inferSchema", "true")
        .load("hdfs://namenode:9000/data/bank-data.csv")
 val selected_Data =  bank_Marketing_Data.select("age", "job",
"marital",   "default", "housing", "loan", "duration",
"previous", "poutcome", "empvarrate", "y").withColumn("age",
bank_Marketing_Data("age").cast(DoubleType))
.withColumn("duration",
bank_Marketing_Data("duration").cast(DoubleType))
.withColumn("previous",
bank_Marketing_Data("previous").cast(DoubleType))
selected_Data.show(5) } }
```

The following is the output:

age	job	marital	default	housing	loan	duration
56.0	housemaid	married	no	no	no	261.0
57.0	services	married	unknown	no	no	149.0
37.0	services	married	no	yes	no	226.0
40.0	admin	married	no	no	no	151.0
56.0	services	married	no	no	yes	307.0

previous	poutcome	empvarrate	y
0.0	nonexistent	1.1	no
0.0	nonexistent	1.1	no
0.0	nonexistent	1.1	no

```
|      0.0 |nonexistent|      1.1 | no |
|      0.0 |nonexistent|      1.1 | no |
+---------+-----------+----------+----+
```

How it works...

The Bank Marketing data is loaded as a csv file, schema is inferred and variables are identified. From the 21 columns available, 10 columns as mentioned in the beginning are considered for running the logistic regression. Once the dataset is loaded, the `age`, `duration` and `previous` columns are converted to double with the statements `.withColumn("age", bank_Marketing_Data("age").cast(DoubleType))`. The `selected_Data.show(5)` line displays the first five records. From this sample data, the independent and dependent variables are identified.

There's more...

In the subsequent recipes, let's see how to explore data and apply feature engineering.

See also

Please refer to the *Data Exploration* and *Feature Engineering* recipes for the following steps.

Data exploration

In this recipe, we'll see how to explore data.

Getting ready

To step through this recipe, you will need a running Spark cluster in any one of the modes, that is, local, standalone, YARN, and Mesos. For installing Spark on a standalone cluster, please refer to `http://spark.apache.org/docs/latest/spark-standalone.html`. Also, include the Spark MLlib package in the `build.sbt` file so that it downloads the related libraries and the API can be used. Install Hadoop (optionally), Scala, and Java.

How to do it…

1. After variable identification, let's try do some data exploration and come up with inferences about the data. Here is the code which does data exploration:

```
/*Summary statistics*/
val summary = selected_Data.describe()
println("Summary Statistics")
summary.show()

/* Unique values for each Field */
val columnNames = selected_Data.columns
val uniqueValues_PerField = columnNames.map{field => field +":"
+selected_Data.select(field).distinct().count()}
println("Unique Values for each Field: ")
uniqueValues_PerField.foreach(println)
  // Frequency of Categories for categorical variables
val frequency_Variables  = columnNames.map{
fieldName =>
if(fieldName == "job" || fieldName == "marital" || fieldName
== "default" ||   fieldName == "housing" || fieldName ==
"poutcome")
Option(fieldName,selected_Data.groupBy(fieldName).count())
else  None }
val seq_Df_WithFrequencyCount =
frequency_Variables.filter(optionalDf =>
optionalDf!=None).map{optionalDf => optionalDf.get}
seq_Df_WithFrequencyCount.foreach{case(fieldName, df) =>
println("Frequency Count of "+fieldName)
df.show()
```

The following is the output:

```
Summary Statistics:
+-------+------------------+------------------+
|summary|             age  |          duration|
+-------+------------------+------------------+
|  count|            41188 |             41188|
|   mean|40.02406040594348 |258.2850101971448 |
|stddev |10.421249980934034|259.27924883646506|
|    min|               17 |                 0|
|    max|               98 |              4918|
+-------+------------------+------------------+


+-------+------------------+-------------------+
|summary|          previous|        empvarrate |
```

```
+-------+-----------------+-------------------+
|  count|       41188     |        41188      |
|   mean|0.17296299893172767|0.08188550063146532 |
|stddev |0.49490107983928977|1.5709597405170272  |
|   min |        0        |        -3.4       |
|   max |        7        |         1.4|
+-------+-----------------+-------------------+
```

```
Unique Values for each Field:
age:78
job:12
marital:4
default:3
housing:3
loan:3
duration:1544
previous:8
poutcome:3
empvarrate:10
y:2
```

```
Frequency Count of job:
+-------------+-----+
|          job|count|
+-------------+-----+
|   unemployed| 1014|
|     services| 3969|
|  blue-collar| 9254|
|      unknown|  330|
|    housemaid| 1060|
| entrepreneur| 1456|
|self-employed| 1421|
|      retired| 1720|
|       admin.|10422|
|   management| 2924|
|   technician| 6743|
|      student|  875|
+-------------+-----+
```

```
Frequency Count of marital:
+--------+-----+
| marital|count|
+--------+-----+
| unknown|   80|
|divorced| 4612|
|  single|11568|
| married|24928|
```

```
+--------+-----+

Frequency Count of default:
+-------+-----+
|default|count|
+-------+-----+
|unknown| 8597|
|     no|32588|
|    yes|    3|
+-------+-----+

Frequency Count of housing:
+-------+-----+
|housing|count|
+-------+-----+
|unknown|  990|
|     no|18622|
|    yes|21576|
+-------+-----+

Frequency Count of loan:
+-------+-----+
|   loan|count|
+-------+-----+
|unknown|  990|
|     no|33950|
|    yes| 6248|
+-------+-----+

Frequency Count of poutcome:
+-----------+-----+
|   poutcome|count|
+-----------+-----+
|nonexistent|35563|
|    failure| 4252|
|    success| 1373|
+-----------+-----+
```

2. From the previous data exploration, we see that the numeric columns age, duration, previous and empvarrate do not have any missing values. Also, the frequency count of the categorical variables reveal that there are no missing values in the nominal variables too.

How it works...

As a part of data exploration, the `selected_Data.describe()` line gives the summary statistics of all the numeric fields. A few observations that we can figure out are:

- The numeric `age`, `duration`, `previous` and `empvarrate` fields do not have any missing values. Next, for each field, we had a number of unique values. The `val columnNames = selected_Data.columns` line generates all column names. Next we iterate through all the columns and generate unique values such as `selected_Data.select(fieldName).distinct().count.toString`. From this, we can understand that the `job`, `marital`, `default`, `housing`, `poutcome` and `loan` variables have a reasonable number of categories. We also explored the frequency of different categories for each nominal attribute as `selected_Data.groupBy(fieldName).count()`. The output provides the following observations:
- The sum of counts of different categories for each nominal variable is `41188` which means the nominal variables do not have any missing values.

There's more...

In the preceding recipe, we saw how to explore data. In the next recipe, let's see how to apply feature engineering.

See also

Please refer to the *Variable identification* recipe to understand the initial steps.

Feature engineering

In this recipe, we'll see how to apply feature engineering on the explored data.

Getting ready

To step through this recipe, you will need a running Spark cluster in any one of the modes, that is, local, standalone, YARN, and Mesos. For installing Spark on a standalone cluster, please refer to http://spark.apache.org/docs/latest/spark-standalone.html. Also, include the Spark MLlib package in the build.sbt file so that it downloads the related libraries and the API can be used. Install Hadoop (optionally), Scala, and Java.

How to do it...

1. After data exploration, the next step is to perform feature engineering. Let's try to convert nominal variables into numeric types. Here is the code which does encoding for the nominal variables:

```
/* Applying One Hot encoding of Categorical Variables */
// One Hot Encoding for Job
val sqlFunc = udf(coder)
val new_Df_WithDummyJob =
create_DummyVariables(selected_Data, sqlFunc,"job",0)
val new_Df_WithDummyMarital =
create_DummyVariables(new_Df_WithDummyJob, sqlFunc,
"marital", 0)
val new_Df_WithDummyDefault =
create_DummyVariables(new_Df_WithDummyMarital, sqlFunc,
"default", 0)
val new_Df_WithDummyHousing =
create_DummyVariables(new_Df_WithDummyDefault, sqlFunc,
"housing", 0)
val new_Df_WithDummyPoutcome =
create_DummyVariables(new_Df_WithDummyHousing, sqlFunc,
"poutcome", 0)
val new_Df_WithDummyLoan =
create_DummyVariables(new_Df_WithDummyPoutcome, sqlFunc,
"loan", 0)
```

2. Here is the function which creates *n* columns for all the categorical variables having *n* distinct categories:

```
def create_DummyVariables(df:DataFrame,
udf_Func:UserDefinedFunction, variableType:String, i:Int ):
DataFrame = {

variableType match {
```

```
       case "job" => if (i == 12) df
              else {
              val df_new = df.withColumn (variableType + "_" +
              i.toString, udf_Func(lit(variableType),col
              ("job"), lit (i) ) )
              create_DummyVariables (df_new, udf_Func,
              variableType, i + 1)
              }
     case "marital" => if(i == 4)  df
              else {
              val df_new = df.withColumn (variableType +
              "_" + i.toString, udf_Func(lit(variableType),
              col ("marital"), lit (i) ) )
              create_DummyVariables (df_new, udf_Func,
              variableType, i + 1)
              }
    case "default" =>  if(i == 3)  df
              else {
              val df_new = df.withColumn (variableType + "_"
              + i.toString, udf_Func(lit(variableType),
              col ("default"), lit (i) ) )
              create_DummyVariables (df_new, udf_Func,
              variableType, i + 1)
              }
  case "housing" =>  if(i == 3)  df
              else {
              val df_new = df.withColumn (variableType +
              "_" + i.toString, udf_Func(lit(variableType),
              col ("housing"), lit (i) ) )
              create_DummyVariables (df_new, udf_Func,
              variableType, i + 1)
              }
  case "poutcome" =>  if(i == 3)  df
               else {
               val df_new = df.withColumn (variableType +
               "_" + i.toString, udf_Func(lit(variableType),
                col ("poutcome"), lit (i) ) )
                create_DummyVariables (df_new, udf_Func,
                variableType, i + 1)
                }
  case "loan" =>  if(i == 3)  df
              else {
              val df_new = df.withColumn (variableType + "_" +
              i.toString, udf_Func(lit(variableType),
              col ("loan"), lit (i) ) )
              create_DummyVariables (df_new, udf_Func,
              variableType, i + 1)
              } } }
```

3. Here is the definition for udf `coder` which returns values 0/1 for every distinct category:

```
val coder  = (variableType:String, columnValue:String,
jobNo:Int) =>
variableType match{
case "job" => columnValue match {
case "unemployed" => if (jobNo == 0) 1.0 else 0.0
case "services" => if (jobNo == 1) 1.0 else 0.0
case "blue-collar" => if (jobNo == 2) 1.0 else 0.0
case "unknown" => if (jobNo == 3) 1.0 else 0.0
case "housemaid" => if (jobNo == 4) 1.0 else 0.0
case "entrepreneur" => if (jobNo == 5) 1.0 else 0.0
case "self-employed" => if (jobNo == 6) 1.0 else 0.0
case "retired" => if (jobNo == 7) 1.0 else 0.0
case "admin." => if (jobNo == 8) 1.0 else 0.0
case "management" => if (jobNo == 9) 1.0 else 0.0
case "technician" => if (jobNo == 10) 1.0 else 0.0
case "student" => if (jobNo == 11) 1.0 else 0.0
}
case "marital" => columnValue match {
case "unknown" => if(jobNo == 0) 1.0 else 0.0
case "divorced" => if(jobNo == 1) 1.0 else 0.0
case "single" => if(jobNo == 2) 1.0 else 0.0
case "married" => if(jobNo == 3) 1.0 else 0.0
}
case "default" => columnValue match {
case "unknown" => if(jobNo == 0) 1.0 else 0.0
case "no" => if(jobNo == 1) 1.0 else 0.0
case "yes" => if(jobNo == 2) 1.0 else 0.0
}
case "housing" => columnValue match {
case "unknown" => if(jobNo == 0) 1.0 else 0.0
case "no" => if(jobNo == 1) 1.0 else 0.0
case "yes" => if(jobNo == 2) 1.0 else 0.0
}
case "poutcome" => columnValue match {
case "nonexistent" => if(jobNo == 0) 1.0 else 0.0
case "failure" => if(jobNo == 1) 1.0 else 0.0
case "success" => if(jobNo == 2) 1.0 else 0.0
}
case "loan" => columnValue match {
case "unknown" => if(jobNo == 0) 1.0 else 0.0
case "no" => if(jobNo == 1) 1.0 else 0.0
case "yes" => if(jobNo == 2) 1.0 else 0.0
} }
```

4. Now, as the dummy variables are created, let's remove the original categorical variables from the final data frame to fit into the logistic regression model:

```
val final_Df = new_Df_WithDummyLoan.drop("job")
       .drop("marital")
       .drop("default")
       .drop("housing").drop("loan").drop("poutcome")
val indexerModel = new StringIndexer()
  .setInputCol("y")
  .setOutputCol("y_Index")
  .fit(final_Df)
val indexedDf = indexerModel.transform(final_Df).drop("y")
indexedDf.show(5)
```

The following is the output:

```
+----+----------+--------+-----------+------+--------+
|age |  duration|previous| empvarrate |job_0 |  job_1|
+----+----------+--------+-----------+------+--------+
|56.0|    261.0 |    0.0|       1.1 |   0.0|    0.0|
|57.0|    149.0 |    0.0|       1.1 |   0.0|    1.0|
|37.0|    226.0 |    0.0|       1.1 |   0.0|    1.0|
|40.0|    151.0 |    0.0|       1.1 |   0.0|    0.0|
|56.0|    307.0 |    0.0|       1.1 |   0.0|    1.0|
+--------------+-----------+----------------+--------+

+------+-----+
|job_2 |job_3|
+------+-----+
|  0.0|   0.0|
|0.0  |  0.0 |
|0.0  |  0.0 |
|0.0  |  0.0 |
|0.0  |  0.0 |
+-----+------+
```

How it works...

Since there is no missing value treatment, we directly applied feature engineering. As a part of this, since the categorical variables have reasonable categories, there is no need to create broader category fields out of any nominal field. Next, all the categorical variables need to be converted to numeric types. For this, a create_DummyVariables(df:DataFrame, udf_Func:UserDefinedFunction, variableType:String, i:Int): DataFrame function is created which takes the DataFrame, user defined function, categorical variable and iteration count as input.

For each categorical variable job, marital, default, housing, poutcome, and loan, the dummy variables such as `marital_0, marital_1, marital_2, marital_3` are created in an iterative fashion as `val df_new = df.withColumn (variableType + "_" + i.toString, udf_Func (lit(variableType), col ("marital"), lit (i) ) )` and `create_DummyVariables (df_new, udf_Func, variableType, i + 1)`. This is done for all six categorical variables. The user defined function generates values for the dummy variables using a match clause. For example, the housing variable has three unique categories; `unknown, yes` and `no` corresponding to which three variables- `housing_0` (represents 'unknown'), `housing_1` (represents 'no') and `housing_2` (represents 'yes') are created as part of recursive function `create_DummyVariables`.

After this, the categorical variables are dropped using the statement `val final_Df = new_Df_WithDummyLoan.drop("job").drop("marital").drop("default").drop("housing").drop("loan").drop("poutcome")`. Next, for the target variable `y` representing `yes` or `no` we used `StringIndexer` in Spark. The statement `val indexerModel = new StringIndexer().setInputCol("y").setOutputCol("y_Index").fit(final_Df)` creates a `StringIndexerModel` which takes the input column (`nominal variable`) and output column which contains the unique representation for each category.

There's more...

In the above recipe, we saw how to apply feature engineering. In the next recipe, let's see how to apply the algorithm on the final dataset.

See also

Please refer to the *Variable identification* and *Data exploration* recipes to understand the initial steps.

Applying logistic regression

In this recipe, we'll see how to apply Logistic regression.

Getting ready

To step through this recipe, you will need a running Spark cluster in any one of the modes, that is, local, standalone, YARN, and Mesos. For installing Spark on a standalone cluster, please refer to http://spark.apache.org/docs/latest/spark-standalone.html. Also, include the Spark MLlib package in the build.sbt file so that it downloads the related libraries and the API can be used. Install Hadoop (optionally), Scala, and Java.

How to do it...

1. The final step is splitting the DataFrame/RDD into train and test sets and applying logistic regression on the training set:

```
val final_Rdd  =  indexedDf.rdd.map {
row =>
val age = row.getAs[Double]("age")
val duration = row.getAs[Double]("duration")
val previous = row.getAs[Double]("previous")
val empvarrate = row.getAs[Double]("empvarrate")
val job_0 = row.getAs[Double]("job_0")
val job_1 = row.getAs[Double]("job_1")
val job_2 = row.getAs[Double]("job_2")
val job_3 = row.getAs[Double]("job_3")
val job_4 = row.getAs[Double]("job_4")
val job_5 = row.getAs[Double]("job_5")
val job_6 = row.getAs[Double]("job_6")
val job_7 = row.getAs[Double]("job_7")
val job_8 = row.getAs[Double]("job_8")
val job_9 = row.getAs[Double]("job_9")
val job_10 = row.getAs[Double]("job_10")
val job_11 = row.getAs[Double]("job_11")
val marital_0 = row.getAs[Double]("marital_0")
val marital_1 = row.getAs[Double]("marital_1")
val marital_2 = row.getAs[Double]("marital_2")
val marital_3 = row.getAs[Double]("marital_3")
val default_0 = row.getAs[Double]("default_0")
val default_1 = row.getAs[Double]("default_1")
val default_2 = row.getAs[Double]("default_2")
val housing_0 = row.getAs[Double]("housing_0")
val housing_1 = row.getAs[Double]("housing_1")
val housing_2 = row.getAs[Double]("housing_2")
val poutcome_0 = row.getAs[Double]("poutcome_0")
val poutcome_1 = row.getAs[Double]("poutcome_1")
val poutcome_2 = row.getAs[Double]("poutcome_2")
```

```
val loan_0 = row.getAs[Double]("loan_0")
val loan_1 = row.getAs[Double]("loan_1")
val loan_2 = row.getAs[Double]("loan_2")
val label = row.getAs[Double]("y_Index")
val featurecVec = Vectors.dense(Array(age,duration,previous,
empvarrate,job_0,job_1,job_2,job_3,job_4,job_5,job_6,job_7,
job_8,job_9,job_10,job_11,marital_0
marital_1,marital_2,marital_3,
default_0,default_1,default_2,housing_0,housing_1,housing_2,
poutcome_0,poutcome_1,poutcome_2,loan_0,loan_1,loan_2))
LabeledPoint(label,  featurecVec) }
val splits = final_Rdd.randomSplit(Array(0.8,0.2))
val training = splits(0).cache()
val test = splits(1)
val model = new LogisticRegressionWithLBFGS()
.setNumClasses(2)
.run(training)
// Compute raw scores on the test set.
val predictionAndLabels = test.map { case LabeledPoint(label,
features) =>
val prediction = model.predict(features)
(prediction, label) }
// Get evaluation metrics.
val metrics = new MulticlassMetrics(predictionAndLabels)
val precision = metrics.precision
println("Precision = "+precision)
```

The following is the output:

```
Precision = 0.908132347594231
```

How it works...

As a final step of applying the algorithm, the DataFrame is converted to RDD. The output `y_Index` variable is the label and from the remaining variables, dense vector is created. Once the `RDD[LabeledPoint]` is generated, the line `final_Rdd.randomSplit(Array(0.8,0.2))` splits the RDD into training and testing containing 80% and 20% of the records, respectively. The line `val model = new LogisticRegressionWithLBFGS().setNumClasses(2).run(training)` runs the algorithm on the training dataset. From the test set, the model predicts the label from the features as `model.predict(features)`. After this, using `MultiClassMetrics`, the precision of the model is displayed.

There's more...

Once the model is built, the initially created hypothesis will be tested and data needs to be sufficient to test all the scenarios. In the preceding case study, we applied the logistic regression model from MLlib, Spark has support for `ml` pipelines as well which we can use to apply algorithms directly on the DataFrame. Also, there is support for evaluating different models built in the `org.apache.spark.mllib.evaluation` package. There are other flavors of regression such as ridge regression, stepwise regression, **Ordinary Least Squares Regression** (**OLSR**), multivariate regression and so on. Spark MLlib offers several regression algorithms with different estimation techniques.

See also

Please visit the recipes *Working with Spark programming model*, *Working with Spark's Python and Scala shells*, *Working with pair RDDs* in `Chapter 1`, *Big Data Analytics with Spark*. To understand more about statistics, go through the elementary concepts of statistics at `http://www.statsoft.com/Textbook/Elementary-Statistics-Concepts`.

Real-time intrusion detection using streaming k-means

Clustering analysis is the task of grouping a set of objects in such a way that objects in the same group (cluster) are more similar than those in other clusters. It is one of the subjective modeling techniques widely used in the industry. One example of its usage is segmenting customer portfolios based on demographics, transaction behavior, or other behavioral attributes. Clustering generates natural clusters and is not dependent on any of the driving objective functions. Once the clustering does initial profiling of the portfolio, the objective modeling technique can be used to build a specific strategy.

There are a number of clustering algorithms such as hierarchical clustering, k-means clustering, spectral clustering, DBSCAN and so on. This recipe shows how to detect an anomaly from the network data based on the clustering technique.

Variable identification

In this recipe, we'll see how to identify the required variables for analysis and understand their description.

Getting ready

To step through this recipe, you will need a running Spark cluster in any one of the modes, that is, local, standalone, YARN, or Mesos. For installing Spark on a standalone cluster, please refer to `http://spark.apache.org/docs/latest/spark-standalone.html`. Also, include the Spark MLlib package in the `build.sbt` file so that it downloads the related libraries and the API can be used. Install Hadoop (optionally), Scala, and Java.

How to do it...

1. Let's take an example of network data which contains information on network access and a variety of network intrusions. This is the NSL-KDD dataset, which is a refined version of the KDD'99 dataset. Although the dataset has intrusions being represented as labels, we use the k-means clustering algorithm which is an unsupervised learning approach to cluster the dataset into normal and four major attack categories, that is, DoS, Probe, R2L and U2R.

    Please download the dataset from the following location:
   `https://github.com/ChitturiPadma/datasets/blob/master/KDD_Data.csv`

2. Here is a description of some of the variables that we are going to use in our analysis:

Variable	Description
duration	Length (number of seconds) of the connection
protocol_type	Type of the protocol for example, TCP, UDP and so on.
service	Network service at the destination for example, HTTP, telnet and so on.
src_bytes	Number of data bytes from source to destination

dst_bytes	Number of data bytes from destination to source
flag	Normal or error status of the connection
land	1 if connection is from/to same host/port and 0 otherwise
wrong_fragment	Number of wrong fragments
urgent	Number of urgent packets
hot	Number of hot indicators
num_failed_logins	Number of failed login attempts
logged_in	1 if successfully logged in; 0 otherwise

There are a total of 43 variables and 148517 rows. For the description of other variables, please visit:

`https://github.com/ChitturiPadma/datasets/blob/master/FieldNames.`

To learn about the attack types, please refer to:
`https://github.com/ChitturiPadma/datasets/blob/master/Attack_Types`

3. The data resides in HDFS. Let's load the data into Spark and see the values corresponding to different variables:

```
import org.apache.spark._
import org.apache.spark.mllib.linalg.Vectors
import org.apache.spark.sql._
import org.apache.spark.sql.functions._
import org.apache.spark.sql.DataFrameNaFunctions
import org.apache.spark.sql.types._
import org.apache.spark.mllib.stat.
{MultivariateStatisticalSummary, Statistics}
object Variable_Identification {
def main(args:Array[String]): Unit = {
val conf = new SparkConf()
  .setMaster("spark://master:7077")
  .setAppName("Variable_Identification")
val sc = new SparkContext(conf)
val sqlContext = new SQLContext(sc)
import sqlContext.implicits._
//Loading data
val network_data =
sqlContext.read.format("com.databricks.spark.csv")
```

```
    .option("header", "true")
    .option("inferSchema","true")
    .load("hdfs://namenode:9000/KDD_Data.csv")
  network_data.show(5)
  } }
```

The following is the output:

```
+--------+-------------+--------+------+----------+---------+
|duration|protocol_type|service |  flag|src_bytes |dst_bytes|
+--------+-------------+--------+------+----------+---------+
|       0|          tcp|ftp_data|   SF |      491 |        0|
|       0|          udp|other   |   SF |      146 |        0|
|       0|          tcp|private |   S0 |        0 |        0|
|       0|          tcp|http    |   SF |      232 |     8153|
|       0|          tcp|http    |   SF |      199 |      420|
+--------------+----------+---------------+---------------+
```

```
+----+--------------+
|land|wrong_fragment|
+----+--------------+
| 0  |           0  |
| 0  |           0  |
| 0  |           0  |
| 0  |           0  |
| 0  |           0  |
+----+--------------+
```

How it works...

In the preceding code snippet, since the file is of CSV format, we imported the data initially into Spark using the CSV package. The schema is inferred and variables are identified. The `network_data.show(5)` line displays the first five records. From this sample data, the independent and dependent variables are identified. There are in total 41 attributes and a few sample attributes `duration`, `protocol_type`, `service`, `flag`, `src_bytes`, `dst_bytes`, `land` and `wrong_fragment` are displayed in the output.

There's more...

In subsequent recipes, let's look at how to simulate file data as real-time streaming data, explore, and apply online k-means.

Clustering, Classification, and Regression_

See also

Please refer to the *Producer code generating real-time data* and *Apply streaming k-means* recipes for the subsequent steps.

Simulating real-time data

In this recipe, we'll see how to simulate real-time data.

Getting ready

To step through this recipe, you will need Kafka and Zookeeper running on the cluster. Install Scala and Java.

How to do it...

1. Since the data is available in files, let's simulate the data in real time using a producer which writes the data into Kafka. Here is the code:

```
import java.util.{Date, Properties}
import kafka.javaapi.producer.Producer
import kafka.producer.KeyedMessage
import kafka.producer.ProducerConfig
import org.apache.spark.mllib.linalg.Vectors
import scala.io.{BufferedSource, Source}
import scala.util.Random
object KafkaProducer {
   def main(args:Array[String]): Unit ={
      val random:Random = new Random
      val props = new Properties
 props.put("metadata.broker.list","172.22.128.16:9092")
 props.put("serializer.class","kafka.serializer.StringEncoder")
 props.put("request.required.acks","1")
 val config:ProducerConfig =  new ProducerConfig(props)
 val producer:Producer[String,String] = new
 Producer[String,String](config)
 val (fileObject1, fileObject2) =
    getFileObject(hdfs://namenode:9000/KDD_Data.csv")
 val lines = readFile(fileObject1,fileObject2)
    while(true)
       {
```

[160]

```
val record = lines(random.nextInt(148517))
  if(!record.contains("duration")) {
val parts = record.split(",").toBuffer
parts.remove(42)
parts.remove(1,3)
val msg = parts.toArray.mkString(",")
val data:KeyedMessage[String,String] = new
KeyedMessage[String,String]     ("test",msg)
producer.send(data) } }
producer.close
  }
def readFile(buffer1:BufferedSource):List[String]  =
buffer1.getLines().toList
def getFileObject(path1:String)
:BufferedSource=Source.fromFile(path1)
```

How it works...

The `KafkaProducer` code simulates the network intrusion data in real time. For this, kafka and zookeeper must be running on the cluster. The line, `val props = new Properties` creates a properties object. The kafka broker and serializer information is set in the properties object as `props.put("metadata.broker.list","172.22.128.16:9092")`. The file from HDFS is read and a loop is run continuously which reads a random record from the file as `val record = lines(random.nextInt(148517))`. If the record is not the header, the last column representing the unique value for attack is removed as `parts.remove(42)`. The categorical `protocol_type`, `service` and `flag` variables are also removed using the line `parts.remove(1,3)` as k-means clustering needs only numeric fields. Now the record is transformed to a `KeyedMessage` type using the line, `val data:KeyedMessage[String,String] = new KeyedMessage[String,String]("test",msg)`. The message is sent to kafka using the line, `producer.send(data)`. This happens iteratively and sends a random record to Kafka.

There's more...

In the preceding recipe, we saw how to write producer code that simulates the streaming data. In practical scenarios, the data would be coming either from a port, website, or even from a database. The change in records can trigger real-time events. In the next recipe, let's see how to process real-time streaming data and apply a streaming k-means algorithm.

See also

Please refer to the *Applying streaming k-means* recipe for the subsequent steps.

Applying streaming k-means

In this recipe, we'll see how to apply online k-means on streaming data.

Getting ready

To work through this recipe, you will need a running Spark cluster in any one of the modes, that is, local, standalone, YARN, or Mesos. For installing Spark on a standalone cluster, please refer to http://spark.apache.org/docs/latest/spark-standalone.html. Also, include the Spark MLlib package in the build.sbt file so that it downloads the related libraries and the API can be used. Install Hadoop (optionally), Scala, and Java. This recipe also requires Kafka and Zookeeper running on the cluster. We are going to run the algorithm on real data.

How to do it...

1. Let's try to build a real-time network detection system using Spark streaming and MLlib. Here is the code which processes the real time data, performs pre-processing and applies k-means algorithm on live data:

```
import java.net.InetAddress
import _root_.kafka.serializer.StringDecoder
import kafka.server.KafkaApis
import org.apache.spark._
import org.apache.spark.streaming._
import org.apache.spark.streaming.StreamingContext._
import org.apache.spark.streaming.kafka._
import org.apache.spark.broadcast._
import org.apache.spark.mllib.linalg._
import org.apache.spark.mllib.clustering._
import org.apache.spark.rdd.RDD
import org.apache.spark.mllib.regression.LabeledPoint
import org.joda.time.DateTime

object AnomalyDetection_StreamingKMeans {
def distance(featureVector:Vector, centroid:Vector)=
```

```
math.sqrt(featureVector.toArray.zip(centroid.toArray).map{case
(vec1,vec2) => vec1-vec2}.map(diff => diff*diff).sum)

def distToCentroid(featureVector:Vector,
broadCastModel:Broadcast[StreamingKMeansModel]):Double={
val model = broadCastModel.value
val cluster = model.predict(featureVector)
val centroid = model.clusterCenters(cluster)
distance(featureVector, centroid)
  }

def getCurrentDateTime:Long =  DateTime.now.getMillis
def getIpAddress = InetAddress.getLocalHost.getHostAddress

def normalize(dataum:Vector, means:Array[Double],
stdevs:Array[Double]):Vector = {
val normalizedArray = (dataum.toArray, means, stdevs).zipped.map{
(value, mean, stdev ) => if(stdev <=0) (value-mean) else (value-
 mean)/stdev
  }
Vectors.dense(normalizedArray)
  }
def main(args:Array[String]): Unit ={
println("Entering Streaming K-Means Application")
val conf = new SparkConf().setMaster("spark://master:7077")
.setAppName("Anomaly-Detection_System")
val sc = new SparkContext(conf)
val ssc = new StreamingContext(sc, Seconds(6))
val topicName = "test"
val topicSet = topicName.split(",").toSet
val brokerName = getIpAddress+":"+"9092"
val kafkaParams = Map[String,String]("metadata.broker.list" ->
brokerName)
val inputDstream = KafkaUtils.createDirectStream[String, String,
StringDecoder, StringDecoder](ssc, kafkaParams,
topicSet).map(_._2)
val labelsAndData = inputDstream.map{dataPoint => val parts =
dataPoint.split(",").toBuffer
val label = parts.remove(parts.length-1)
val labelModified = label match {
case str:String=> if(str == "back" || str == "neptune" ||
    str == "land" || str == "smurf" || str == "pod" || str ==
    "teardrop" || str == "apache2" || str == "udpstorm" || str ==
    "processtable" || str == "mailbomb" || str == "worm")
    "DoS"

  else if(str == "nmap" || str == "ipsweep" || str == "satan" ||
    str == "portsweep" || str == "mscan" || str == "saint")
```

```
  "Probe"
  else if(str == "multihop" || str == "ftp_write" || str ==
  "guess_passwd" || str == "phf" || str == "spy" || str ==
  "warezclient" || str == "imap" || str == "warezmaster" || str
  == "snmpgetattack" || str == "snmpguess"  || str ==
  "httptunnel" || str == "sendmail" || str == "xlock" || str ==
  "named" || str == "xsnoop")
    "R2L"

  else if (str == "loadmodule" || str == "rootkit" || str ==
  "buffer_overflow" || str == "perl" || str == "xterm" || str ==
  "sqlattack" || str == "ps" )
    "U2R"
  else if(str=="normal") "normal"
  else "unknown"
 }
val vector = Vectors.dense(parts.map(_.toDouble).toArray)
(labelModified, (dataPoint,vector))
}
val normalizedDStream =
labelsAndData.transform{labelsAndVectorsRdd
=>
val rddVector = labelsAndVectorsRdd.values.values
val dataAsArray =  rddVector.map(_.toArray)
val n = dataAsArray.count
val sums = dataAsArray.reduce((a,b) => a.zip(b).map
(t => t._1 +t._2))
val means = sums.map(_/n)
val meanBroadcasted = sc.broadcast(means)
val dataWithMeanDiffSquared =  dataAsArray.map{features => val
meanValue =  meanBroadcasted.value
val length = features.length
val featuresMapped = (0 to length-1).map{i => val diff =
features(i)-meanValue(i)
diff*diff}
featuresMapped.toArray}
val squaredSumReduced = dataWithMeanDiffSquared.reduce((a,b) =>
a.zip(b).map(t =>
t._1+t._2) )
val variance = squaredSumReduced.map(_/n)
val stdevs = variance.map(ele => math.sqrt(ele))
val stdevBroadcasted = sc.broadcast(stdevs)
val normalizedData = labelsAndVectorsRdd.map{case(label,
(original,vector)) =>
val meanValue = meanBroadcasted.value
val stdevValue = stdevBroadcasted.value
(label,(original,normalize(vector, meanValue, stdevValue)))
  }
```

```
normalizedData
    }.cache()
 val streaming_k_means = new StreamingKMeans()
 .setK(5)
 .setDecayFactor(1.0)
 .setRandomCenters(38,0.0)
 streaming_k_means.trainOn(normalizedDStream.map(_._2).map(_._2))
 val model = streaming_k_means.latestModel()
 val broadCastedKMeans = sc.broadcast(model)
 normalizedDStream.foreachRDD{
 labelsAndVectorsRdd =>
 val distances =  labelsAndVectorsRdd.map{
 case(label, (original, dataVector)) =>
 distToCentroid(dataVector,broadCastedKMeans) }
 val threshold = distances.top(100).last
 val detectedAnomalies = labelsAndVectorsRdd.filter{
 case(label, (original, dataVector)) =>
 distToCentroid(dataVector,broadCastedKMeans) > threshold
 }
 val mappedDetectedAnomalies = detectedAnomalies.map{case(label,
 (original, dataVector)) => (label, "anomaly")}
 val detectedAnomalyCount =
 mappedDetectedAnomalies.count.toDouble
 val realAnomalies =
 mappedDetectedAnomalies.filter{case(originalLabel,
 predictedLabel) => originalLabel!="normal"}
 val correctAnomalyCount = realAnomalies.count.toDouble
 println("Accuracy is:"+correctAnomalyCount/detectedAnomalyCount)
 }
  ssc.start()
  ssc.awaitTermination()
  ssc.stop()
 }
}
```

The following is the output:

Entering streaming k-means application

```
Accuracy is : 0.7575757575757576
Accuracy is : 0.6868686868686869
Accuracy is : 0.7474747474747475
Accuracy is : 0.7474747474747475
Accuracy is : 0.7777777777777778
Accuracy is : 0.7070707070707071
Accuracy is : 0.696969696969697
Accuracy is : 0.7676767676767676
Accuracy is : 0.7272727272727273
Accuracy is : 0.7878787878787878
Accuracy is : 0.7575757575757576
Accuracy is : 0.7676767676767676
Accuracy is : 0.7474747474747475
Accuracy is : 0.7373737373737373
Accuracy is : 0.8181818181818182
```

How it works...

The `AnomalyDetection_StreamingKMeans` code initializes the `Dstream` to read data from `Kafka` using the line, `KafkaUtils.createDirectStream[String, String, StringDecoder, StringDecoder](ssc, kafkaParams, topicSet).map(_._2)`. Next, the `Dstream` is transformed such that the line, `val label = parts.remove(parts.length-1)` removes the label and the label is mapped to four major attack categories; `DoS`, `Probe`, `U2R`, `R2L` and `normal`. The features are mapped to a dense vector as `val vector = Vectors.dense(parts.map(_.toDouble).toArray)` and the `Dstream` `labelsAndData` contains a modified label, original record and vector. The Dstream `labelsAndData` is transformed to perform the following operation-the line `val sums = dataAsArray.reduce((a,b) => a.zip(b).map(t => t._1 +t._2))` adds all the feature vectors to a single vector (represented as array) and mean is calculated as `valmeans = sums.map(_/n)`. For each vector in the `rdddataAsArray`, the square of difference from the mean is calculated as `val featuresMapped = (0 to length-1).map{i => val diff = features(i)-meanValue(i).diff*diff`.

From the calculated difference, variance is calculated using the lines, `val squaredSumReduced = dataWithMeanDiffSquared.reduce((a,b) => a.zip(b).map(t => t._1+t._2) )` and `val variance = squaredSumReduced.map(_/n)`. Also, standard deviation is calculated using the line, `val stdevs = variance.map(ele => math.sqrt(ele))`. Using the calculated standard deviation and mean, the feature vectors are normalized with the `formula (x-mu)/sigma`. This is performed in the function, `normalize(dataum:Vector, means:Array[Double], stdevs:Array[Double]):Vector`. The streaming k-means object is initialized as `val streaming_k_means = new StreamingKMeans().setK(3).setDecayFactor(1.0).setRandomCenters(38,0.0)`.

Now the algorithm is applied on the `normalizedDStream` as `streaming_k_means.trainOn(normalizedDStream.map(_._2).map(_._2))`. Using the built model, the distance of each feature vector to its centroid as `distToCentroid(dataVector,broadCastedKMeans)`. The threshold distance is defined as `val threshold = distances.top(100).last`. Any feature vector (data point) whose distance to centroid greater than the threshold is the anomaly and this is done using the following line: `distToCentroid(dataVector,broadCastedKMeans) > threshold`. Finally, to calculate the accuracy, the count of predicted labels which are the same as the original label is found out (which are not normal) and the `correctAnomalyCount/detectedAnomalyCount` ratio gives the percentage of correct anomalies detected.

There's more...

For the preceding dataset, although there is no missing value treatment, there is feature engineering applied, which created a broader category-four attacks instead of having the actual labels, which are 21 in number. The interesting point is that we applied streaming k-means which is mini batch k-means available in Python Scikit learn. MLlib includes a variation called streaming k-means, which can update a clustering incrementally as new data arrives in a `StreamingKMeansModel`. This could be used to continuously learn, approximately, how new data affects the clustering and not just assess new data against existing clusters. It integrates with Spark streaming.

Here we applied the simplistic model. For example, the Euclidean distance is used in this example because it is the only distance function supported by Spark MLlib at this time. In future, it may be possible to use distance functions that can better account for the distributions of, and correlations between, features, such as the Mahalanobis distance. Coming to the model evaluation part, there are more sophisticated cluster quality evaluation metrics that could be applied, even without labels, to pick k, such as the Silhouette coefficient. These tend to evaluate not just closeness of points within one cluster, but closeness of points to other clusters.

Finally, different models could be applied too, instead of simple k-means clustering; for example, a Gaussian mixture model or DBSCAN could capture more subtle relationships between data points and the cluster centers.

See also

Please visit the earlier *Working with Spark programming model, Work with Spark's Python and Scala shells, Working with pair RDDs* recipes from `Chapter 1`, *Big Data Analytics with Spark* to become more familiar with Spark. Also, to learn how to work with linear and logistic regression, please refer to the earlier *Apply regression analysis for sales data* and *Apply logistic regression on bank marketing data* recipes. To understand more about statistics, go through the elementary concepts in statistics from `http://www.statsoft.com/Textbook/Elementary-Statistics-Concepts`.

5
Working with Spark MLlib

In this chapter, you will learn about the MLlib component of Spark. We will cover the following recipes:

- Implementing Naive Bayes classification
- Implementing decision trees
- Building a recommendation system
- Implementing logistic regression using Spark ML pipelines

Introduction

MLlib is the **machine learning** (**ML**) library that is provided with Apache Spark, the in-memory, cluster-based, open source data processing system. In this chapter, I will examine the functionality of algorithms provided within the MLlib library in terms of areas of machine learning tasks such as classification, recommendation, and neural processing. For each algorithm, we'll provide working examples that tackle real problems. We will take a step-by-step approach in describing how the following algorithms can be used, and what they are capable of doing.

Big data and machine learning takes place in three steps-collect, analyze and predict. For this purpose, the Spark ecosystem supports a wide range of workloads, including batch applications, iterative algorithms, interactive queries, and stream processing. The Spark MLlib component offers a variety of ML algorithms which are scalable.

Working with Spark ML pipelines

Spark MLlib's goal is to make practical ML scalable and easy. Similar to Spark Core, MLlib provides APIs in three languages that is, Python, Scala, and Java–with example code which will ease the learning curve for users coming from different backgrounds. The pipeline API in MLlib provides a uniform set of high-level APIs built on top of DataFrames that helps users create and tune practical ML pipelines. This API is under a new package with name `spark.ml`.

MLlib standardizes APIs for machine learning algorithms to make it easier to combine multiple algorithms into a single pipeline or workflow. Let's see the key terms introduced by the pipeline API:

- **DataFrame**: The ML API uses DataFrame from Spark SQL as an ML dataset, which can hold a variety of data types. For example, a DataFrame could have different columns storing text, feature vectors, true labels and predictions.
- **Transformer**: A transformer is an algorithm which can transform one DataFrame into another DataFrame. For example, an ML model is a transformer which transforms a DataFrame with features into a DataFrame with predictions.
- **Estimator**: An estimator is an algorithm which can be fit on a DataFrame to produce a Transformer. For example, a learning algorithm is an Estimator which trains on a DataFrame and produces a model.
- **Pipeline**: A pipeline chains multiple transformers and estimators together to specify an ML workflow.
- **Parameter**: All transformers and estimators share a common API for specifying parameters.

The following are the pipeline components:

- **Transformer**: It is an abstraction which includes feature transformers and learned models. A transformer internally implements a `transform()` method which converts one DataFrame into another by appending one or more columns. For example:
  - A feature transformer might take a DataFrame, read a column, map it into a new column (feature vectors) and output a new DataFrame with the mapped column appended.
  - A learning model might take a DataFrame, read the column containing feature vectors, predict the label for the each feature vector and results in a DataFrame with predicted labels as a field.

- **Estimator**: It abstracts the concept of a learning algorithm or any algorithm that fits or trains on data. An estimator implements the `fit()` method which accepts a DataFrame and produces the model (which is a transformer).

Implementing Naive Bayes' classification

Naive Bayes is a simple probabilistic classifier based on the Bayes theorem. This classifier is capable of calculating the most probable output depending on the input. It is possible to add new raw data at runtime and have a better probabilistic classifier. The Naive Bayes model is typically used for classification. There will be a bunch of features $X1, X2,....Xn$ observed for an instance. The goal is to infer to which class among the limited set of classes the particular instance belongs. This model makes the assumption that every pair of features Xi and Xj is conditionally independent given the class. This classifier is a sub-class of Bayesian networks. For more information about the classifier, please refer to `http://www.statsoft.com/textbook/naive-bayes-classifier`.

This recipe shows how to run the Naive Bayes classifier on the `weather` dataset using the Naive Bayes classifier algorithm available in the Spark MLlib package. The code is written in Scala.

Getting ready

To step through this recipe, you will need a running Spark cluster in any one of the modes, that is, local, standalone, YARN, or Mesos. For installing Spark on a standalone cluster, please refer `http://spark.apache.org/docs/latest/spark-standalone.html`. Also, include the Spark MLlib package in the `build.sbt` file so that it downloads the related libraries and the API can be used. Install Hadoop (optionally), Scala, and Java. Please download the dataset from the following location: `https://github.com/ChitturiPadma/datasets/blob/master/weather.csv`.

How to do it...

1. Let us see how to implement Naive Baye's classification:

```
import org.apache.spark.{SparkContext, SparkConf}
import org.apache.spark.mllib.classification.{NaiveBayes,
NaiveBayesModel}
import org.apache.spark.mllib.linalg.Vectors
```

```
import org.apache.spark.mllib.regression.LabeledPoint
object NaiveBayesSample {
def main (args:Array[String]): Unit =
{
val conf = new SparkConf
conf.setMaster("spark://master:7077").setAppName
("NaiveBayesSample")
val sc = new SparkContext(conf)
val data =
sc.textFile("hdfs://namenode:9000/datasets/weather.csv")
val parsedData = data.map{line => val parts = line.split(",")
val label = if(parts(0)=="overcast") 0.0 else
if(parts(0)=="rainy") 1.0 else 2.0
val feature1 = parts(1).toDouble
val feature2 = parts(2).toDouble
val feature3 = if(parts(3)=="FALSE") 0.0 else 1.0
LabeledPoint(label,
Vectors.dense(Array(feature1,feature2,feature3)))}
// Split data into training (60%) and test (40%)
val splits = parsedData.randomSplit(Array(0.6,0.4), seed = 11L)
val training = splits(0)
val test = splits(1)
val model = NaiveBayes.train(training, lambda = 1.0, modelType =
"multinomial")
val predictionAndLabel = test.map(p =>
(model.predict(p.features), p.label))
val accuracy = 1.0*predictionAndLabel.filter(x => x._1 ==
x._2).count()/test.count()
println("Accuracy is..."+accuracy)
//Save and Load model
model.save(sc, "hdfs://namenode:9000/models/myNaiveBayesModel")
val sameModel = NaiveBayesModel.load(sc,
"hdfs://namenode:9000/models/myNaiveBayesModel")
    }
}
```

2. The weather dataset `weather.txt` looks like this:

Season	Temperature	Humidity	Windy
overcast	83	86	FALSE
overcast	64	65	TRUE
overcast	72	90	TRUE
overcast	81	75	FALSE
rainy	70	96	FALSE

rainy	68	80	FALSE
rainy	65	70	TRUE
rainy	75	80	FALSE
rainy	71	91	TRUE
sunny	85	85	FALSE
sunny	80	90	TRUE
sunny	72	95	FALSE
unny	69	70	FALSE
sunny	75	70	TRUE

3. Convert the data into numerics as follows:

Season	Temperature	Humidity	Windy
0	83	86	0
0	64	65	1
0	72	90	1
0	81	75	0
1	70	96	0
1	68	80	0
1	65	70	1
1	75	80	0
1	71	91	1
2	85	85	0
2	80	90	1
2	72	95	0
2	69	70	0
2	75	70	1

How it works...

The preceding code snippet `NaiveBayesSample` implements multinomial Naive Bayes. It takes an RDD of `LabeledPoint` and an optional smoothing parameter `lambda` as input and also an optional model type parameter `multinomial`. It outputs `NaiveBayesModel`, which is used for evaluation and prediction. `LabeledPoint` is a class that represents the features and labels of a data point. These labeled points are used in supervised leaning algorithms such as regression and classification. For multiclass classification, labels should be of class indices starting from 0, 1, 2, ... Hence, the weather data is converted to numeric and is given as input for the algorithm.

There's more...

The labeled point takes a label and local vector either dense or sparse as input. To get familiar with local vectors, labeled points and so on, please refer to `http://spark.apache.org/docs/latest/mllib-data-types.html` in Spark MLlib package. Also, refer `http://spark.apache.org/docs/latest/mllib-statistics.html` for information on basic statistics.

See also

Please visit the *Working with the Spark programming model, Working with Spark's Python and Scala shells* and *Working with pair RDDs* recipes in `Chapter 1`, *Big Data Analytics with Spark* to get familiar with Spark. To understand more about statistics, go through the elementary concepts in statistics from `http://www.statsoft.com/Textbook/Elementary-Statistics-Concepts`.

Implementing decision trees

Decision trees are the most widely used data mining machine learning algorithm in practice for classification and regression. They are easy to interpret, handle categorical features and extend to the multiclass classification. This decision tree model, which is a powerful, non-probabilistic technique, captures more complex nonlinear patterns and feature interactions. Their outcome is quite understandable. They are not hard to use since it's not required to tweak a lot of parameters.

This recipe shows how to run the decision tree on web content which evaluates a large set of URLs and classifies them as *ephemeral* (that is, short-lived and will cease being popular soon) or *evergreen* (that last for longer time). It is available in the Spark MLlib package. The code is written in Scala.

Getting ready

To step through this recipe, you will need a running Spark cluster in any one of the modes, that is, local, standalone, YARN, or Mesos. For installing Spark on a standalone cluster, please refer to `http://spark.apache.org/docs/latest/spark-standalone.html`. Also, include the Spark MLlib package in the `build.sbt` file so that it downloads the related libraries and the API can be used. Install Hadoop (optionally), Scala, and Java. Please download the dataset from `http://www.kaggle.com/c/stumbleupon/data`. Download the training data (`train.tsv`); you will need to accept the terms and conditions before downloading the dataset.

How to do it...

1. Before we begin, remove the column name header from the first line of the file. Change to the directory in which you downloaded the data and run the following to remove the first line and pipe the result to a new file called `train_noheader.tsv`:

    ```
    sed 1d train.tsv > train_noheader.tsv
    ```

2. Here is the code that implements Decision trees:

    ```
    import org.apache.spark.{SparkContext, SparkConf}
    import org.apache.spark.mllib.tree.DecisionTree
    import org.apache.spark.mllib.tree.model.DecisionTreeModel
    import org.apache.spark.mllib.tree.impurity._
    import org.apache.spark.mllib.linalg.Vectors
    import org.apache.spark.mllib.regression.LabeledPoint
    import org.apache.spark.mllib.tree.configuration.Algo
    object DecisionTreeSample {
    def main(args:Array[String])
    {
    val conf = new SparkConf
    conf.setMaster("spark://master:7077")
      .setAppName("DecisionTreeSample")
    ```

```
val sc = new SparkContext(conf)
val rawData = sc.textFile("hdfs://namenode:9000/datsets/
              train_noheader.tsv")
val records = rawData.map(line => line.split("\t"))
val data = records.map{record =>
val trimmed = record.map(_.replaceAll("""", ""))
val label = trimmed(record.size-1).toInt
val features = trimmed.slice(4,record.size-1).map(d =>
    if(d=="?")  0.0 else    d.toDouble)
LabeledPoint(label, Vectors.dense(features))}
val maxTreeDepth = 5
val dtModel = DecisionTree.train(data, Algo.Classification,
Entropy, maxTreeDepth)
val predictions = dtModel.predict(data.map(lp => lp.features))
predictions.take(5).foreach(println)
    }
}
```

The following is the output:

```
0.0
0.0
 .0
0.0
1.0
```

How it works...

The dataset contains the URL and ID of the page in the first two columns. The other columns contain textual content and the final column contains the target – 1 is evergreen, while 0 is non-evergreen. All the available numeric features are used directly. Initially, data cleaning is done by trimming out the extra quotation ". For the missing values denoted by "?", zero is assigned to these missing values.

In the preceding code snippet, the label variable is extracted from the last column and an array of features for columns 5 to 25 (after cleaning and dealing with missing values). The Label is converted to a `Int` value and the features to an `Array[Double]`. Now, the label and the features are wrapped in a `LabeledPoint`, converting the features into a MLlib vector. The data `(RDD[LabeledPoint])` is trained using `DecisionTree`. Finally, `predictions` are made using the `DecisiconTreeModel`.

There's more...

The tree complexity has a crucial effect on its accuracy. The decision tree is a top-down approach that begins at a root node (or feature) and then selects at each step the feature that gives the best split of the dataset, as measured by the information gain of this split. The information gain is computed from the node impurity (which is the extent to which the labels at the node are similar, or homogenous) minus the weighted sum of the impurities for the two child nodes that would be created by the split. For classification tasks, there are two measures to select the best split – Gini impurity and entropy.

When we make predictions using the model, we should be able to evaluate how well the model performs. Hence, prediction error and accuracy could be calculated. The performance of the model is determined by calculating the average classification accuracy as the total number of correctly classified instances divided by the total number of data points.

See also

For more about decision trees, please refer the Spark documentation at `http://spark.apac he.org/docs/latest/mllib-decision-tree.html`. The earlier *Implementing Naive Bayes classification* recipe also talks about classification based on Bayes' theorem.

Building a recommendation system

Recommendation engines are one of the types of machine learning algorithms. Often, people might have experienced them using the popular websites such as Amazon, Netflix, YouTube, Twitter, LinkedIn and Facebook. The idea behind recommendation engines is to predict what people might like and to uncover relationships between the items to aid in the discovery process.

Recommender systems are widely studied and there are many approaches such as – content-based filtering and collaborative filtering. Other approaches, such as ranking models, have also gained popularity. Since Spark's recommendation models only include an implementation of matrix factorization, this recipe shows how to run **matrix factorization** on rating datasets from the MovieLens website.

The algorithm is available in the Spark MLLib package. The code is written in Scala.

Getting ready

To step through this recipe, you will need a running Spark cluster in any one of the modes, that is, local, standalone, YARN, or Mesos. For installing Spark on a standalone cluster, please refer to http://spark.apache.org/docs/latest/spark-standalone.html. Also, include the Spark MLlib package in the build.sbt file so that it downloads the related libraries and the API can be used. Install Hadoop (optionally), Scala, and Java. Please download the dataset from
http://files.grouplens.org/datasets/movielens/ml-100k.zip. This is a 100k dataset, which is a set of 100,000 data points related to ratings given by a set of users to a set of movies. It also contains movie metadata and user profiles.

How to do it...

1. In the following code snippet, **alternating least squares** (**ALS**), which solves matrix factorization problems, is used to train the model. This ALS achieves good performance and it's also easy to implement in a parallel fashion. Develop a Spark standalone application using the Eclipse IDE as follows:

```
import org.apache.spark.{SparkContext, SparkConf}
import org.apache.spark.mllib.recommendation.ALS
import org.apache.spark.mllib.recommendation.Rating
object RecommendationSample {
def main(args:Array[String]): Unit =
{
//Initalize SparkConf and SparkContext
val conf = new SparkConf
conf.setMaster("spark://master:7077")
.setAppName("Alternating_Least_Squares")
val sc = new SparkContext(conf)
//Load and parse the data
val rawData = sc.textFile("hdfs://namenode:9000/datsets/u.data")
val ratings = rawData.map(line => line.split("\t").take(3) match
{
case Array(userid, movieid, rating) => Rating(userid.toInt,
movieid.toInt, rating.toDouble)
})
val rank = 10
val numIterations = 10
val model = ALS.train(ratings, rank, numIterations, 0.01)
val userId = 789
val movieId = 123
val predictedRating = model.predict(userId, movieId)
```

```
val K=10
val topKRecs = model.recommendProducts(userId, K)
println("Predicted Rating: " +predictedRating+" for User:
"+userId)
println("top-K recommended Items:")
println(topKRecs.mkString("\n"))
//Evaluate the model on training data
val userProducts = ratings.map{case Rating(user, product, rate) =>
(user,product)}
val predictions = model.predict(userProducts).map{case
Rating(user,product,rate) =>    ((user,product), rate)}
val ratesAndPreds = ratings.map{case Rating(user,product,rate) =>
((user,product),    rate)}.join(predictions)
val meanSquaredError = ratesAndPreds.map{case ((user,product),
(r1,r2)) =>
val err = r1 -r2
    err*err}.mean
println("Mean Squared Error: "+meanSquaredError)
    }
}
```

The following is the output:

```
Predicted Rating: 3.7145698398131506 for User: 789
top-K recommended Items:
Rating(789,634,10.417101374782789)
Rating(789,390,9.698498529021368)
Rating(789,793,9.075930316942125)
Rating(789,1093,8.939263466151157)
Rating(789,1184,8.758673390571044)
Rating(789,1316,8.247478149972812)
Rating(789,1496,8.020321930691964)
Rating(789,962,7.638944782465387)
Rating(789,1283,7.638183734722482)
Rating(789,624,7.629865917211151)
Mean Squared Error: 0.48259870392275334
```

How it works...

The dataset consists of user ID, movie ID, rating, and timestamp fields separated by tabs (\t). The val ratings = rawData.map(line => line.split("\t").take(3) match {case Array(userid, movieid, rating) => Rating(userid.toInt, movieid.toInt, rating.toDouble)}) line extracts the first three fields using split and transform the array of IDs and ratings into a Rating object. The Rating class is a wrapper around user ID, movie ID and the actual rating arguments.

Now, the `ALS.train` method (trains the ALS model) requires parameters such as `rank` (number of factors in ALS model), `iterations` (number of iterations to run) and `lambda` (controls the regularization of the model).

The `model.predict` computes the predicted score for a given `user` and `item`. The `model.recommendProducts` generates top-K recommended items for a user. Finally mean-squared error is calculated, which gives the performance of the ALS model.

There's more...

As said in the beginning, the most prevalent recommendation model is content-based filtering, which uses the content or attributes of an item, finds similarity between two pieces of content and generates items similar to a given item. The other one is collaborative filtering, in which there is a user-based approach and an item-based approach. The matrix factorization model takes a 2-D matrix with users as rows and items as columns. This 2-D matrix is represented as the product of two smaller matrices (factor matrices) and the prediction happens by computing the dot product between row of a user-factor matrix and the relevant row of an item-factor matrix. There is also the implicit matrix factorization method, which takes implicit feedback and computes the recommendation.

Once the model is generated, it is essential to evaluate its predictive capability or accuracy. There are some direct measures that determine how well a model predicts such as mean squared error. The Mean average precision determines how best the model performs at predicting things, which is not directly optimized in the model.

See also

For more about collaborative filtering, please refer to the Spark documentation `http://spark.apache.org/docs/latest/mllib-collaborative-filtering.html`. The documentation also contains references to the papers that underlie the ALS algorithm implemented on each component of explicit and implicit data. The earlier *Implementing decision trees* recipe also talks about classification models.

Implementing logistic regression using Spark ML pipelines

In this recipe, let's see how to run logistic regression algorithms using Spark ML pipelines.

Getting ready

To step through this recipe, you will need a running Spark cluster in any one of the modes, that is, local, standalone, YARN, or Mesos. For installing Spark on a standalone cluster, please refer http://spark.apache.org/docs/latest/spark-standalone.html. Also, include the Spark MLlib package in the build.sbt file so that it downloads the related libraries and the API can be used. Install Hadoop (optionally), Scala, and Java.

> Please download the dataset from the following location: https://github
> .com/ChitturiPadma/datasets/blob/master/Community_Dataset.csv.

How to do it...

1. Let's have a look at some of the records in the dataset. The first column corresponds to the label and the other three columns are the features:

PA	640	5	6
PA	140	2	5.5
PA	405	2	7.5
PA	389	3	7
PA	359	3	5.7
PA	349	2	6.3
PA	388	3	5

2. Here is the code which creates a DataFrame out of the previous data and creates an instance for LogisticRegression:

   ```
   import org.apache.spark._
   import org.apache.spark.rdd._
   import org.apache.spark.sql._
   import org.apache.spark.sql.functions._
   ```

```
import org.apache.spark.mllib.linalg._
import org.apache.spark.ml.classification.LogisticRegression
import org.apache.spark.ml.param.ParamMap
import org.apache.spark.sql.Row
object LogisticRegression_MLPipeline {
def main(args:Array[String]): Unit = {
val conf = new SparkConf()
  .setMaster("spark://master:7077")
  .setAppName("Logistic_MLPipeline")
val sc = new SparkContext(conf)
val sqlContext = new SQLContext(sc)
import sqlContext.implicits._

//Loading data
val community_data =
sqlContext.read.format("com.databricks.spark.csv")
  .option("inferSchema", "true")
.load("hdfs://namenode:9000/Community_Dataset.csv")
/* function that returns 0.0 is string is "PA" and 1.0 if string
  is "MP" */
val func = udf((s:String) => if(s== "PA") 0.0 else 1.0)
val final_data = community_data.withColumn("label",func($"C0")
.as("label")).drop("C0")
final_data.show(5) } }
```

The following is the output:

```
+---+---+---+-----+
| C1| C2| C3|label|
+---+---+---+-----+
|640|  5|6.0|  0.0|
|140|  2|5.5|  0.0|
|405|  2|7.5|  0.0|
|389|  3|7.0|  0.0|
|359|  3|5.7|  0.0|
+---+---+---+-----+
```

3. Let's now create DataFrame from the `final_data` RDD and also an instance for `LogisticRegression` as follows:

```
val training = final_data.rdd.map{
row => val feature1 = row.getInt(0).toDouble
val feature2 = row.getInt(1).toDouble
val feature3 = row.getDouble(2)
val label = row.getAs[Double]("label")
(label,Vectors.dense(feature1,feature2,feature3))
  }.toDF("label","features")
//Create instance for the LogisticRegression
```

```
val lr = new LogisticRegression()

//Display the parameters and any any default values
println("LogisticRegression parameters:\n" + lr.explainParams()
+ "\n")
```

The following is the output:

```
LogisticRegression parameters:
elasticNetParam: the ElasticNet mixing parameter, in range [0, 1].
For alpha = 0, the penalty is an L2 penalty. For alpha = 1,
it is an
L1 penalty (default:   0.0)
featuresCol: features column name (default: features)
fitIntercept: whether to fit an intercept term (default: true)
labelCol: label column name (default: label)
maxIter: maximum number of iterations (>= 0) (default: 100)
```

4. Let's set the parameters and try to fit the model for the DataFrame training as follows:

```
//Set the parameters
lr.setMaxIter(10)
.setRegParam(0.01)
//Fit the model
val model1 = lr.fit(training)
println("Model 1 was fit using parameters: " +
model1.parent.extractParamMap)
```

The following is the output:

```
Model 1 was fit using parameters: {
  logreg_584f918c00a8-elasticNetParam: 0.0,
  logreg_584f918c00a8-featuresCol: features,
  logreg_584f918c00a8-fitIntercept: true,
  logreg_584f918c00a8-labelCol: label,
  logreg_584f918c00a8-maxIter: 10,
  logreg_584f918c00a8-predictionCol: prediction,
  logreg_584f918c00a8-probabilityCol: probability,
  logreg_584f918c00a8-rawPredictionCol: rawPrediction,
  logreg_584f918c00a8-regParam: 0.01,
  logreg_584f918c00a8-standardization: true,
  logreg_584f918c00a8-threshold: 0.5,
  logreg_584f918c00a8-tol: 1.0E-6,
  logreg_584f918c00a8-weightCol: }
```

5. There is also an alternative way of specifying the parameters using a `ParamMap` and learning a new model as follows:

```
//Alternative way of specifying the parameters using a ParamMap
val paramMap = ParamMap(lr.maxIter -> 20)
.put(lr.maxIter, 30)
// Specify 1 Param. This overwrites the  original maxIter.
.put(lr.regParam -> 0.1, lr.threshold -> 0.55)
// Specify multiple Params.
// Also can combine ParamMaps.
val paramMap2 = ParamMap(lr.probabilityCol -> "myProbability")
// Change output column name.
val paramMapCombined = paramMap ++ paramMap2
//Learn a new model using the paramMapCombined parameters.
/* paramMapCombined overrides all parameters set earlier via
lr.set* methods */
val model2 = lr.fit(training, paramMapCombined)
println("Model 2 was fit using parameters: " +
model2.parent.extractParamMap)
```

The following is the output:

```
Model 2 was fit using parameters: {
    logreg_5d7f5ebdfbc2-elasticNetParam: 0.0,
    logreg_5d7f5ebdfbc2-featuresCol: features,
    logreg_5d7f5ebdfbc2-fitIntercept: true,
    logreg_5d7f5ebdfbc2-labelCol: label,
    logreg_5d7f5ebdfbc2-maxIter: 30,
    logreg_5d7f5ebdfbc2-predictionCol: prediction,
    logreg_5d7f5ebdfbc2-probabilityCol: myProbability,
    logreg_5d7f5ebdfbc2-rawPredictionCol: rawPrediction,
    logreg_5d7f5ebdfbc2-regParam: 0.1,
    logreg_5d7f5ebdfbc2-standardization: true,
    logreg_5d7f5ebdfbc2-threshold: 0.55,
    logreg_5d7f5ebdfbc2-tol: 1.0E-6,
    logreg_5d7f5ebdfbc2-weightCol: }
```

6. Now let's prepare the test data and make predictions using the `Transformer.transform()` method. Here is the code for the same:

```
// Prepare test data.
val test = sqlContext.createDataFrame(Seq(
    (1.0, Vectors.dense(400, 5, 8.7)),
    (0.0, Vectors.dense(500, 5, 11.9)),
    (1.0, Vectors.dense(650, 6, 7.8))
)).toDF("label", "features")
model2.transform(test)
```

```
   .select("features", "label", "myProbability", "prediction")
   .collect()
   .foreach { case Row(features: Vector, label: Double, prob:
Vector, prediction:Double) =>
   println(s"($features, $label) -> prob=$prob,
prediction=$prediction")
   }
```

The following is the output:

```
([400.0,5.0,8.7], 1.0) -> prob=
[0.2179020321435895,0.7820979678564105], prediction=1.0
([500.0,5.0,11.9], 0.0) -> prob=
[0.29104102896280887,0.7089589710371911], prediction=1.0
([650.0,6.0,7.8], 1.0) -> prob=
[0.1620630814622409,0.8379369185377591],   prediction=1.0
```

How it works...

In the preceding code snippet, we saw how to run `LogisticRegression` using an ML pipeline. Initially, the data is loaded using the Spark CSV package and a column `label` is created which contains `0.0` when the string in the column `C0` is `PA` and `1.0` when the string is `MP`. From the DataFrame `final_data`, the DataFrame `training` is obtained, which contains the variable `label` and feature `vector` (using `Vectors.dense`).

Next, an instance of `LogisticRegression` is created as `val lr = new LogisticRegression()`. The default parameters of the `lr` are displayed as `lr.explainParams()`. The parameters, such as the maximum number of iterations and regularization parameter are set as `lr.setMaxIter(10).setRegParam(0.01)`. The model is fit on the `training` data as `val model1 = lr.fit(training)`. The parameters of the model are displayed as `model1.parent.extractParamMap`. We also saw alternative ways of specifying the parameters using `ParamMap`. The test data is prepared and the `transform` method (which uses the `features` column) outputs the probability as `myProbability` and the respective prediction.

There's more...

A pipeline is a sequence of stages where each stage is either a transformer or an estimator. The stages run in order, and the input DataFrame is transformed as it passes through each stage. For transformer stages, the `transform()` method is called on the DataFrame. For estimator stages, the `fit()` method is called to produce a transformer (which becomes part of the `PipelineModel`, or fitted `Pipeline`), and that transformer's `transform()` method is called on the DataFrame.

A pipeline's stages are specified as an ordered array. It is possible to create linear as well as nonlinear pipelines as long as the data flow graph forms a **Directed Acyclic Graph (DAG)**. Since pipelines can operate on DataFrames with varied types, they cannot use compile-time type checking. `Pipelines` and `PipelineModels` instead do runtime checking before actually running the pipeline. This type checking is done using the DataFrame schema, a description of the data types of columns in the DataFrame. Also, a pipeline's stages should be unique instances.

See also

The algorithms, such as decision tree, random forest, gradient-boosted tree and so on have implementations in Spark ML pipelines.

6
NLP with Spark

In this chapter, we will see how to run NLP algorithms over Spark. You will learn the following recipes:

- Installing NLTK on Linux
- Installing Anaconda on Linux
- Anaconda for cluster management
- POS tagging with PySpark on an Anaconda cluster
- Named Entity Recognition with IPython over Spark
- Implementing openNLP – chunker over Spark
- Implementing openNLP – sentence detector over Spark
- Implementing stanford NLP – lemmatization over Spark
- Implementing sentiment analysis using stanford NLP over Spark

Introduction

The study of natural language processing is called NLP. It is about the application of computers on different language nuances and building real-world applications using NLP techniques. NLP is analogous to teaching a language to a child. The most common tasks, such as understanding words and sentences, forming grammatically and structurally correct sentences are natural to humans. In NLP, some of these tasks translate to tokenization, chunking, parts of speech tagging, parsing, machine translation and speech recognition and these are tough challenges for computers.

Currently, NLP is one of the rarest skill sets that is required in the industry. With the advent of big data, the major challenge is that there is a need for people who are good with not just structured, but also with semi or unstructured data. Petabytes of weblogs, tweets, Facebook feeds, chats, e-mails and reviews are generated continuously. Companies are collecting all these different kinds of data for better customer targeting and to gather meaningful insights. To process all these unstructured data at large scale, people need to understand NLP as well as get acquainted with processing data in distributed fashion (big data processing). In order to achieve functionalities of NLP applications such as spelling correction (MS Word), search engines (Google, Bing), news feeds (Google, Yahoo!) and any other applications that perform basic NLP tasks preprocessing, there are many tools available, such as GATE, Mallet, Open NLP, UMA, Stanford ToolKit and **Natural Language ToolKit** (**NLTK**).

NLTK is a comprehensive Python library for natural language processing and text analytics. It is often used for rapid prototyping of text processing programs and it can even be used in production applications. The different areas of application are as follows:

- **Searching:** This identifies specific elements of text. It simply finds occurrence of a name in a document or involves finding synonyms and alternates spelling/mis-spelling to find entries which are close to the original search string.
- **Machine translation:** This involves translating one natural language to another.
- **Summation:** This summarizes paragraphs, articles, documents or collections.
- **Named Entity Recognition (NER):** This extracts names, locations, people and things from text.
- **Parts of Speech Tagging (POS):** This splits up the text into different grammatical elements such as nouns and verbs useful in analyzing text further.
- **Sentiment analysis:** People's feelings and attitudes regarding movies, books and other products is determined using this technique. It is useful in providing automated feedback on how well a product is perceived.
- **Speech recognition:** This is responsible for recognizing text from the speech.

Installing NLTK on Linux

In this recipe, we will see how to install NLTK on Linux. Before proceeding with the installation, let's consider the version of Python we're going to use. There are two versions or flavors of Python, namely Python 2.7.x and Python 3.x. Although the latest version, Python 3.x, appears to be the better choice, for scientific, numeric, or data analysis work, Python 2.7 is recommended.

Getting ready

To step through this recipe, you need Ubuntu 14.04 (Linux flavor) installed on the machine. Python comes pre-installed. The `python --version` command gives the version of the Python installed. If the version seems to be 2.6.x, upgrade it to Python 2.7 as follows:

```
sudo apt-get install python2.7
```

How to do it...

Let's see the installation process for NLTK:

1. Once the Python 2.7.x version is available, install NLTK as follows:

    ```
    sudo pip install -U nltk
    ```

2. The preceding installation may throw an error such as the following:

    ```
    Could not find any downloads that satisfy the requirement nltk
    Cleaning up...
    No distributions at all found for nltk
    Storing debug log for failure in /home/padmac/.pip/pip.log
    ```

3. If so, please try to install `nltk` as follows:

    ```
    sudo pip install nltk
    DownloaDing/unpacking nltk
    Cannot fetch index base URL https://pypi.python.org/
    Downloading nltk-3.2.tar.gz (1.2MB): 1.2MB downloaded
    Running setup.py (path:/tmp/pip_build_root/
    warning: no files found matching 'Makefile' under directory
    '*.txt'
    warning: no previously-included files matching '*~' found
    anywhere in distribution
    Installing collected packages: nltk
    Running setup.py install for nltk
    warning: no files found matching 'Makefile' under directory
    '*.txt'
    warning: no previously-included files matching '*~' found
    anywhere in distribution
    Successfully installed nltk
    Cleaning up...
    ```

4. The `numpy` package is optional to install:

```
sudo pip install -U numpy
```

5. Now test the installation by invoking Python interpreter and type the following:

```
python
Python 2.7.6 (default, Mar 22 2014, 22:59:56)
[GCC 4.8.2] on linux2
Type "help", "copyright", "credits" or "license" for more
information.
>>> import nltk
>>>
```

How it works...

The preceding commands install the `nltk` and `numpy` (optional) libraries. For older versions of Python, it might be necessary install setup tools (see `http://pypi.python.org/pypi/setuptools`) and to install pip (`sudo easy_install pip`).

There's more...

The NLTK library is available as a part of Anaconda (continuum analytics). Anaconda is a Python distribution for data analytics. It supports a variety of numerical and scientific packages, such as `numpy`, `pandas`, `scipy`, `matpotlib` and `ipython`, with over 250 more packages available via a simple `conda install <package-name>`. Please refer to the following recipes below for installing Anaconda and Anaconda for cluster management.

See also

Please refer to `Chapter 2`, *Tricky Statistics with Spark* to know how to work with Pandas on the Spark framework. Similarly, refer to `Chapter 1`, *Big Data Analytics with Spark* to get familiar with Spark.

Installing Anaconda on Linux

Anaconda is a free, enterprise-ready Python distribution for data analytics, processing and scientific computing. In this recipe, we will see how to install Anaconda on Linux. Before proceeding with the installation, let's consider the version of Python we're going to use. There are two versions or flavors of Python, namely Python 2.7.x and Python 3.x. Although the latest version, Python 3.x, appears to be the better choice, for scientific, numeric, or data analysis work, Python 2.7 is recommended.

Getting ready

To step through this recipe, you need Ubuntu 14.04 (Linux flavor) installed on the machine. Python comes pre-installed. `python --version` gives the version of the Python installed. If the version is 2.6.x, upgrade it to Python 2.7 as follows:

```
sudo apt-get install python2.7
```

How to do it...

Once Python version 2.7.x is available, download the Anaconda installer from `https://www.continuum.io/downloads` and type the following in the terminal window at the path where Anaconda has been downloaded:

```
bash ~/path/Anaconda2-2.5.0-Linux-x86_64.sh
```

How it works...

The preceding command installs Anaconda and the following line is added in `.bashrc` by the Anaconda installer as follows:

```
export PATH="/home/padma/anaconda2/bin:$PATH"
```

Now close and reopen the terminal for the changes to take effect. In order to ensure that `conda` is successfully installed, enter the following `conda -version` command which results in the version as `conda 3.19.1`.

To update `conda` to the current version, use the `update` command to update conda:

```
conda 3.19.1
```

There's more...

Anaconda includes an easy installation of Python and updates over scientific and analytic Python packages that include `numpy`, `pandas`, `scipy`, `matpotlib`, and `ipython`, with over 250 more packages available via a simple `conda install <package-name>`. The Anaconda platform is language-specific as well as extensible. It provides integrations such as Cloudera, Amazon AWS, Microsoft Azure, Docker, VM Depot, Vagrant and so on.

See also

For more details on Anaconda (continuum analytics), please visit `http://docs.continuum.io/anaconda/index`.

Anaconda for cluster management

Anaconda for cluster management provides resource management tools which allow users to easily create, provision and manage bare-metal or cloud-based clusters. It enables the management of conda environments on clusters and provides integration, configuration and setup management of Hadoop services. This can be installed alongside enterprise Hadoop distributions such as Cloudera CDH or Hortonworks HDP and this is used to manage conda packages and environments across a cluster.

Getting ready

To step through this recipe, you need Ubuntu 14.04 (Linux flavor) installed on the machine. Python comes pre-installed. `python --version` gives the version of Python installed. If the version is 2.6.x, upgrade it to Python 2.7 as follows:

```
sudo apt-get install python2.7
```

For installing Anaconda, please refer to the earlier *Installing Anaconda on Linux* recipe.

How to do it...

Let's look at the installation process for installing Anaconda for cluster management:

1. You can create a new environment in conda with Python 2.7 using the following command:

   ```
   conda create -n acluster python=2.7
   ```

2. Activate the `acluster` environment as follows:

   ```
   source activate acluster
   ```

3. Install the command-line client for Anaconda cloud as follows:

   ```
   conda install anaconda-client
   ```

4. Log in to your Anaconda cloud account as follows:

   ```
   (acluster)padma@padma$ anaconda login
   Using Anaconda Cloud api site https://api.anaconda.org
   Username: padma
   padma's Password:
   login successful
   ```

   If the login is unsuccessful, visit `https://anaconda.org/account/register` and register the account by providing the necessary details. Now try to log in with the created credentials:

5. Now install Anaconda for cluster management on the local machine using the following command:

   ```
   conda install anaconda-cluster -c anaconda-cluster
   ```

6. The preceding code creates the `~/.acluster` directory which contains sample `~/.acluster/providers.yaml` and an example profile file located in `~/.acluster/profiles.d/`.

7. Edit the `~/.acluster/providers.yaml` file and replace the `private_key` location:

   ```
   private_key: ~/.ssh/id_rsa
   ```

8. Edit `~/.acluster/profiles.d/aws_profile_sample` file and configure the following fields:

```
name: padma
provider: aws_east
num_nodes: 4
node_id: bare_metal  # Ubuntu 14.04, us-east-1 region
node_type: bare_metal
user: ubuntu
anaconda_url: http://localhost/miniconda/Miniconda-latest-
Linux-x86_64.sh
machines:
  head:
    - 192.168.1.1
  compute:
    - 192.168.1.2
    - 192.168.1.3
    - 192.168.1.4
plugins:
  - spark-yarn
  - notebook
default_channels: http://localhost/conda/anaconda
conda_channels:
  - defaults
  - anaconda-cluster
  - blaze
  - pypi
  - username
  - https://conda.anaconda.org/username/
security:
  disable_selinux: false
  flush_iptables: false
```

9. Rename `aws_profile_sample` to `profile-name`, `aws_profile_sample.yaml` to `profile-name.yaml`, `aws_profile_sample_spark_yarn.yaml` to `profile-name_spark_yarn.yaml` and `aws_profile_sample_spark_standalone.yaml` to `profile-name_spark_standalone.yaml`. Now create `demo_cluster` as follows:

```
acluster create demo_cluster --profile padma
```

10. Install the following `conda` packages:

```
acluster conda install numpy scipy pandas nltk
```

11. Also, the plugin for Ipython notebook is installed as follows:

```
acluster install notebook
```

How it works...

The preceding commands show various steps to install Anaconda for cluster management, create an Anaconda cloud account, run the cluster with a specified number of instances and install packages such as `numpy`, `scipy` and `nltk`. If at any step of setting up the cluster, there is a failure then trace the dependency packages to be installed and install them.

There's more...

There are a variety of packages supported by Anaconda; please visit `http://docs.continuum.io/anaconda/pkg-docs` to see the list of packages supported. There are also plugins available to export Python objects to Excel and import the contents of Excel spreadsheets to perform calculations or visualizations in Python. Also, IDEs such as Spyder, PyCharm, Eclipse and PyDev can be integrated to run in Anaconda. For details, please refer to `http://docs.continuum.io/anaconda/ide_integration`.

See also

For more details on Anaconda (continuum analytics), please visit `http://docs.continuum.io/anaconda/index`.

POS tagging with PySpark on an Anaconda cluster

Parts-of-speech tagging is the process of converting a sentence in the form of a list of words, into a list of tuples, where each tuple is of the form (word, tag). The **tag** is a part-of-speech tag and signifies whether the word is a noun, adjective, verb and so on. This is a necessary step before chunking. With parts-of-speech tags, a chunker knows how to identify phrases based on tag patterns. These POS tags are used for grammar analysis and word sense disambiguation.

Getting ready

To step through this recipe, you will need a running Spark cluster either in pseudo distributed mode or in one of the distributed modes, that is, standalone, YARN, or Mesos. Also, have PySpark and Anaconda installed on the Linux machine, that is, Ubuntu 14.04. For installing Anaconda, please refer the earlier recipes.

How to do it...

Let's see how to implement POS tagging using PySpark:

1. Activate the Anaconda cluster as follows:

    ```
    source activate acluster
    ```

2. Install the Spark + YARN plugin on the cluster as follows:

    ```
    acluster install spark-yarn
    ```

3. Once the installation of the plugin is done, we can view the YARN UI as follows:

    ```
    acluster open yarn
    ```

4. Install the NLTK library as follows:

    ```
    acluster conda install nltk
    ```

5. The following output is seen from each node, which indicates that the package was successfully installed across the cluster:

```
Node "ip-192-168-0-1.ec2.internal":
Successful actions: 1/1
Node "ip-192-168-0-2.ec2.internal":
Successful actions: 1/1
Node "ip-192-168-0-3.ec2.internal":
Successful actions: 1/1
```

6. Now, download data for the NLTK project as follows:

```
acluster cmd 'sudo /opt/anaconda/bin/python -m
nltk.downloader -d /usr/share/nltk_data all'
```

7. After a few minutes, the output is as below:

```
Execute command "sudo /opt/anaconda/bin/python -m
nltk.downloader -d /usr/share/nltk_data all" target: "*" cluster:
"d"
All nodes (x3) response: [nltk_data] Downloading collection 'all'
[nltk_data]    |
[nltk_data]    | Downloading package abc to
/usr/share/nltk_data...
[nltk_data]    |   Unzipping corpora/abc.zip.
[nltk_data]    | Downloading package alpino to
/usr/share/nltk_data...
[nltk_data]    |   Unzipping corpora/alpino.zip.
[nltk_data]    | Downloading package biocreative_ppi to
[nltk_data]    |     /usr/share/nltk_data...
. . . .
[nltk_data]    |   Unzipping models/bllip_wsj_no_aux.zip.
[nltk_data]    | Downloading package word2vec_sample to
[nltk_data]    |     /usr/share/nltk_data...
[nltk_data]    |   Unzipping models/word2vec_sample.zip.
[nltk_data]    |
[nltk_data]   Done downloading collection all
```

8. Now create a script in order to run NLTK's POS-tagger as follows:

```
# spark-nltk.py
from pyspark import SparkConf
from pyspark import SparkContext
conf = SparkConf()
conf.setMaster('yarn-client')
conf.setAppName('spark-nltk')
sc = SparkContext(conf=conf)
data =
```

```
sc.textFile('file:///usr/share/nltk_data/corpora/state_union/
1972-Nixon.txt')
import nltk
words = data.flatMap(lambda x: nltk.word_tokenize(x))
print words.take(10)
pos_word = words.map(lambda x: nltk.pos_tag([x]))
print pos_word.take(5)
```

9. Run the script on the Spark Cluster:

```
Using Spark's default log4j profile: org/apache/spark/log4j-
defaults.properties
15/06/13 05:14:29 INFO SparkContext: Running Spark version 1.6.0
[...]
['Address',
    'on',
    'the',
    'State',
    'of',
    'the',
    'Union',
    'Delivered',
        'Before',
     'a']
[...]
[[('Address', 'NN')],
    [('on','IN')],
    [('the', 'DT')],
    [('State', 'NNP')],
    [('of', 'IN')]]
```

The output shows the words that were returned from the Spark script, including the results from the `flatMap` operation and the POS-tagger.

How it works...

First, SparkContext is created. Note that Anaconda for cluster management will not create a SparkContext by default. In the preceding example, we use the YARN resource manager. After SparkContext is created, `sc.textFile('file:///usr/share/nltk_data/corpora/state_union/1972-Nixon.txt')` is used to load the data. Next, `nltk` is imported and the text is mapped to the `word_tokenize` function in NLTK. Finally, NLTK's POS-tagger, `nltk.pos_tag([x])`, is used to find the parts of speech for each word.

There's more...

Apart from the POS tagger, the significant NLP tasks such as chunker, **Named Entity Recognition (NER)**, text classification using naive Bayes classifier, decision tree classifier, and maximum entropy classifier can be performed on large datasets as the framework Spark provides distributed computation. For details on NLP, please refer `https://en.wikipedia.org/wiki/Natural_language_processing` and `http://nlp.stanford.edu/`.

See also

Please refer *Installing Anaconda on Linux* and *Anaconda for cluster management* recipes to get familiar with installations and continuum analytics.

NER with IPython over Spark

Apart from POS, one of the most common labeling problems is finding entities in the text. Typically, NER constitutes name, location and organizations. There are NER systems that tag more entities than just these three such as labeling and named entities using the context and other features. There is a lot more research going on in this area of NLP, where people are trying to tag biomedical entities, product entities, and so on.

Getting ready

To step through this recipe, you will need a running Spark cluster either in pseudo distributed mode or in one of the distributed modes, that is, standalone, YARN, or Mesos. Also, have PySpark and Ipython installed on the Linux machine, that is, Ubuntu 14.04. For installing IPython, please refer to the *Using IPython with PySpark* recipe in the Chapter 2, *Tricky Statistics with Spark*.

How to do it...

1. Download and install NLTK data correctly as follows:

```
ipython console -profile=pyspark
In [1]:
In [1]: from pyspark import SparkConf, SparkContext
```

```
Welcome to
      ____              __
     / __/__  ___ _____/ /__
    _\ \/ _ \/ _ `/ __/  '_/
   /__ / .__/\_,_/_/ /_/\_\   version 1.6.0
      /_/

Using Python version 2.7.11 (default, Dec  6 2015 18:08:32)
SparkContext available as sc, HiveContext available as
sqlContext.
In [2]: import nltk
In [3]: nltk.download('averaged_perceptron_tagger')
[nltk_data] Downloading package averaged_perceptron_tagger to
[nltk_data]     /home/padma/nltk_data...
[nltk_data]   Unzipping taggers/averaged_perceptron_tagger.zip.
Out[3]: True
In [4]: nltk.download('maxent_ne_chunker')
[nltk_data] Downloading package maxent_ne_chunker to
[nltk_data]     /home/padma/nltk_data...
[nltk_data]   Unzipping chunkers/maxent_ne_chunker.zip.
Out[4]: True
In [5]: nltk.download('words')
[nltk_data] Downloading package words to /home/padma/nltk_data...
[nltk_data]   Unzipping corpora/words.zip.
Out[5]: True
In [6]: from pyspark import SparkConf, SparkContext
In [7]: import nltk
In [8]: from nltk import word_tokenize, ne_chunk
In [9]: data = sc.parallelize("Mark is studying at Stanford
University in California")
In [10]: words = data.flatMap(lambda x: word_tokenize(x))
In [11]: pos_tags = words.map(lambda x: nltk.pos)
In [12]: ne_chunks = pos_tags.map(lambda x: ne_chunk(x,
binary=False))
In [13]: ne_chunks.take(2)
16/03/09 09:36:04 INFO spark.SparkContext: Starting job:
runJob at PythonRDD.scala:393
16/03/09 09:36:04 INFO scheduler.DAGScheduler: Got job 1 (runJob
at PythonRDD.scala:393) with 1 output partitions
16/03/09 09:36:04 INFO scheduler.DAGScheduler: Final stage:
ResultStage 1 (runJob at PythonRDD.scala:393)
16/03/09 09:36:04 INFO scheduler.DAGScheduler: Parents of final
stage: List()
16/03/09 09:36:04 INFO scheduler.DAGScheduler: Missing parents:
List()
16/03/09 09:36:04 INFO scheduler.DAGScheduler: Submitting
ResultStage 1 (PythonRDD[2] at RDD at PythonRDD.scala:43), which
has no missing parents
16/03/09 09:36:04 INFO storage.MemoryStore: Block broadcast_1
```

```
stored as values in memory (estimated size 4.5 KB, free 11.6 KB)
16/03/09 09:36:04 INFO storage.MemoryStore: Block
broadcast_1_piece0 stored as bytes in memory (estimated size 3.0
KB, free 14.6 KB)
16/03/09 09:36:04 INFO storage.BlockManagerInfo: Added
broadcast_1_piece0 in memory on localhost:39038 (size: 3.0 KB,
free: 511.5 MB)
16/03/09 09:36:04 INFO spark.SparkContext: Created broadcast 1
from broadcast at DAGScheduler.scala:1006
16/03/09 09:36:04 INFO scheduler.DAGScheduler: Submitting 1
missing tasks from ResultStage 1 (PythonRDD[2] at RDD at
PythonRDD.scala:43)
16/03/09 09:36:04 INFO scheduler.TaskSchedulerImpl: Adding task
set 1.0 with 1 tasks
16/03/09 09:36:04 INFO scheduler.TaskSetManager: Starting task
0.0 in stage 1.0 (TID 1, localhost, partition 0,PROCESS_LOCAL,
2107 bytes)
16/03/09 09:36:04 INFO executor.Executor: Running task 0.0 in
stage 1.0 (TID 1)
16/03/09 09:36:07 INFO python.PythonRunner: Times: total = 3267,
boot = 4, init = 363, finish = 2900
16/03/09 09:36:07 INFO executor.Executor: Finished task 0.0 in
stage 1.0 (TID 1). 1112 bytes result sent to driver
16/03/09 09:36:07 INFO scheduler.TaskSetManager: Finished task
0.0 in stage 1.0 (TID 1) in 3284 ms on localhost (1/1)
16/03/09 09:36:07 INFO scheduler.TaskSchedulerImpl: Removed
TaskSet 1.0, whose tasks have all completed, from pool
16/03/09 09:36:07 INFO scheduler.DAGScheduler: ResultStage 1
(runJob at PythonRDD.scala:393) finished in 3.286 s
16/03/09 09:36:07 INFO scheduler.DAGScheduler: Job 1 finished:
runJob at PythonRDD.scala:393, took 3.302134 s
Out[13]: [Tree('S', [('M', 'NN')]), Tree('S', [('a', 'DT')])]
```

2. The following code snippet shows the use of the stanford NER tagger:

```
In [14]: from nltk.tag.stanford import NERTagger
In [15]: st = NERTagger('<PATH>/stanford-
ner/classifiers/all.3class.distsim.crf.ser.gz',...'<PATH>
/stanford-ner/stanford-ner.jar')
dataForStanford = sc.parallelize('Rami Eid is studying at Stony
Brook University in NY')
wordsSt = dataForStanford.flatMap(lambda x: x.split())
wordsTagged = wordsSt.map(lambda x: st.tag(x))
Out [15]: [('Rami', 'PERSON'), ('Eid', 'PERSON'), ('is', 'O'),
('studying', 'O'), ('at', 'O'), ('Stony', 'ORGANIZATION'),
('Brook', 'ORGANIZATION'), ('University', 'ORGANIZATION'), ('in',
'O'), ('NY', 'LOCATION')]
```

How it works...

NLTK provides a method for named entity extraction, that is, `ne_chunk`. The preceding code snippet demonstrated how to use it for tagging any sentence. This method will require you to preprocess the text to tokenize for sentences, tokens and POS tags in the same order to be able to tag for named entities. NLTK used `ne_chunking`, where chunking is nothing but tagging multiple tokens to a call it a meaningful entity.

The `ne_chunking` method recognizes people (names), places (location) and organizations. If binary is set to `True` then it provides the output for the entire sentence tree and tags everything. Setting it to `False` will give us detailed person, location, and organization information.

Similar to the POS tagger, NLTK also has a wrapper around Stanford NER. This NER tagger has better accuracy. If you observe closely, even with a very small test sentence, we can say the Stanford tagger outperformed the NLTK `ne_chunk` tagger.

There's more...

There are two ways of tagging the NER using NLTK. One is by using the pre-trained NER model that just scores the test data, the other is to build a machine learning based model. NLTK provides the `ne_chunk()` method and a wrapper around the Stanford NER tagger for NER. The above taggers are a nice solution for a generic kind of entity tagging, but we have to train our own tagger, when it comes to tagging domain-specific entities such as biomedical and product names, so we have to build our own NER system. The NER Calais tagger is a recommended one. It has ways of tagging not just typical NER, but also some more entities. The performance of this tagger is also very good.

See also

There are also pre-trained taggers such as the Sequential tagger, N-gram tagger, Regex tagger, and Brill tagger. The internals of either the NLTK or Stanford taggers are still a black box. For example, `pos_tag` internally uses a **Maximum Entropy Classifier** (**MEC**), while the `StanfordTagger` also uses a modified version of Maximum Entropy. These are discriminatory models. While there is **Hidden Markov Model** (**HMM**) and **Conditional Random Field** (**CRF**) based taggers, these are generative models. Please refer to the NLP class `https://www.coursera.org/course/nlp` for greater understanding of these concepts.

Implementing openNLP – chunker over Spark

Chunking is shallow parsing, where instead of retrieving deep structure of the sentence, we try to club some chunks of the sentences that constitute some meaning. A chunk is defined as the minimal unit that can be processed. The conventional pipeline in chunking is to tokenize the POS tag and the input string, before they are given to any chunker.

Getting ready

To step through this recipe, you will need a running Spark cluster either in pseudo distributed mode or in one of the distributed modes, that is, standalone, YARN, or Mesos. For installing Spark on a standalone cluster, please refer to
`http://spark.apache.org/docs/latest/spark-standalone.html`. Install Hadoop (optionally), Scala, and Java.

How to do it...

Let's see how to run OpenNLP-Chunker over Spark:

1. Let's start an application named SparkNLP. Initially specify the following libraries in the `build.sbt` file:

```
libraryDependencies ++= Seq(
"org.apache.spark" %% "spark-core" % "1.6.0",
"org.apache.spark" %% "spark-mllib" % "1.6.0",
"org.apache.spark" %% "spark-sql" % "1.6.0",
"org.apache.spark" %% "spark-streaming" % "1.6.0",
"org.apache.opennlp" % "opennlp-tools" % "1.6.0",
"org.apache.opennlp" % "opennlp-uima" % "1.6.0"
 )
```

2. Here is the code for the Chunker which runs on the each record of Spark RDD and identifies the parts of speech:

```
import java.io.File
import opennlp.tools.chunker.{ChunkerME, ChunkerModel}
import opennlp.tools.tokenize.WhitespaceTokenizer
import org.apache.spark.SparkConf
import org.apache.spark.SparkContext
import opennlp.tools.cmdline.postag.POSModelLoader
```

```
import opennlp.tools.postag.POSModel
import opennlp.tools.postag.POSSample
import opennlp.tools.postag.POSTaggerME
object Chunker_Demo {
def main(args:Array[String]): Unit ={
val conf = new SparkConf()
.setAppName("Chunker_Application")
.setMaster("spark://master:7077")
.set("spark.serializer",
"org.apache.spark.serializer.KryoSerializer")
val sc = new SparkContext(conf)
val textInput = sc.makeRDD(Array("I am Padma working in Fractal
Analytics Company","I am a big data enthusiast",
"I love cooking"),1)
val modelFile = new File("/home/padmac/opennlp_models/en-pos-
 maxent.bin")
val chunkerModelFile = new File("/home/padmac/opennlp_models/en
chunker.bin")
val model = new POSModelLoader().load(modelFile)
val tagger = new POSTaggerME(model)
val chunkerModel = new ChunkerModel(chunkerModelFile)
val chunkerME= new ChunkerME(chunkerModel)
val broadCastedChunkerME = sc.broadcast(chunkerME)
val broadCastedTagger = sc.broadcast(tagger)
val resultsAndSpan = textInput.map{sentence =>
val tokenizedLines =
WhitespaceTokenizer.INSTANCE.tokenize(sentence)
val tags = broadCastedTagger.value.tag(tokenizedLines)
val result = broadCastedChunkerME.value.
chunk(tokenizedLines,tags)
val span = broadCastedChunkerME.value
.chunkAsSpans(tokenizedLines,tags)
(result,span)}
val results = resultsAndSpan.flatMap{case(results,spans) =>results}
val spans = resultsAndSpan.flatMap{case(results,spans) =>spans}
println("Resultant Strings: ")
results.foreach(println)
println("Spans: ")
spans.foreach(println)
}
}
```

The following is the output:

Resultant strings:

```
B-NP
B-VP
B-NP
I-NP
B-PP
B-NP
I-NP
I-NP
B-NP
B-VP
B-NP
I-NP
I-NP
I-NP
B-NP
B-VP
I-VP
Spans:
[0..1) NP
[1..2) VP
[2..4) NP
[4..5) PP
[5..8) NP
[0..1) NP
[1..2) VP
[2..6) NP
[0..1) NP
[1..3) VP
```

How it works...

In the preceding code snippet, the models `en-pos-maxent.bin` (POS tagger model with tag dictionary) and `en-chunker.bin` (chunker model) are downloaded from the location h `ttp://opennlp.sourceforge.net/models-1.5/`. The `POSModelLoader().load(modelFile)` line loads the POS Model. Next, the `POSTaggerME(model)` line initializes the `POSTagger` from the model. Also, `ChunkerModel(chunkerModelFile)` loads the chunker model and passing this as parameter, `ChunkerME` is initialized.

When broadcasting these models they might result in serialization exceptions. Hence setting the property, `org.apache.spark.serializer.KryoSerializer` serializes the models.Next, for each sentence in the RDD, `WhitespaceTokenizer.INSTANCE.tokenize` generates tokens. The generated array of tokens are passed to `POSTaggerME` which tags the parts of speech.

Now, `broadCastedChunkerME.value.chunk(tokenizedLines,tags)` generates chunks from the tokens and the corresponding tags. Finally from the tokenized sentences and tags, spans are generated as `broadCastedChunkerME.value.`

```
chunkAsSpans(tokenizedLines,tags)
```

There's more...

Chunker partitions a sentence into a set of chunks using the tokens generated by the tokenizer. For example, for the sentence *President speaks about the health care reforms* can be broken into two chunks, one is *the President,* which is noun dominated, and hence is called a **noun phrase** (**NP**). The remaining part of the sentence is dominated by a verb; hence it is called a **verb phrase** (**VP**). There is one more sub-chunk in the part that is, *speaks about the health care reforms.* Here, one more NP exists that can be broken down again in *speaks about* and *health care reforms.* Chunking is also a processing interface to identify non-overlapping groups in unrestricted text. Regular chunker used the rule NP/VP, which defines different POS patterns called as verb/noun phrase.

Regular expression based chunkers rely on chunk rules defined manually to chunk the string. So, if we are able to write a universal rule that can incorporate most of the noun phrase patterns, we can use regex chunkers. Unfortunately, it's hard to come up with those kind of generic rules; the other approach is to use a machine learning way of doing chunking.

See also

Please refer to *POS tagging with PySpark on an Anaconda cluster* and *NER with IPython over Spark* recipes to know details on implementing POS tagging and NER using NLTK over Spark.

Implementing openNLP – sentence detector over Spark

Partitioning text into sentences is called **Sentence Boundary Disambiguation (SBD)** or Sentence Detection. This process is useful for many downstream NLP tasks, which require analysis within sentences; for instance POS and phrase analysis. This Sentence Detection process is language dependent. Most search engines are not concerned with Sentence Detection. They are only interested in query's tokens and their respective positions. POS taggers and other NLP tasks that perform extraction of data will frequently process individual sentences. The detection of sentence boundaries will help separate phrases that might appear to span sentences.

Getting ready

To step through this recipe, you will need a running Spark cluster either in pseudo distributed mode or in one of the distributed modes, that is, standalone, YARN, or Mesos. For installing Spark on a standalone cluster, please refer to `http://spark.apache.org/docs/latest/spark-standalone.html.`. Install Hadoop (optionally), Scala, and Java.

How to do it...

Let's see how to detect sentences using OpenNLP over Spark:

1. Let's start an application named SparkNLP. Initially specify the following libraries in the `build.sbt` file:

```
libraryDependencies ++= Seq(
"org.apache.spark" %% "spark-core" % "1.6.0",
"org.apache.spark" %% "spark-mllib" % "1.6.0",
"org.apache.spark" %% "spark-sql" % "1.6.0",
"org.apache.spark" %% "spark-streaming" % "1.6.0",
"org.apache.opennlp" % "opennlp-tools" % "1.6.0",
"org.apache.opennlp" % "opennlp-uima" % "1.6.0"
)
```

2. Here is the code for the Sentence Detector which runs on the each record of Spark RDD and identifies the sentence:

```
import java.io.File
import opennlp.tools.sentdetect.{SentenceDetectorME,
SentenceModel}
import org.apache.spark.SparkConf
import org.apache.spark.SparkContext
object SentenceDetector_Demo {
def main(args:Array[String]): Unit ={
val conf = new SparkConf()
.setAppName("SentenceDetector_Application")
.setMaster("spark:master:7077")
.set("spark.serializer",
"org.apache.spark.serializer.KryoSerializer")
val sc = new SparkContext(conf)
val textInput = sc.makeRDD(Array("Hi Padma ! How are you ?",
"He saw him in Boston at McKenzie's pub. At 3:00 where he",
"He was the last person. To see Fred."),1)
val sentenceDetectorModelFile = new
File("/home/padmac/opennlp_models/en- sent.bin")
val model = new SentenceModel(sentenceDetectorModelFile)
val sdetector = new SentenceDetectorME(model)
val broadCastedsdector = sc.broadcast(sdetector)
val broadCastedsdector = sc.broadcast(sdetector)
val results = textInput.map{record =>
(broadCastedsdector.value.sentDetect(record),
broadCastedsdector.value.getSentenceProbabilities)
}
val detectedSentences = results.keys.flatMap(x => x)
val probabilities = results.values.flatMap(x => x)
println("Detected Sentences: ")
detectedSentences.collect().foreach(println)
println("Probabilities : ")
probabilities.collect().foreach(println)
 }
}
```

The following is the output:

Detected sentences:

```
Hi Padma !
How are you ?
He saw him in Boston at McKenzie's pub.
At 3:00 where he
He was the last person.
To see Fred.
```

Probabilities:

```
0.8702580316569011
0.94117302373681
0.9863984646806333
1.0
0.999763703383087
0.9347401492739993
```

How it works...

Initially the model `en-sent.bin` is downloaded from `http://opennlp.sourceforge.net/models-1.5/`. The `SentenceModel(sentenceDetectorModelFile)` line, loads the `SentenceModel`. Next, the `SentenceDetectorME(model)` line initializes the `SenetenceDetectorME` from the model. The `SenetenceDetectorME` created, is broadcasted which might result in serialization issues. Hence setting the property, `che.spark.sorg.apaerializer.KryoSerializer` serializes the model.

For each element in the RDD, `broadCastedsdector.value.sentDetect(record)` generates detected array of sentences. The `getSentenceProbabilities` method returns an array of doubles representing the confidence of the sentences detected from the last use of the `sentDetect` method. The detected sentences and the respective probabilities are finally displayed on console.

There's more...

Common approaches to detect sentences are to include a set of rules to train a model for detection. The simple rules could be that text should be terminated by a period, question mark or exclamation mark and also the period should not be preceded by an abbreviation or followed by a digit and so on. The detection of sentence boundaries helps separate phrases that might appear to span sentences. However, breaking text into sentences is difficult because punctuation is frequently ambiguous, abbreviations often contain periods and also sentences may be embedded within each other by the use of quotes.

See also

Please refer *POS tagging with PySpark on an Anaconda cluster, NER with IPython over Spark* and*Implemeting OpenNLP-Chunkerover Spark* recipes to know details on implementing POS tagging, NER and Chunker using NLTK and OpenNLP over Spark.

Implementing stanford NLP – lemmatization over Spark

Lemmatization is one of the pre-processing steps which is a more methodical way of converting all the grammatical/inflected forms of the root of the word. It uses context and parts of speech to determine the inflected form of the word and applies different normalization rules for each part of speech to get the word (lemma). In this recipe, we'll see lemmatization of text using Stanford API.

Getting ready

To step through this recipe, you will need a running Spark cluster either in pseudo distributed mode or in one of the distributed modes, that is, standalone, YARN, or Mesos. For installing Spark on a standalone cluster, please refer to `http://spark.apache.org/docs/latest/spark-standalone.html.`. Install Hadoop (optionally), Scala, and Java.

How to do it...

Let's see how to apply lemmatization using Stanford NLP over Spark:

1. Let's start an application named SparkCoreNLP. Initially specify the following libraries in `build.sbt` file:

```
libraryDependencies ++= Seq(
"org.apache.spark" %% "spark-core" % "1.6.0",
"org.apache.spark" %% "spark-mllib" % "1.6.0",
"org.apache.spark" %% "spark-sql" % "1.6.0",
"org.apache.spark" %% "spark-streaming" % "1.6.0",
"org.apache.opennlp" % "opennlp-tools" % "1.6.0",
"org.apache.opennlp" % "opennlp-uima" % "1.6.0"
"edu.stanford.nlp" % "stanford-corenlp" % "3.6.0",
"com.google.protobuf" % "protobuf-java" % "2.6.1"
)
```

2. Here is the code for the Lemmatization using Stanford NLP API:

```
import java.util._
import edu.stanford.nlp.ling.CoreAnnotations._
import edu.stanford.nlp.ling.CoreAnnotations.TokensAnnotation
import edu.stanford.nlp.ling.CoreAnnotations
.LemmaAnnotation
import edu.stanford.nlp.pipeline.StanfordCoreNLP
import scala.collection.JavaConverters._
object Lemmatization_Stanford {
def main(args: Array[String]): Unit = {
val conf = new SparkConf()
.setMaster("spark:master:7077")
.setAppName("Lemmatization_Demo")
.set("spark.serializer",
"org.apache.spark.serializer.KryoSerializer")
val sc = new SparkContext(conf)
val textInput = sc.makeRDD(Array("Hi Padma ! How are you ?", "He
saw him in Boston at McKenzie's pub. At 3:00 where he", "He was the
last person. To see Fred."), 1)
val props = new Properties()
props.put("annotators", "tokenize, ssplit, pos, lemma")
val pipeline = new StanfordCoreNLP(props)
val broadCastedPipeline = sc.broadcast(pipeline)
val lemmas = textInput.flatMap{
record =>
val document = broadCastedPipeline.value.process(record)
val sentences =
document.get(classOf[SentencesAnnotation]).asScala.toList
```

```
    val tokens = sentences.flatMap{sentence =>
    sentence.get(classOf[TokensAnnotation]).asScala.toList}
    tokens.map{token =>
    val word = token.get(classOf[TextAnnotation])
    val lemma = token.get(classOf[LemmaAnnotation])
    (word,lemma) }
      }
    lemmas.foreach(println)
      }
      }
```

How it works...

The preceding code snippet shows how to use Stanford NLP API over Spark to lemmatize the text. Initially, properties object is created and the annotators `tokenize`, `ssplit`, `pos` and `lemma` are specified. `tokenize` performs tokenization, `ssplit` performs sentence splitting, `pos` does POS tagging and `lemma` performs lemmatization. The line `new StanfordCoreNLP(props)` creates `StanforCoreNLP` object which is the pipeline. Now, this `StanfordCoreNLP` instance is broadcasted. For each sentence in the RDD, the line `broadCastedPipeline.value.process(record)` generates `Annotation`. Using the generated `Annotation`, the line `document.get(classOf[SentencesAnnotation]).asScala.toList` generates sentences of the form `List[CoreMap]`. For each sentence in turn, tokens are generated in the form – `List[CoreLabel]`. The generated tokens are iterated and for each token, `token.get(classOf[TextAnnotation])` returns the word and `token.get(classOf[LemmaAnnotation])` returns lemma.

There's more...

The goal of stemming and lemmatization is to reduce inflectional forms and sometimes derivationally related forms of a word to a common base form. Stemming usually refers to a crude heuristic process that chops off the ends of words in the hope of achieving this goal correctly, and often includes the removal of derivational affixes. Lemmatization usually refers to doing things properly with the use of a vocabulary and morphological analysis of words, normally aiming to remove inflectional endings only and to return the base or dictionary form of a word, which is known as the lemma.

If confronted with the token 'saw', stemming might return just 's', whereas lemmatization would attempt to return either 'see' or 'saw' depending on whether the use of the token is verb or a noun. These two may also differ in a way that – stemming most commonly collapses derivationally related words, whereas lemmatization commonly collapses the different inflectional forms of a lemma. Linguistic processing for stemming or lemmatization is often done by an additional plug-in component to the indexing process, and a number of such components exist, in both commercial and open-source

See also

Please refer to *Implemeting OpenNLP-Chunkerover Spark* and *Implemeting OpenNLP – sentence detector over Spark* recipes to know details on running Chunker and sentence detector using OpenNLP.

Implementing sentiment analysis using stanford NLP over Spark

Sentiment analysis or opinion mining involves building a system to collect and categorize opinions about a product. This can be used in several ways that help marketers evaluate the success of an ad-campaign or new product launch, determine which versions of product or service are popular and also identify demographics that like or dislike product features. In this recipe we will see how the Stanford NLP API performs sentiment analysis.

Getting ready

To step through this recipe, you will need a running Spark cluster either in pseudo distributed mode or in one of the distributed modes, that is, standalone, YARN, or Mesos. For installing Spark on a standalone cluster, please refer to `http://spark.apache.org/docs/latest/spark-standalone.html`. Install Hadoop (optionally), Scala, and Java.

How to do it...

Let's see how to apply sentiment analysis using Stanford NLP over Spark:

1. Let's start an application named SparkCoreNLP. Initially specify the following libraries in the `build.sbt` file:

```
libraryDependencies ++= Seq(
"org.apache.spark" %% "spark-core" % "1.6.0",
"org.apache.spark" %% "spark-mllib" % "1.6.0",
"org.apache.spark" %% "spark-sql" % "1.6.0",
"org.apache.spark" %% "spark-streaming" % "1.6.0",
"org.apache.opennlp" % "opennlp-tools" % "1.6.0",
"org.apache.opennlp"
% "opennlp-uima" % "1.6.0"
"edu.stanford.nlp" % "stanford-corenlp" % "3.6.0",
"com.google.protobuf" % "protobuf-java" % "2.6.1"
)
```

2. Here is the code for the sentiment analysis using stanford NLP API:

```
import edu.stanford.nlp.ling.CoreAnnotations
import edu.stanford.nlp.neural.rnn.RNNCoreAnnotations
import edu.stanford.nlp.sentiment.
SentimentCoreAnnotations
import org.apache.spark.SparkConf
import org.apache.spark.SparkContext
import java.util._
import edu.stanford.nlp.pipeline.{Annotation, StanfordCoreNLP}
import scala.collection.JavaConverters._
object SentimentAnalysis_StanfordAPI {
def main(args:Array[String]): Unit =
{
val conf = new SparkConf()
.setMaster("spark:master:7077")
.setAppName("SentimentAnalysis_Demo")
.set("spark.serializer","org.apache.spark.serializer.
KryoSerializer")
val sc = new SparkContext(conf)
val textInput = sc.makeRDD(Array("An overly sentimental film with a
somewhat problematic message, but its sweetness and charm are
occasionally enough to approximate true depth and grace.",
"Sam was an odd sort of fellow. Not prone to angry and not prone to
merriment. Overall, an odd fellow.", "Mary thought that custard pie
was the best pie in the world. However, she loathed chocolate
pie"), 1)
val sentimentText = scala.collection.immutable.List("Very
```

```
Negative", "Negative", "Neutral", "Positive", "Very Positive")
val props = new Properties()
props.put("annotators", "tokenize, ssplit, parse, sentiment")
val pipeline = new StanfordCoreNLP(props)
val broadCastedPipeline = sc.broadcast(pipeline)
val broadCastedSentimentText = sc.broadcast(sentimentText)
val scoredSentiments = textInput.flatMap{
record => val annotation = new Annotation(record)
pipeline.annotate(annotation)
val sentenceList =
annotation.get(classOf[CoreAnnotations.SentencesAnnotation])
.asScala.toList; sentenceList.map{sentence =>
val tree sentence.get(classOf[SentimentCoreAnnotations.
SentimentAnnotatedTree])
val score = RNNCoreAnnotations.getPredictedClass(tree)
broadCastedSentimentText.value(score)
}
}
scoredSentiments.foreach(println)
}
}
```

The following is the output:

```
Positive
Neutral
Negative
Neutral
Positive
Neutral
```

How it works...

The preceding code snippet shows how to use Stanford NLP API with Spark to extract sentiment out of the text. The textInput RDD contains different possible sentences. The list sentimentText holds strings for different possible sentiments. The properties object is created and the annotators–tokenize, ssplit, parse and sentiment are specified. tokenize performs tokenization, ssplit performs sentence splitting, parse does Parsing and sentiment extracts sentiment out of the text.

The `new StanfordCoreNLP(props)` line creates a `StanforCoreNLP` object which is the pipeline. Now, this `StanfordCoreNLP` instance is broadcasted. For each sentence in the RDD, the `new Annotation(record)` line creates annotation and then `pipeline.annotate(annotation)` line performs the actual processing behind the scene. The `Annotation` class get method returns list of objects of type `CoreMap` which represents the results of splitting the input text into sentences. For each sentence in turn, `sentence.get(classOf[SentimentCoreAnnotations.SentimentAnnotatedTree])` line generates an instance of `Tree` object which represents the tree structure containing parse of the text for the sentiment. The `getPredictedClass` method returns an index into the `sentimentText` array reflecting the sentiment of the text. Finally the sentiments are displayed on the console.

There's more...

Apart from sentiment analysis which is the most common use case, there are others like – spam classification, e-mail categorization, news categorization etc. Sentiment analysis is extremely useful in social media monitoring as it allows us to gain an overview of the wider public opinion behind certain topics. The applications of sentiment analysis are broad and powerful. The ability to extract insights from social data is a practice that is being widely adopted by organizations across the world. Shifts in sentiment on social media have been shown to correlate with shifts in the stock market.

See also

Please refer *Implementing OpenNLP – chunker over Spark, Implemeting OpenNLP – sentence detector* and *Implementing stanford NLP – lemmatizationover Spark* recipes to know details on running Chunker, sentence detector and lemmatization using OpenNLP and stanford NLP

7

Working with Sparkling Water - H2O

In this chapter, you will learn the following recipes:

- Working with H2O on Spark

    Downloading and installing H2O

    Using H2O API in Spark

- Implementing k-means using H2O over Spark
- Implementing spam detection with Sparkling Water
- Deep learning with airlines and weather data
- Implementing a crime detection application
- Running SVM with H2O over Spark

Introduction

H2O is a fast, scalable, open-source machine learning and deep learning library for smarter applications. Using in-memory compression, H2O handles billions of data rows in memory, even with a small cluster. In order to create complete analytic workflows, H2O's platform includes interfaces for R, Python, Scala, Java, JSON and CoffeeScript/JavaScript flows, as well as a built-in web interface. H2O is designed to run in standalone mode on Hadoop, or within a Spark Cluster. It includes many common machine learning algorithms, such as generalized linear modeling (linear regression, logistic regression, and so on), Naive Bayes, principal components analysis, k-means clustering and others.

H2O also implements best-in-class algorithms at scale, such as distributed random forest, gradient boosting and deep learning. Users can build thousands of models and compare the results to get the best predictions.

Sparkling Water allows users to combine the fast, scalable machine learning algorithms of H2O with the capabilities of Spark. With Sparkling Water, users can drive computation from Scala, R, or Python and use the H2O flow UI, providing an ideal machine learning platform for application developers. This integrates the two open source environments, namely Spark, which is an elegant and powerful general-purpose, open-source, in-memory platform and H2O, an in-memory application for machine learning.

Features

Sparkling Water provides transparent integration for the H2O engine and its machine learning algorithms into Spark platforms, which enables the following:

- Use of H2O algorithms in the Spark workflow
- Transformation between H2O and Spark data structures
- Use of Spark RDDs and DataFrames as input for H2O algorithms
- Use of H2O frames as input for MLlib algorithms
- Transparent execution of Sparkling Water applications on top of Spark

Working with H2O on Spark

Sparkling Water is executed as a regular Spark application. It provides a way to initialize H2O services on each node in the Spark Cluster and to access data stored in the data structures of Spark and H2O. The Sparkling Water application is launched inside a spark executor created after submitting the application. At this point, H2O starts the services, including the distributed **key value** (**KV**) storage and the memory manager.

Getting ready

To step through this recipe, you will need a running Spark Cluster in any one of the following modes: Local, standalone, YARN, Mesos. You must also include the Spark MLlib package in the `build.sbt` file so that it downloads the related libraries and the API can be used. Install Hadoop (optionally), Scala, and Java.

How to do it...

In this recipe, we'll learn how to download and install H2O services in a Spark Cluster. We'll also use the H2O API in Spark.

The list of sub-recipes in this section is as follows:

- Downloading and installing H2O
- Using H2O API in Spark

The following are the steps for downloading and installing H2O:

1. Please download the Sparkling Water 1.6.1 from the following location: `http://h2o-release.s3.amazonaws.com/sparkling-water/rel-1.6/1/index.html`.
2. As per the latest addition of H2O, the compatible version of Spark is 1.6.0. The pre-requisite is to download and install Spark 1.6.0, point `SPARK_HOME` to the existing installation of Spark and also specify the `MASTER` variable in the `sparkling-env.sh` as follows:

```
export MASTER="spark://172.22.225.174:7077"
export SPARK_HOME="/home/padmac/bigdata/spark-1.6.0-bin-hadoop2.6"
export SPARK_LOG_DIR="${tmpdir}spark/logs"
#export SPARK_WORKER_DIR="${tmpdir}spark/work"
export SPARK_LOCAL_DIRS="${tmpdir}spark/work"
export SPARK_WORKER_DIR="~/bigdata/sparkworkerdir"
```

3. Now invoke `sparkling-shell` as follows:

```
./bin/sparkling-shell --conf "spark.executor.memory=1g"
```

```
Spark master (MASTER)     : spark://172.22.225.174:7077
Spark home   (SPARK_HOME) : /home/padmac/bigdata/spark-1.6.0-bin-hadoop2.6
H2O build version         : 3.8.1.3 (turan)
Spark build version       : 1.6.1

16/10/23 13:09:36 WARN NativeCodeLoader: Unable to load native-hadoop library for your platform... using builtin-java classes where applicable
16/10/23 13:09:37 INFO SecurityManager: Changing view acls to: padmac
16/10/23 13:09:37 INFO SecurityManager: Changing modify acls to: padmac
16/10/23 13:09:37 INFO SecurityManager: SecurityManager: authentication disabled; ui acls disabled; users with view permissions: Set(padmac); use
rs with modify permissions: Set(padmac)
16/10/23 13:09:37 INFO HttpServer: Starting HTTP Server
16/10/23 13:09:38 INFO Utils: Successfully started service 'HTTP class server' on port 45583.
Welcome to
      ____              __
     / __/__  ___ _____/ /__
    _\ \/ _ \/ _ `/ __/  '_/
   /___/ .__/\_,_/_/ /_/\_\   version 1.6.0
      /_/
```

```
16/10/23 13:00:26 WARN ObjectStore: Failed to get database default, returning NoSuchObjectException
16/10/23 13:00:27 INFO HiveMetaStore: Added admin role in metastore
16/10/23 13:00:27 INFO HiveMetaStore: Added public role in metastore
16/10/23 13:00:27 INFO HiveMetaStore: No user is added in admin role, since config is empty
16/10/23 13:00:27 INFO HiveMetaStore: 0: get_all_databases
16/10/23 13:00:27 INFO audit: ugi=padmac        ip=unknown-ip-addr      cmd=get_all_databases
16/10/23 13:00:27 INFO HiveMetaStore: 0: get_functions: db=default pat=*
16/10/23 13:00:27 INFO audit: ugi=padmac        ip=unknown-ip-addr      cmd=get_functions: db=default pat=*
16/10/23 13:00:27 INFO Datastore: The class "org.apache.hadoop.hive.metastore.model.MResourceUri" is tagged as "embedded-only" so does not have i
ts own datastore table.
16/10/23 13:00:29 INFO SessionState: Created HDFS directory: /tmp/hive-padmac/padmac/65eeb4ce-e42b-408b-b286-77b32af47b38
16/10/23 13:00:29 INFO SessionState: Created local directory: /tmp/hive-padmac/padmac/65eeb4ce-e42b-408b-b286-77b32af47b38
16/10/23 13:00:29 INFO SessionState: Created HDFS directory: /tmp/hive-padmac/padmac/65eeb4ce-e42b-408b-b286-77b32af47b38/_tmp_space.db
16/10/23 13:00:29 INFO SparkILoop: Created sql context (with Hive support)..
SQL context available as sqlContext.

scala>
```

4. Let's create `H2OContext` inside the Sparkling shell, as shown in the following screenshot:

```
scala> import org.apache.spark.h2o._
import org.apache.spark.h2o._

scala> val h2oContext = new H2OContext(sc).start()
16/10/23 13:13:21 WARN H2OContext: Increasing 'spark.locality.wait' to value 30000
16/10/23 13:13:21 WARN H2OContext: The property 'spark.scheduler.minRegisteredResourcesRatio' is not specified!
We recommend to pass `--conf spark.scheduler.minRegisteredResourcesRatio=1`
16/10/23 13:13:21 INFO H2OContext: Starting H2O services: Sparkling Water configuration:
  workers        : None
  cloudName      : sparkling-water-padmac_-751800580
  flatfile       : true
  clientBasePort : 54321
  nodeBasePort   : 54321
  cloudTimeout   : 60000
  h2oNodeLog     : INFO
  h2oClientLog   : WARN
  nthreads       : -1
  drddMulFactor  : 10
16/10/23 13:13:21 INFO SparkContext: Starting job: collect at SpreadRDDBuilder.scala:110
```

```
  Open H2O Flow in browser: http://192.168.0.5:54323 (CMD + click in Mac OSX)

h2oContext: org.apache.spark.h2o.H2OContext =

Sparkling Water Context:
 * H2O name: sparkling-water-padmac_-751800580
 * number of executors: 1
 * list of used executors:
  (executorId, host, port)
  ------------------------
  (0,192.168.0.5,54321,192.168.0.5)
  ------------------------

  Open H2O Flow in browser: http://192.168.0.5:54323 (CMD + click in Mac OSX)

scala>

scala> import h2oContext._
import h2oContext._
```

5. The `sparkling-shell` can also be launched on the `yarn-client` with specified executor properties, as follows:

```
bin/sparkling-shell --num-executors 3 --executor-memory 4g --
driver-memory 4g    --master yarn-client
```

The following are the steps for using H2O API in Spark:

1. Let's see how to use the H2O API in a standalone Spark application. Specify the following libraries in the `build.sbt` file:

```
libraryDependencies ++= Seq(
"ai.h2o" % "sparkling-water-core_2.10" % "1.6.4",
"ai.h2o" % "sparkling-water-ml_2.10" % "1.6.4" )
```

2. Please download the dataset from the following location
   `https://github.com/ChitturiPadma/datasets/blob/master/chicagoCrimes.cs`
   v. Here is the sample code which depicts the usage of H2O API:

```
import org.apache.spark._
import org.apache.spark.sql._
import org.apache.spark.h2o._
import org.apache.spark.h2o.H2OContext
object H2OSample_Demo {
  def main(args:Array[String]): Unit = {
  val conf = new SparkConf()
  .setMaster("spark://master:7077")
  .setAppName("H2O_SampleDemo")
  val sc = new SparkContext(conf)
  val sqlContext = new SQLContext(sc)
  val h2oContext = H2OContext.getOrCreate(sc)
  import h2oContext._
  import h2oContext.implicits._
  import sqlContext.implicits._
  val chicagoCrimesData =
  sqlContext.read.format("com.databricks.spark.csv")
  .option("header", "true")
  .option("inferSchema",
  "true").load("hdfs://namenode:9000/chicagoCrimes.csv")
  val h2oFrame = h2oContext.asH2OFrame(chicagoCrimesData)
  val means_H2OFrame = h2oFrame.means()
  means_H2OFrame.foreach(println)
    }
  }
}
```

The following is the output:

```
0.29282928292829286
0.15231523152315232
1159.6180618061808
11.348988512757956
22.954095409540987
37.44764476447647
```

How it works...

Initially, to install Sparkling Water, the version compatible with Spark 1.6.0 is downloaded and in the `sparkling-env.sh` file, the variables, such as `SPARK_HOME`, `MASTER` and `SPARK_WORKER_DIR`, are set and the Sparkling shell is invoked. This then initializes both `SparkContext` and `SQLContext` (as in `spark-shell`), and the corresponding H2O API is available from the shell by importing the `org.apache.spark.h2o` package.

Next, for a standalone application, the dependencies`sparkling-water-core_2.10` and `sparkling-water-ml_2.10` are included in the `build.sbt` file. In the preceding code snippet, the line `H2OContext.getOrCreate(sc)` creates the `H2OContext` if it doesn't exist, and retrieves if it already exists. Using the `SQLContext`, the CSV file is read and the line `h2oContext.asH2OFrame(chicagoCrimesData)` creates the `H2OFrame`. Finally, `h2oFrame.means()` displays the mean of the respective columns of the frame.

There's more...

In the next recipes, we'll see how we can run some of the machine learning algorithms using the H2O API.

See also

For more details, please refer to the H2O documentation at `http://docs.h2o.ai`.

Implementing k-means using H2O over Spark

In this recipe, we'll look at how to run a k-means clustering algorithm on a dataset of figures concerning prostate cancer. Please download the dataset from `https://github.com/ChitturiPadma/datasets/blob/master/prostate.csv`. This is prostate cancer data that came from a study that examined the correlation between the level of prostate-specific antigen and a number of other clinical measures in men.

Getting ready

To step through this recipe, you will need a running Spark Cluster in any one of the following modes: Local, standalone, YARN, Mesos. Include the Spark MLlib package in the `build.sbt` file so that it downloads the related libraries and the API can be used. Install Hadoop (optionally), Scala, and Java. Also, install Sparkling Water as discussed in the preceding recipe.

How to do it...

1. The sample rows in the `prostate.csv` look like the following:

ID	CAPSULE	AGE	RACE	DPROS	DCAPS	PSA	VOL	GLEASON
1	0	65	1	2	1	1.4	0	6
2	0	72	1	3	2	6.7	0	7
3	0	70	1	1	2	4.9	0	6
4	0	76	2	2	1	51.2	20	7
5	0	69	1	1	1	12.3	55.9	6

2. Here is the code to run k-means on the preceding dataset:

```
import org.apache.spark._
import org.apache.spark.sql._
import org.apache.spark.h2o._
import hex.kmeans.KMeansModel.KMeansParameters
import hex.kmeans.{KMeans, KMeansModel}
import water._
import water.support.SparkContextSupport
object H2O_KmeansDemo {
def main(args:Array[String]): Unit = {
val conf = new SparkConf()
.setMaster("spark://master:7077")
.setAppName("H2O_KmeansDemo")
val sc = new SparkContext(conf)
val sqlContext = new SQLContext(sc)
val h2oContext = H2OContext.getOrCreate(sc)
import h2oContext._
import h2oContext.implicits._
import sqlContext.implicits._
val prostateDf =
```

```
sqlContext.read.format("com.databricks.spark.csv")
.option("header", "true")
.option("inferSchema",
 "true").load("hdfs://namenode:9000/prostate.csv")
prostateDf.registerTempTable("prostate_table")
val result = sqlContext.sql("SELECT * FROM prostate_table
WHERE CAPSULE=1")
val h2oFrame = h2oContext.asH2OFrame(result)
/* Build a KMeans model, setting model parameters via a
Properties */
val model = runKmeans(h2oFrame)
println(model)
// Shutdown Spark cluster and H2O
h2oContext.stop(stopSparkContext = true) }

def runKmeans[T](trainDataFrame: H2OFrame): KMeansModel = {
val params = new KMeansParameters
params._train = trainDataFrame._key
params._k = 3
// Create a builder
val job = new KMeans(params)
// Launch a job and wait for the end.
val kmm = job.trainModel.get
// Print the JSON model
println(new String(kmm._output.writeJSON(new
AutoBuffer()).buf()))

// Return a model
kmm
 }
}
```

The following is the output:

```
Model Metrics Type: Clustering
Description: N/A
model id: KMeans_model_1477245204509_1
frame id: frame_rdd_16
MSE: NaN
total sum of squares: 1216.0
total within sum of squares: 927.4515
total between sum of squares: 288.54852
per cluster sizes: [32, 57, 64]
per cluster within sum of squares: [293.8000208794267, 324.00423677789296, 309.647229009292]
Model Summary:
Number of Rows Number of Clusters Number of Categorical Columns Number of Iterations Within Cluster Sum of Squares Total Sum of Squares Between
Cluster Sum of Squares
            153                 3                             0                    7              927.45149           1216.00000
        288.54851
Scoring History:
            Timestamp   Duration Iteration Avg. Change of Std. Centroids Within Cluster Sum Of Squares
2016-10-23 23:23:37  0.075 sec         0                            NaN                    2426.68984
2016-10-23 23:23:38  0.232 sec         1                        9.40828                    1000.31544
2016-10-23 23:23:38  0.235 sec         2                        0.08238                     978.39570
2016-10-23 23:23:38  0.238 sec         3                        0.05895                     961.27869
2016-10-23 23:23:38  0.241 sec         4                        0.10461                     938.94383
2016-10-23 23:23:38  0.245 sec         5                        0.09135                     927.77160
2016-10-23 23:23:38  0.248 sec         6                        0.00283                     927.45149
```

How it works...

Initially `SparkContext`, `SQLContext` and `H2OContext` are initialized and the `prostate.csv` file is loaded using the `sqlContext.read.format("com.databricks.spark.csv")` statement from HDFS. From the `prostateDf` DataFrame, a temporary table is created as `prostateDf.registerTempTable("prostate_table")`. The `sqlContext.sql("SELECT * FROM prostate_table WHERE CAPSULE=1")` statement fetches all the rows where `CAPSULE` is equal to 1. Next, `H2OFrame` is created from the `h2oContext.asH2OFrame(result)` statement.

The `runKmeans` function takes an `H2OFrame` as parameter, creates an instance of `KmeansParameters` and initializes the properties `_train` and `_k`. Next, the `Kmeans` object is created as a new `Kmeans(params)`. The `job.trainModel.get` line retrieves the `KmeansModel` and returns it.

The `runKmeans(h2oFrame)` line in the main function passes `H2OFrame` as the input, runs the `Kmeans` algorithm and returns `KmeansModel`. Finally, the `h2oContext.stop(stopSparkContext = true)` statement stops the `H2OContext` and also the `SparkContext`.

There's more...

After submitting the resulting Sparkling Water application into a Spark Cluster, the application can create `H2OContext`, which initializes the H2O services on top of the Spark nodes. The application can then use any functionality provided by H2O, including its algorithms and interactive UI. H2O uses its own data structure called **H2OFrame** to represent tabular data, but `H2OContext` allows H2O to share data with Spark's RDDs.

Also, the H2O API supports loading data directly into the H2OFrame from file(s) stored on local filesystems, HDFS, S3 and HTTP/HTTPS. Sparkling Water can read data stored in the CSV, SVMLight, and ARFF formats.

See also

Please visit the *Working with H2O on Spark* recipe to learn about the details of installing Sparkling Water and writing standalone Sparkling Water applications. For more details, please refer to the H2O documentation at `http://docs.h2o.ai`.

Implementing spam detection with Sparkling Water

In this recipe, we'll look at how to implement a spam detector by extracting data, transforming and tokenizing messages, building Spark's Tf-IDF model, and expanding messages to feature vectors. We'll also create and evaluate H2O's deep learning model. Lastly, we will use the models to detect spam messages.

Getting ready

To step through this recipe, you will need a running Spark Cluster in any one of the following modes: Local, standalone, YARN, Mesos. Include the Spark MLlib package in the `build.sbt` file so that it downloads the related libraries and the API can be used. Install Hadoop (optionally), Scala, and Java. Also, install Sparkling Water as discussed in the preceding recipe.

How to do it...

1. Please download the dataset from
   `https://github.com/ChitturiPadma/datasets/blob/master/smsData.txt`. The records in the dataset look like the following:

   ```
   ham    Ok... But they said i've got wisdom teeth hidden inside n
   mayb need 2 remove.
   ham    U thk of wat to eat tonight.
   ham    I dunno until when... Lets go learn pilates...
   spam Someonone you know is trying to contact you via our dating
   service! To find out who it could be call from your mobile or
   landline 09064015307 BOX334SK38ch
   ham    Ok c u then.
   spam   URGENT! We are trying to contact U. Todays draw shows that
   you have won a £800 prize GUARANTEED. Call 09050003091 from land
   line. Claim C52. Valid12hrs only spam  Not heard from U4 a
   while. Call 4 rude chat private line 01223585334 to cum. Wan 2C
   pics of me gettin shagged then text PIX to 8552. 2End send STOP
   8552 SAM xxx
   ham    staff.science.nus.edu.sg/~phyhcmk/teaching/pc1323
   ham    Thank god they are in bed!
   ```

2. Here is the code for spam detection:

   ```
   import hex.ModelMetricsBinomial
   import hex.deeplearning.{DeepLearning, DeepLearningModel}
   import hex.deeplearning.DeepLearningModel.DeepLearningParameters
   import org.apache.spark.h2o._
   import org.apache.spark.mllib.feature.{HashingTF, IDF, IDFModel}
   import org.apache.spark.rdd.RDD
   import org.apache.spark.sql.{DataFrame, SQLContext}
   import org.apache.spark.{SparkConf, SparkContext, mllib}
   import water.support.{H2OFrameSupport, ModelMetricsSupport,
   SparkContextSupport}
   ```

```
object H2O_SpamDetector extends SparkContextSupport with
ModelMetricsSupport   with H2OFrameSupport {
case class SMS(target: String, fv: mllib.linalg.Vector)
val TEST_MSGS = Seq(
"Michal, beer tonight in MV?",
"We tried to contact you re your reply to our offer of a Video
Handset? 750 anytime any networks mins? UNLIMITED TEXT?")
def main(args:Array[String]): Unit = {
val conf = new SparkConf()
        .setMaster("spark://master:7077")
        .setAppName("H2O_Spam_Detector")
val sc = new SparkContext(conf)
implicit val h2oContext = H2OContext.getOrCreate(sc)
implicit val sqlContext = new SQLContext(sc)
import h2oContext._
import h2oContext.implicits._
import sqlContext.implicits._
// Loading Data
val dataRdd = sc.textFile("hdfs://namenode:9000/smsData.txt")
.map(l => l.split("\t")).filter(r => !r(0).isEmpty)
//Extract response spam or ham
val hamSpamRdd = dataRdd.map(r => r(0))
val messageRdd = dataRdd.map(r => r(1))
// Tokenize message content
val tokensRdd = tokenize(messageRdd)

// Build IDF model
val (hashingTF, idfModel, tfidf) = buildIDFModel(tokensRdd)

// Merge response with extracted vectors
val resultDf: DataFrame = hamSpamRdd.zip(tfidf).map(v => SMS(v._1,
v._2)).toDF

val table:H2OFrame = h2oContext.asH2OFrame(resultDf)
// Transform target column into
table.replace(table.find("target"),
table.vec("target").toCategoricalVec).remove()

// Split table
val keys = Array[String]("train.hex", "valid.hex")
val ratios = Array[Double](0.8)
val frs = split(table, keys, ratios)
val (train, valid) = (frs(0), frs(1))
table.delete()
// Build a model
val dlModel = buildDLModel(train, valid)
// Collect model metrics
val trainMetrics = modelMetrics[ModelMetricsBinomial](dlModel,
```

```
train)
val validMetrics = modelMetrics[ModelMetricsBinomial](dlModel,
valid)
println(
  s"""
      |AUC on train data = ${trainMetrics.auc}
      |AUC on valid data = ${validMetrics.auc}
    """.stripMargin)
// Detect spam messages
TEST_MSGS.foreach(msg => {
 println(s""" |"$msg" is ${if (isSpam(msg,sc, dlModel, hashingTF,
   idfModel)) "SPAM" else    "HAM"}
   """.stripMargin)
   })
 // Shutdown Spark cluster and H2O
h2oContext.stop(stopSparkContext = true)
}
def tokenize(data: RDD[String]): RDD[Seq[String]] = {
val ignoredWords = Seq("the", "a", "", "in", "on", "at", "as",
 "not", "for")
val ignoredChars = Seq(',', ':', ';', '/', '<', '>', '"', '.',
'(', ')', '?', '-',    ''','!','0', '1')
val texts = data.map( r=> {
var smsText = r.toLowerCase
for( c <- ignoredChars) {
   smsText = smsText.replace(c, ' ')
 }
 val words =smsText.split(" ").filter(w =>
 !ignoredWords.contains(w) && w.length>2).distinct
 words.toSeq
 })
 texts
}

/* Buil tf-idf model representing a text message. */
def buildIDFModel(tokens: RDD[Seq[String]],
               minDocFreq:Int = 4,
               hashSpaceSize:Int = 1 << 10): (HashingTF, IDFModel,
               RDD[mllib.linalg.Vector]) = {
// Hash strings into the given space
val hashingTF = new HashingTF(hashSpaceSize)
val tf = hashingTF.transform(tokens)
// Build term frequency-inverse document frequency
val idfModel = new IDF(minDocFreq = minDocFreq).fit(tf)
val expandedText = idfModel.transform(tf)
(hashingTF, idfModel, expandedText)
 }
 /** Builds DeepLearning model. */
```

```scala
def buildDLModel(train: Frame, valid: Frame,
        epochs: Int = 10, l1: Double = 0.001, l2: Double = 0.0,
        hidden: Array[Int] = Array[Int](200, 200))
        (implicit h2oContext: H2OContext): DeepLearningModel = {
import h2oContext.implicits._
// Build a model
val dlParams = new DeepLearningParameters()
dlParams._train = train
dlParams._valid = valid
dlParams._response_column = 'target
dlParams._epochs = epochs
dlParams._l1 = l1
dlParams._hidden = hidden
// Create a job
val dl = new DeepLearning(dlParams,water.Key.make("dlModel.hex"))
dl.trainModel.get
  }
/* Spam detector */
def isSpam(msg: String,
        sc: SparkContext,
        dlModel: DeepLearningModel,
        hashingTF: HashingTF,
        idfModel: IDFModel,
        hamThreshold: Double = 0.5)
        (implicit sqlContext: SQLContext, h2oContext:
        H2OContext):Boolean = {
import h2oContext.implicits._
import sqlContext.implicits._
val msgRdd = sc.parallelize(Seq(msg))
val msgVector: DataFrame = idfModel.transform(
hashingTF.transform (tokenize (msgRdd))).map(v =>
SMS("?", v)).toDF
val msgTable: H2OFrame = msgVector
msgTable.remove(0) // remove first column
val prediction = dlModel.score(msgTable)
//println(prediction)
prediction.vecs()(1).at(0) < hamThreshold
  }
}
```

The following is the output:

```
AUC on train data = 0.9998817765671698
AUC on valid data = 0.9821645021645021
"Michal, beer tonight in MV?" is HAM
"We tried to contact you re your reply to our offer of a Video
  Handset? 750 anytime any networks mins? UNLIMITED TEXT?" is SPAM
```

How it works...

Initially, all the required libraries are imported. The `SparkContext` and `SQLContext` are initialized and the `smsData.txt` file is loaded using the `sc.textFile("hdfs://namenode:9000/smsData.txt").map(l => l.split("\t")).filter(r => !r(0).isEmpty)` line. The dataset consists of two columns, the first one being the label (`ham` or `spam`) and the second one being the message itself. The H2O services are started using the `implicit val h2oContext = H2OContext.getOrCreate(sc)` line. Once the data is loaded, the first and second columns from the data are extracted as `val hamSpamRdd = dataRdd.map(r => r(0))` and `val messageRdd = dataRdd.map(r => r(1))`.

Next, the `messageRDD` is sent as a parameter to the `tokenize` method, which then removes the stop words and some special characters. Once the messages are tokenized, the `tokensRDD` is sent as a parameter to `buildIDFModel`. This method instantiates Spark's `HashingTF` and vectorizes the words. The inverse document frequency object `IDF` is created as a new `IDF(minDocFreq = minDocFreq).fit(tf)`, and it creates a numerical representation of how much information a given word provides in the whole message. The extracted vectors are merged with hamSpamRDD as `hamSpamRdd.zip(tfidf).map(v => SMS(v._1, v._2)).toDF`. The H2OFrame is created from the `h2oContext.asH2OFrame(result)` statement.

The dataset is split and the splits with specified keys are stored in H2O's distributed storage. The ratios are specified as `val ratios = Array[Double](0.8)`. Now, the table is split as per the specified keys and ratios using the `val frs = split(table, keys, ratios)` line. As per the split, `frs`, which is of the type `Array[Frame]`, contains two elements where the first element has 80% of the data and second element has 20% of the data. The 80% of the data becomes train and the remaining 20% becomes valid.

The `buildDLModel` method creates `DeepLearningParmeters` as `val dlParams = new DeepLearningParameters()`. Next, the properties of the `DeepLearningParmeters` are specified as `dlParams._train = train` and `dlParams._valid = valid`. The deep learning model is created as `val dl = new DeepLearning(dlParams, water.Key.make("dlModel.hex"))` and the trained model is returned as `dl.trainModel.get`. The model metrics from the training data (`train`) and from the validation data (`valid`) are obtained using the `val trainMetrics = modelMetrics[ModelMetricsBinomial](dlModel, train)` line.

The `isSpam` method predicts the unlabeled data. It uses the model generated by the pipeline. To make a prediction, we call the `transform` method. The prediction is obtained using the `dlModel.score(msgTable)` line, where `msgTable` is the `H2OFrame` created from the `msgVector` DataFrame.

There's more...

Sparkling Water enables transformation between different types of RDDs and H2O's H2OFrame, and vice versa. When converting from an H2OFrame to an RDD, a wrapper is created around the H2OFrame to provide an RDD-like API. In this case, data is not duplicated but served directly from the underlying H2OFrame. Converting from an RDD DataFrame to an H2OFrame requires data duplication because it transfers data from the RDD storage into the H2OFrame. However, data stored in an H2OFrame is heavily compressed and does not need to be preserved in RDD.

The `H2OContext` contains the necessary information for running H2O services and exposes methods for data transformation between the Spark RDD or DataFrame and the H2OFrame. Starting `H2OContext` involves a distributed operation that contacts all accessible Spark executor nodes and initializes H2O services.

See also

Please visit the earlier *Working with H2O on Spark* recipe to learn about the details of installing Sparkling Water and writing standalone Sparkling Water applications. You can also refer to the *Implementing k-means using H2O over Spark* recipe. For more details, please refer to the H2O documentation at `http://docs.h2o.ai`.

Deep learning with airlines and weather data

In this recipe, we'll see how to run deep learning models on an airlines dataset.

Getting ready

To step through this recipe, you will need a running Spark Cluster in any one of the following modes: Local, standalone, YARN, Mesos. Include the Spark MLlib package in the `build.sbt` file so that it downloads the related libraries and the API can be used. Install Hadoop (optionally), Scala, and Java. Also, install Sparkling Water as discussed in the preceding recipe.

How to do it...

1. Please download the dataset from
   `https://github.com/ChitturiPadma/datasets/blob/master/allyears2k_heade`
   `rs.csv`. The sample records (with a few columns) in the dataset look like the following:

Year	Month	Day of Month	DayOfWeek	DepTime	CRSDepTime	ArrTime	CRSArrTime
1987	10	14	3	741	730	912	849
1987	10	15	4	729	730	903	849
1987	10	17	6	741	730	918	849
1987	10	18	7	729	730	847	849
1987	10	19	1	749	730	922	849

2. Here is the code for loading the airline data and fetching records with the specific destination SFO:

```
import hex.deeplearning.DeepLearning
import hex.deeplearning.DeepLearningModel.DeepLearningParameters
import org.apache.spark.{SparkContext, SparkConf, SparkFiles}
import org.apache.spark.h2o.{DoubleHolder, H2OContext, H2OFrame}
import org.apache.spark.sql.{SQLContext, Dataset}
import water.support.{SparkContextSupport}
object H2O_DeepLearning_AirlinesData {
def main(args:Array[String]): Unit ={
val conf = new SparkConf()
  .setMaster("spark://master:7077")
  .setAppName("H2O_DeepLearning_AirlinesData")
val sc = new SparkContext(conf)
val h2oContext = H2OContext.getOrCreate(sc)
val sqlContext = new SQLContext(sc)
import h2oContext._
import h2oContext.implicits._
import sqlContext.implicits._
//Loading Data
val airlinesData =
sqlContext.read.format("com.databricks.spark.csv")
    .option("header", "true")
    .option("inferSchema",
"true").load("hdfs://namenode:9000/allyears2k_headers.csv")
//Create temporary table or view
airlinesData.registerTempTable("airlinesTable")
val result : H2OFrame = sqlContext.sql("SELECT * FROM
airlinesTable WHERE Dest    LIKE 'SFO'")
println(" Number of flights with destination in SFO:
"+result.numRows())
  } }
```

The following is the output:

```
Number of flights with destination in SFO: 1331
```

3. Now, let's see the code used to run the deep learning:

```
// Run Deep Learning
// Training data
val train = result('Year, 'Month, 'DayofMonth, 'DayOfWeek,
'CRSDepTime, 'CRSArrTime,'UniqueCarrier, 'FlightNum, 'TailNum,
'CRSElapsedTime, 'Origin,   'Dest,'Distance, 'IsDepDelayed )
train.replace(train.numCols()-1
train.lastVec().toCategoricalVec
train.update()

// Configure Deep Learning algorithm
val dlParams = new DeepLearningParameters()
dlParams._train = train
dlParams._response_column = 'IsDepDelayed
val dl = new DeepLearning(dlParams)
val dlModel = dl.trainModel.get

// Use model for scoring
println("Making prediction with help of DeepLearning model")
val predictionH2OFrame = dlModel.score(result)
predictions.vecs().map(_.at(0)).foreach(println)

// Shutdown H2O
h2oContext.stop(stopSparkContext = true)
```

The following is the output:

```
Making prediction with help of DeepLearning model
1.0
0.04475814491848565
0.9552418550815144
```

How it works...

Initially, all the required libraries are imported. The `SparkContext` and `SQLContext` are initialized and the `allyears2k_headers.csv` file is loaded using the `sqlContext.read.format("com.databricks.spark.csv")` line from HDFS. From the `airlinesData` DataFrame, a temporary table is created as `airlinesData.registerTempTable("airlinesTable")`. The `sqlContext.sql("SELECT * FROM airlinesTable WHERE Dest LIKE 'SFO'")` statement fetches all the airlines records whose `Dest` is `SFO`. Next, the result `H2OFrame` is created from the query result.

Next, for the model training, fields such as `'Year, 'Month, 'DayofMonth, 'DayOfWeek,` `'CRSDepTime, 'CRSArrTime,'UniqueCarrier, 'FlightNum, 'TailNum,` `'CRSElapsedTime, 'Origin, 'Dest, 'Distance` and `'IsDepDelayed` are selected from the `H2OFrame` result. The `DeepLearningParameters` is created as `val dlParams = new` `DeepLearningParameters()`. Next, the properties of the `DeepLearningParameters` are specified as `dlParams._train = train` and `dlParams._response_column =` `'IsDepDelayed`. From the `DeepLearningParameters`, the deep learning model is created as `val dl = new DeepLearning(dlParams)`. The trained model is obtained as `dl.trainModel.get`. The predictions are obtained using the line `dlModel.score(result)`, and finally the predictions are displayed.

There's more...

When launching Sparkling Water applications, both Spark and H2O are in-memory processes and all computation occurs in memory with minimal writing to disk, occurring only when specified by the user. Because all the data used in the modeling process needs to read into memory, the recommended method of launching Spark and H2O is through YARN, which dynamically allocates available resources. When the job is finished, you can tear down the Sparkling Water cluster and free up resources for other jobs.

All Spark and Sparkling Water applications launched with YARN will be tracked and listed in the history server that you can launch on Cloudera Manager. YARN will allocate the container to launch the application master in and when you launch with yarn-client, the Spark driver runs in the client process and the application master submits a request to the resource manager to spawn the Spark executor JVMs. Finally, after creating a Sparkling Water cluster, you have access to HDFS to read data into either H2O or Spark.

See also

Please visit the earlier *Working with H2O on Spark* recipe to find out about the details of installing Sparkling Water and writing standalone Sparkling Water applications. You can also refer to the recipes *Implementing k-means using H2O over Spark* and *Implementing spam detection with Sparkling Water*. For more details, please refer to the H2O documentation at `http://docs.h2o.ai`.

Implementing a crime detection application

In this recipe, we'll see how to run deep learning models on various sets of data to detect crime in the city of Chicago.

Getting ready

To step through this recipe, you will need a running Spark Cluster in any one of the following modes: Local, standalone, YARN, Mesos. Include the Spark MLlib package in the `build.sbt` file so that it downloads the related libraries and the API can be used. Install Hadoop (optionally), Scala, and Java. Also, install Sparkling Water as discussed in the preceding recipe.

How to do it...

1. Please download the following datasets from the following locations:

   Weather data:
   `https://github.com/ChitturiPadma/datasets/blob/master/chicagoAllWeather.csv`.

   Census data:
   `https://github.com/ChitturiPadma/datasets/blob/master/chicagoCensus.csv`.

   Crime data:
   `https://github.com/ChitturiPadma/datasets/blob/master/chicagoCrimes10k.csv`.

2. The sample records (with a few columns) in the datasets look as follows:

   The sample rows in weather data:

date	month	day	year	maxTemp	meanTemp	minTemp
1/1/01	1	1	2001	23	14	6
1/2/01	1	2	2001	18	12	6
1/3/01	1	3	2001	28	18	8
1/4/01	1	4	2001	30	24	19

The sample rows in census data:

Community Area Number	COMMUNITY AREA NAM	PERCENT OF HOUSING CROWDED	PERCENT HOUSEHOLDS BELOW POVERTY
1	Rogers Park	7.7	23.6
2	West Ridge	7.8	17.2
3	Uptown	3.8	24
4	Lincoln Square	3.4	10.9

The sample rows in crime data:

ID	Case Number	Date	Block	IUCR	Primary Type
9955810	HY144797	02/08/2015 11:43:40 PM	081XX S COLESAVE	1811	NARCOTICS
9955861	HY144838	02/08/2015 11:41:42 PM	118XX S STATE ST	486	BATTERY
9955801	HY144779	02/08/2015 11:30:22 PM	002XX S LARAMIE AVE	2026	NARCOTICS
9956197	HY144787	02/08/2015 11:30:23 PM	006XX E 67TH ST	1811	NARCOTICS

3. Include the dependency `ai.h2o" % "h2o-genmodel" % "3.10.0.7` in the `build.sbt` file.
4. The code for loading the datasets and fetching the required records for joining the preceding datasets `chicagoAllWeather.csv`, `chicagoCensus.csv`, `chicagoCrimes10k.csv` looks like the following:

```
import hex.deeplearning.DeepLearningModel
import hex.deeplearning.DeepLearningModel.DeepLearningParameters
import hex.deeplearning.DeepLearningModel.DeepLearningParameters
.Activation
import hex.tree.gbm.GBMModel
import hex.{Model, ModelMetricsBinomial}
import org.apache.spark.SparkContext
import org.apache.spark.h2o.{H2OContext, H2OFrame}
import org.apache.spark.sql.{DataFrame, SQLContext}
import org.joda.time.DateTimeConstants._
import org.joda.time.format.DateTimeFormat
import org.joda.time.{DateTimeZone, MutableDateTime}
import water.MRTask
import water.fvec.{Chunk, NewChunk, Vec}
import water.parser.{BufferedString, ParseSetup}
import water.support.{H2OFrameSupport, ModelMetricsSupport,
SparkContextSupport, SparklingWaterApp}
import java.net._
import org.apache.spark._
```

```
class RefineDateColumn(val datePattern: String,
                       val dateTimeZone: String) extends
                       MRTask[RefineDateColumn] {
// Entry point
def doIt(col: Vec): H2OFrame = {
val inputCol = if (col.isCategorical) col.toStringVec else col
val result = new H2OFrame(
doAll(Array[Byte](Vec.T_NUM, Vec.T_NUM, Vec.T_NUM, Vec.T_NUM,
Vec.T_NUM, Vec.T_NUM, Vec.T_NUM, Vec.T_NUM),
inputCol).outputFrame(
Array[String]("Day", "Month", "Year", "WeekNum", "WeekDay",
"Weekend", "Season","HourOfDay"),
Array[Array[String]](null, null, null, null, null, null,
H2O_ChicagoCrimeAppNew_H2O.SEASONS, null)))
   if (col.isCategorical) inputCol.remove()
result
}

override def map(cs: Array[Chunk], ncs: Array[NewChunk]): Unit =
{
/* Initialize DataTime convertor (cannot be done in setupLocal
since it is not H2O serializable */
val dtFmt = DateTimeFormat.forPattern(datePattern)
.withZone(DateTimeZone.forID(dateTimeZone))
// Get input and output chunks
val dateChunk = cs(0)
val (dayNC, monthNC, yearNC, weekNC, weekdayNC, weekendNC,
seasonNC, hourNC)
= (ncs(0), ncs(1), ncs(2), ncs(3), ncs(4), ncs(5), ncs(6),
ncs(7))
val valStr = new BufferedString()
val mDateTime = new MutableDateTime()
for(row <- 0 until dateChunk.len()) {
  if (dateChunk.isNA(row)) {
    addNAs(ncs)
  } else {
  // Extract data
    val ds = dateChunk.atStr(valStr, row).toString
    if (dtFmt.parseInto(mDateTime, ds, 0) > 0) {
    val month = mDateTime.getMonthOfYear
    dayNC.addNum(mDateTime.getDayOfMonth, 0)
    monthNC.addNum(month, 0)
    yearNC.addNum(mDateTime.getYear, 0)
    weekNC.addNum(mDateTime.getWeekOfWeekyear)
    val dayOfWeek = mDateTime.getDayOfWeek
    weekdayNC.addNum(dayOfWeek)
    weekendNC.addNum(if (dayOfWeek == SUNDAY || dayOfWeek ==
    SATURDAY) 1 else 0, 0)
```

```scala
seasonNC.addNum(ChicagoCrimeAppNew_H2O.getSeason(month), 0)
hourNC.addNum(mDateTime.getHourOfDay)
} else {
addNAs(ncs)
} } } }
private def addNAs(ncs: Array[NewChunk]): Unit =
ncs.foreach(nc => nc.addNA())
}
object ChicagoCrimeAppNew_H2O {
def SEASONS = Array[String]("Spring", "Summer", "Autumn",
"Winter")
def getSeason(month: Int) =
if (month >= MARCH && month <= MAY) 0 // Spring
else if (month >= JUNE && month <= AUGUST) 1 // Summer
else if (month >= SEPTEMBER && month <= OCTOBER) 2 // Autumn
else 3 // Winter
def loadData(datafile: String, modifyParserSetup: ParseSetup
=> ParseSetup =   identity[ParseSetup]): H2OFrame = {
val uri = java.net.URI.create(datafile)
val parseSetup =
modifyParserSetup(water.fvec.H2OFrame.parserSetup(uri))
new H2OFrame(parseSetup, new java.net.URI(datafile))
}


def createWeatherTable(datafile: String): H2OFrame = {
val table = loadData(datafile)
// Remove first column since we do not need it
table.remove(0).remove()
table.update()
table
}


def createCensusTable(datafile: String): H2OFrame = {
val table = loadData(datafile)
// Rename columns: replace ' ' by '_'
val colNames = table.names().map( n => n.trim.replace(' ',
'_').replace('+','_'))
table._names = colNames
table.update()
table
}
def createCrimeTable(datafile: String): H2OFrame = {
val table = loadData(datafile, (parseSetup: ParseSetup) => {
val colNames = parseSetup.getColumnNames
val typeNames = parseSetup.getColumnTypes
colNames.indices.foreach { idx =>
if (colNames(idx) == "Date") typeNames(idx) = Vec.T_STR
}
```

```scala
  parseSetup
  })
  // Refine date into multiple columns
  val dateCol = table.vec(2)
  table.add(new RefineDateColumn("MM/dd/yyyy hh:mm:ss a",
  "Etc/UTC").doIt(dateCol))
  // Update names, replace all ' ' by '_'
  val colNames = table.names().map( n => n.trim.replace(' ',
   '_'))
  table._names = colNames
  // Remove Date column
  table.remove(2).remove()
  // Update in DKV
  table.update()
  table
  }
def main(args:Array[String]): Unit = {
val conf = new SparkConf()
.setMaster("spark://master:7077")
.setAppName("H2O_ChicagoCrimeApp")
val sc = new SparkContext(conf)
implicit val h2oContext = H2OContext.getOrCreate(sc)
implicit val sqlContext = new SQLContext(sc)
import h2oContext._
import h2oContext.implicits._
import sqlContext.implicits._
// Loading Weather Data
val weatherDataTable = asDataFrame(createWeatherTable
("hdfs://namenode:9000/chicagoAllWeather.csv"))
val censusDataTable = asDataFrame(createCensusTable
("hdfs://namenode:9000/chicagoCensus.csv"))
val crimeDataTable = asDataFrame(createCrimeTable
("hdfs://namenode:9000/chicagoCrimes10k.csv"))
weatherDataTable.registerTempTable("chicagoWeather")
censusDataTable.registerTempTable("chicagoCensus")
crimeDataTable.registerTempTable("chicagoCrime")
val crimeWeather = sqlContext.sql(
"""SELECT
|a.Year, a.Month, a.Day, a.WeekNum, a.HourOfDay, a.Weekend,
a.Season, a.WeekDay,
|a.IUCR, a.Primary_Type, a.Location_Description,
a.Community_Area, a.District,
|a.Arrest, a.Domestic, a.Beat, a.Ward, a.FBI_Code,
|b.minTemp, b.maxTemp, b.meanTemp,
|c.PERCENT_AGED_UNDER_18_OR_OVER_64, c.PER_CAPITA_INCOME,
c.HARDSHIP_INDEX,
|c.PERCENT_OF_HOUSING_CROWDED,
c.PERCENT_HOUSEHOLDS_BELOW_POVERTY,
```

```
      |c.PERCENT_AGED_16__UNEMPLOYED,
      c.PERCENT_AGED_25__WITHOUT_HIGH_SCHOOL_DIPLOMA
      |FROM chicagoCrime a
      |JOIN chicagoWeather b
      |ON a.Year = b.year AND a.Month = b.month AND a.Day = b.day
      |JOIN chicagoCensus c
      |ON a.Community_Area = c.Community_Area_Number""".stripMargin)
      val crimeWeatherDF:H2OFrame = crimeWeather
      // Transform all string columns into categorical
      val crimeWeatherDataFrame = asDataFrame(crimeWeatherDF)
      crimeWeatherDataFrame.select("Year","Month","Day","WeekNum",
      "Season","IUCR").show(10)
        }
      }
```

The following is the output:

```
+----+-----+---+-------+------+----+
|Year|Month|Day|WeekNum|Season|IUCR|
+----+-----+---+-------+------+----+
|2015|    1| 23|      4|Winter|null|
|2015|    1| 23|      4|Winter|4625|
|2015|    1| 23|      4|Winter| 320|
|2015|    1| 23|      4|Winter|1310|
|2015|    1| 23|      4|Winter| 610|
|2015|    1| 23|      4|Winter|2210|
|2015|    1| 23|      4|Winter| 470|
|2015|    1| 23|      4|Winter|1305|
|2015|    1| 23|      4|Winter| 486|
|2015|    1| 23|      4|Winter| 820|
+----+-----+---+-------+------+----+
```

Now, let's try to run the GBM model on the `crimeWeatherDF` and collect the model metrics with the following code:

```
def main(args:Array[String]) {
// Previous code
H2OFrameSupport.allStringVecToCategorical(crimeWeatherDF)
val keys = Array[String]("train.hex", "test.hex")
val ratios = Array[Double](0.8, 0.2)
val frs = H2OFrameSupport.split(crimeWeatherDF, keys, ratios)
val (train, test) = (frs(0), frs(1))

// Build GBM model and collect model metrics
val gbmModel = GBMModel(train, test, 'Arrest)
val (trainMetricsGBM, testMetricsGBM) = binomialMetrics(gbmModel, train,
test)
```

```
println(
  s"""Model performance:
     |  GBM:
     |    train AUC = ${trainMetricsGBM.auc}
     |    test  AUC = ${testMetricsGBM.auc}
  """.stripMargin) }

def GBMModel(train: H2OFrame, test: H2OFrame, response: String,
ntrees:Int =   10, depth:Int = 6, family: DistributionFamily =
DistributionFamily.bernoulli)
          (implicit h2oContext: H2OContext) : GBMModel = {
  import h2oContext.implicits._
  import hex.tree.gbm.GBM
  import hex.tree.gbm.GBMModel.GBMParameters
  val gbmParams = new GBMParameters()
  gbmParams._train = train
  gbmParams._valid = test
  gbmParams._response_column = response
  gbmParams._ntrees = ntrees
  gbmParams._max_depth = depth
  val gbm = new GBM(gbmParams)
  val model = gbm.trainModel.get
  model
}
def binomialMetrics[M <: Model[M,P,O], P <: hex.Model.Parameters, O <:
hex.Model.Output]
  (model: Model[M,P,O], train: H2OFrame, test:
H2OFrame):(ModelMetricsBinomial,   ModelMetricsBinomial) = {
    (ModelMetricsSupport.modelMetrics(model,train),
ModelMetricsSupport.modelMetrics(model, test))
  }
```

The following is the output:

```
Model performance:
GBM:
  train AUC = 0.9182010072171471
  test  AUC = 0.9366698161864178
```

In the following code snippet, we train a deep neural network to predict the likelihood of an arrest for a given crime as follows:

```
def main(args:Array[String]) {
// Previous code
// Build Deep Learning model and collect model metrics
val dlModel = DLModel(train, test, 'Arrest)
val (trainMetricsDL, testMetricsDL) = binomialMetrics(dlModel, train,
test)
```

```
println(
  s"""Model performance:
     |  DL:
     |     train AUC = ${trainMetricsDL.auc}
     |     test  AUC = ${testMetricsDL.auc}
  """.stripMargin) }
def DLModel(train: H2OFrame, test: H2OFrame, response: String,
            epochs: Int = 10, l1: Double = 0.0001, l2: Double = 0.0001,
            activation: Activation = Activation.RectifierWithDropout,
hidden:Array[Int] =   Array(200,200))
           (implicit h2oContext: H2OContext) : DeepLearningModel = {
  import h2oContext.implicits._
  import hex.deeplearning.DeepLearning
  val dlParams = new DeepLearningParameters()
  dlParams._train = train
  dlParams._valid = test
  dlParams._response_column = response
  dlParams._epochs = epochs
  dlParams._l1 = l1
  dlParams._l2 = l2
  dlParams._activation = activation
  dlParams._hidden = hidden
  // Create a job
  val dl = new DeepLearning(dlParams)
  val model = dl.trainModel.get
  model }
```

The output is as follows:

```
Model performance:
DL:
train AUC = 0.9032203563709825
test AUC = 0.9358068689123377
```

Let's look at the last building block of the application, which predicts the arrest rate probability for a new crime. The function combines the Spark API to enrich each incoming crime event with census information with H2O's deep learning model, which scores the event:

```
case class Crime(Year: Short, Month: Byte, Day: Byte, WeekNum: Byte,
HourOfDay:Byte,
             Weekend:Byte, Season: String, WeekDay: Byte,
             IUCR: Short,
             Primary_Type: String,
             Location_Description: String,
             Domestic: String,
             Beat: Short,
             District: Byte,
```

```scala
                Ward: Byte,
                Community_Area: Byte,
                FBI_Code: Byte,
                minTemp: Option[Byte],
                maxTemp: Option[Byte],
                meanTemp: Option[Byte])
    object Crime {
    def apply(date:String,
            iucr: Short,
            primaryType: String,
            locationDescr: String,
            domestic: Boolean,
            beat: Short,
            district: Byte,
            ward: Byte,
            communityArea: Byte,
            fbiCode: Byte,
            minTemp: Option[Byte] = None,
            maxTemp: Option[Byte] = None,
            meanTemp: Option[Byte] = None,
            datePattern: String = "MM/dd/yyyy hh:mm:ss a",
            dateTimeZone: String = "Etc/UTC"):Crime = {
    val dtFmt = DateTimeFormat.forPattern(datePattern).withZone
    (DateTimeZone.forID(dateTimeZone))
    val mDateTime = new MutableDateTime()
    dtFmt.parseInto(mDateTime, date, 0)
    val month = mDateTime.getMonthOfYear.toByte
    val dayOfWeek = mDateTime.getDayOfWeek
    Crime(mDateTime.getYear.toShort,
      month,
      mDateTime.getDayOfMonth.toByte,
      mDateTime.getWeekOfWeekyear.toByte,
      mDateTime.getHourOfDay.toByte,
      if (dayOfWeek == SUNDAY || dayOfWeek == SATURDAY) 1 else 0,
      ChicagoCrimeAppNew_H2O.SEASONS(ChicagoCrimeAppNew_H2O.getSeason
      (month)),
      mDateTime.getDayOfWeek.toByte,
      iucr, primaryType, locationDescr,
      if (domestic) "true" else "false" ,
      beat, district, ward, communityArea, fbiCode,
      minTemp, maxTemp, meanTemp)  } }

    def scoreEvent(crime: Crime, model: Model[_,_,_], censusTable:
    DataFrame)
(implicit sqlContext: SQLContext, h2oContext: H2OContext): Float = {
import h2oContext.implicits._
import sqlContext.implicits._
// Create a single row table
```

```
val srdd: DataFrame =
sqlContext.sparkContext.parallelize(Seq(crime)).toDF
// Join table with census data
val row: H2OFrame = censusTable.join(srdd).where('Community_Area ===
'Community_Area_Number) //.printSchema
// Transform all string columns into categorical
H2OFrameSupport.allStringVecToCategorical(row)
val predictTable = model.score(row)
val probOfArrest = predictTable.vec("true").at(0)
probOfArrest.toFloat }

 def main(args:Array[String]) {
// Previous code

// Test the arrest rate probability for a new Crime.
val crimeExamples = Seq(
Crime("02/08/2015 11:43:58 PM", 1811, "NARCOTICS", "STREET",false,
422, 4, 7, 46, 18),
Crime("02/08/2015 11:00:39 PM", 1150, "DECEPTIVE PRACTICE",
"RESIDENCE",false, 923, 9, 14, 63, 11))
for (crime <- crimeExamples) {
val arrestProbGBM = 100*scoreEvent(crime,
gbmModel,
censusDataTable)(sqlContext, h2oContext)
val arrestProbDL = 100*scoreEvent(crime,
dlModel,
censusDataTable)(sqlContext, h2oContext)
println(
  s"""
     |Crime: $crime
     |  Probability of arrest best on DeepLearning: ${arrestProbDL} %
     |  Probability of arrest best on GBM: ${arrestProbGBM} %
     |
  """.stripMargin)
} }
```

The following is the output:

```
Crime:
Crime(2015,2,8,6,23,1,Winter,7,1811,NARCOTICS,STREET,false,422,4,
7,46,18,None,None,None)
Probability of arrest best on DeepLearning: 99.97552 %
Probability of arrest best on GBM: 74.49276 %

Crime: Crime(2015,2,8,6,23,1,Winter,7,1150,DECEPTIVE
PRACTICE,RESIDENCE,false,923,9,14,63,11,None,None,None)
Probability of arrest best on DeepLearning: 1.6130093 %
Probability of arrest best on GBM: 12.061813 %
```

How it works...

Initially, all the required libraries are imported. The `SparkContext` and `SQLContext` are initialized and the `chicagoAllWeather.csv`, `chicagoCensus.csv` and `chicagoCrimes10k.csv` files are loaded using the `hdfs://namenode:9000/chicagoAllWeather.csv` line. The `createWeatherTable`, `createCensusTable`, and `createCrimeTable` methods invoke `loadData`, which creates an `H2OFrame` from the `java.net.URI`.

The `RefineDateColumn` class formats the date and extracts the year, month and day. The `crimeWeatherDF` is an `H2OFrame` created by selecting the required fields from the DataFrame, and all strings are converted to categorical variables using the `H2OFrameSupport.allStringVecToCategorical(crimeWeatherDF)` line.

The dataset is split and the splits with specified keys are stored into H2O's distributed storage. The ratios are specified as `val ratios = Array[Double](0.8)`. Now, the table is split as per the specified keys and ratios using the `val frs = H2OFrameSupport.split(crimeWeatherDF, keys, ratios)` line. As per the split, `frs`, which is of the type `Array[Frame]`, contains two elements where the first element has 80% of the data and the second element has 20% of the data. The 80% of the data becomes train and the remaining 20% becomes valid.

The `GBMModel` is built from the train and test datasets and the model metrics are obtained by invoking the `binomialMetrics(dlModel, train, test)` method. Also, a deep neural network is trained to predict the likelihood of an arrest for a given crime. Finally, the `GBMModel` and `DLModel` accuracy is displayed.

Once the models are ready, the `scoreEvent` method is invoked, which predicts the arrest rate probability for a new crime using both `GBMModel` and `DeepLearningModel`.

There's more...

There are some incredible applications of deep learning with respect to image recognition and machine translation, but the preceding specific use case shows how deep learning can be used to fight crime in the forward-thinking cities of San Francisco and Chicago. Since both are open cities, anybody can access city data ranging from transportation information to building maintenance records. The cities' data is joined with other external data, such as weather and socio-economic statistics, to predict the probability of an arrest for a crime.

See also

Please visit the earlier *Working with H2O on Spark* recipe to learn about the details of installing Sparkling Water and writing standalone Sparkling Water applications. You can also refer to the *Implementing k-means using H2O over Spark* and *Deep learning with airlines and weather data* recipes. For more details, please refer to the H2O documentation at `http://docs.h2o.ai`.

Running SVM with H2O over Spark

In this recipe, we'll see how to run SVM to predict or classify a cancer.

Getting ready

To step through this recipe, you will need a running Spark Cluster in any one of the following modes: Local, standalone, YARN, Mesos. Include the Spark MLlib package in the `build.sbt` file so that it downloads the related libraries and the API can be used. Install Hadoop (optionally), Scala, and Java. Also, install Sparkling Water as discussed in the preceding recipe.

How to do it...

Please download the dataset from `https://github.com/ChitturiPadma/datasets/blob/master/Breast_CancerData.csv`. While including the dependencies `sparkling-water-core` and `sparkling-water-ml`, please change the version to 1.6.8.

The sample records in the data (with a few columns) look as follows:

clump_thickness	uniformity_cell_size	uniformity_cell_shape	marginal_adhesion	single_epithelial_cell_size	bare_nuclei	bland_chromation	normal_nucleoli	mitoses	label
5	1	1	1	2	1	3	1	1	B
5	4	4	5	7	10	3	2	1	B
3	1	1	1	2	2	3	1	1	B
6	8	8	1	3	4	3	7	1	B
4	1	1	3	2	1	3	1	1	B

Here, the last column `label` indicates whether the person has breast cancer (represented by B).

The code that runs SVM on the data is as follows:

```
import java.io._
import org.apache.spark.ml.spark.models.svm._
import org.apache.spark.h2o.H2OContext
import org.apache.spark.sql.SQLContext
import org.apache.spark.{SparkConf, SparkContext, SparkFiles}
import water.fvec.H2OFrame
import water.support.SparkContextSupport

object H2O_SVM {
  def main(args: Array[String]): Unit = {
    val conf = new SparkConf()
      .setMaster("spark://master:7077")
      .setAppName("H2O_SVMDemo")
    val sc = new SparkContext(conf)
    implicit val h2oContext = H2OContext.getOrCreate(sc)
    implicit val sqlContext = new SQLContext(sc)
    val breastCancerData = new H2OFrame(new File)

    // Training data
breastCancerData.replace(breastCancerData.numCols()-1,
breastCancerData.lastVec().toCategoricalVec)
breastCancerData.update()

// Configure DeepLearning Algorithm
    val parms = new SVMParameters
    parms._train = breastCancerData.key

parms._response_column = "label"
val svm = new SVM(parms, h2oContext)
val svmModel = svm.trainModel.get


  // Use model for scoring
  val predictionH2OFrame = svmModel.score(breastCancerData)
  val predictionsFromModel =
  h2oContext.asDataFrame(predictionH2OFrame).collect
  println(predictionsFromModel.mkString("\n===> Model predictions: ",
  ",\n",   ", ...\n"))
  h2oContext.stop(stopSparkContext = true)} }
```

The following is the output:

```
===> Model predictions: [B,-1.1509096730692234,-2.1509096730692234],
[M,-0.07034367987592904,0.9296563201240071],
[B,-0.38250343368714734,-1.3825034336871473],
[M,4.437234562767544,5.437234562767544],
[B,-0.8396775949800639,-1.839677594980064],
[M,3.4288945842797744,4.4288945842797744],
[M,1.0699717275197926,2.0699717275197926],
[B,-0.5191292110606585,-1.5191292110606585],
[B,-0.7746193963925296,-1.7746193963925296],
[B,0.17214830634585576,-0.8278516936541442],
[B,0.2769424962749667,-0.7230575037250333],
[B,-0.18873784770583413,-1.1887378477058341],
[M,-0.20616411116305644,0.7938358888369436],
[B,0.38590280569492896,-0.614097194305071],
[M,0.9036110712837497,1.9036110712837497],
[B,-1.3026190368790118,-2.302619036879012],
[B,-0.5737056696843581,-1.573705669684358],
[B,-0.9584257620799614,-1.9584257620799614],
[M,2.492379623351675,3.492379623351675],
[B,-1.3433935840584859,-2.343393584058486],
```

How it works...

Initially, all the required libraries are imported. The `SparkContext` and `H2OContext` are initialized and the file `Breast_CancerData.csv` is loaded using the `new H2OFrame(new File "(hdfs://namenode:9000/Breast_CancerData.csv")) ` line. The `label` column is replaced with a categorical vector using the `breastCancerData.replace(breastCancerData.numCols()-1, breastCancerData.lastVec().toCategoricalVec)` line.

The `SVMParameters` is created, and the properties, such as `_train` and `_reponse_column`, are initialized. The object SVM is created as `val svm = new SVM(parms, h2oContext)`, and the `SVMModel` is obtained as `val svmModel = svm.trainModel.get`. The model is used for scoring the data as `val predictionH2OFrame = svmModel.score(breastCancerData)`. The predicted scores are obtained as `val predictionsFromModel = h2oContext.asDataFrame(predictionH2OFrame).collect`.

There's more...

In the preceding recipe, we saw how to implement SVMModel on the data, which obtains the scores for the target variable.

See also

You can look again at the earlier *Working with H2O on Spark* recipe to learn about the details of installing Sparkling Water and writing standalone Sparkling Water applications. You can also refer to the *Deep learning with airlines and weather data* and *Implementing crime detection application* recipes. For more details, please refer to the H2O documentation at http://docs.h2o.ai.

8
Data Visualization with Spark

In this chapter, you will learn the following recipes:

- Visualization using Zeppelin
- Creating scatter plots with Bokeh-Scala
- Creating a time series MultiPlot with Bokeh-Scala
- Creating plots with the lightning visualization server
- Visualizing machine learning models with Databricks notebook

Introduction

Visualizing large data is challenging. There are more data points than possible pixels and manipulating distributed data can take a long time. Along with the increase in volume, there are new kinds of datasets which are becoming more and more mainstream. The need to analyze user comments, sentiments, customer calls and various unstructured data has resulted in the use of new kinds of visualizations. The use of graph databases and visualization to represent unstructured data is an example of how things are changing because of increased variety.

There are a variety of tools developed recently which allow interactive analysis with Spark by reducing query latency to the range of human interactions through caching. Additionally, Spark's unified programming model and diverse programming interfaces enable smooth integration with popular visualization tools. We can use these to perform both exploratory and expository visualization over large data. In this chapter, we are going to look at the most widely used visualization techniques with Spark, such as Apache Zeppelin, Lightning, and highly active Scala bindings (Bokeh-Scala).

Visualization using Zeppelin

Apache Zeppelin is a nifty web-based tool that helps us visualize and explore large datasets. From a technical standpoint, Apache Zeppelin is a web application on steroids. We aim to use this application to render some neat, interactive, and shareable graphs and charts.

The interesting part of Zeppelin is that it has a bunch of built-in interpreters–ones that can interpret and invoke all API functions in Spark (with a SparkContext) and Spark SQL (with a SQLContext). The other interpreters that are built in are for Hive, Flink, Markdown and Scala. It also has the ability to run remote interpreters (outside of Zeppelin's own JVM) via Thrift. To look at the list of built-in interpreters, you can go through `conf/interpreter.json` in the Zeppelin installation directory. Alternatively, you can view and customize the interpreters from `http://localhost:8080/#/interpreter` once you start the Zeppelin daemon.

Getting ready

To step through this recipe, you will need a running Spark Cluster in any one of the modes, that is, local, standalone, YARN, or Mesos. Also, include the Spark MLlib package in the `build.sbt` file so that it downloads the related libraries and the API can be used. Install Hadoop (optionally), Scala, and Java. For installing Zeppelin, choose a cluster node that does not contain the DataNode or NameNode. This is to ensure that Zeppelin has enough processing resources on that node. The prerequisites for installing Zeppelin are as follows:

- Git
- Java 1.7
- OS Ubuntu 14.x
- Apache Maven
- Hadoop client
- Spark

How to do it...

In this recipe, we'll be using the built-in SparkContext and SQLContext inside Zeppelin and transforming data using Spark. At the end, we'll register the transformed data as a table and use Spark SQL to query the data and visualize it.

The list of sub-recipes in this section are as follows:

- Installing Zeppelin
- Customizing Zeppelin's server and websocket port
- Visualizing data on HDFS – parameterizing inputs
- Using custom functions during visualization
- Adding external dependencies to Zeppelin
- Pointing to an external Spark Cluster

Installing Zeppelin

Zeppelin supports binary build as well as source build. Let's see how to build it from source. We just ought to run one command to install it to our local machine. At the end of this recipe, we'll see how to connect Zeppelin to an external Spark master. Here is the code:

```
git clone https://github.com/apache/zeppelin.git
cd zeppelin/
mvn clean package -Pspark-1.6 -Phadoop-2.6 -Pyarn -Ppyspark -Psparkr -
Pscala-2.10 -DskipTests

[INFO] Reactor Summary:
[INFO]
[INFO] Zeppelin .......................................... SUCCESS
[1:39.666s]
[INFO] Zeppelin: Interpreter ............................. SUCCESS
[1:40.830s]
[INFO] Zeppelin: Zengine ................................. SUCCESS
[2:46.084s]
[INFO] Zeppelin: Display system apis ..................... SUCCESS
[2:03.322s]
[INFO] Zeppelin: Spark dependencies ...................... SUCCESS
[14:30.613s]
[INFO] Zeppelin: Spark ................................... SUCCESS
[1:27.082s]
[INFO] Zeppelin: Markdown interpreter .................... SUCCESS [8.820s]
[INFO] Zeppelin: Angular interpreter .................... SUCCESS [0.558s]
[INFO] Zeppelin: Shell interpreter ...................... SUCCESS [0.817s]
[INFO] Zeppelin: Livy interpreter ....................... SUCCESS
[1:04.855s]
[INFO] Zeppelin: HBase interpreter ...................... SUCCESS
[4:38.000s]
[INFO] Zeppelin: PostgreSQL interpreter ................. SUCCESS
[36.218s]
```

```
[INFO] Zeppelin: JDBC interpreter ...................... SUCCESS
[49.480s]
[INFO] Zeppelin: File System Interpreters .............. SUCCESS
[37.278s]
[INFO] Zeppelin: Flink ................................. SUCCESS
[1:59.856s]
[INFO] Zeppelin: Apache Ignite interpreter ............. SUCCESS
[36.267s]
[INFO] Zeppelin: Kylin interpreter ..................... SUCCESS [1.000s]
[INFO] Zeppelin: Python interpreter .................... SUCCESS [5.144s]
[INFO] Zeppelin: Lens interpreter ...................... SUCCESS
[2:06.158s]
[INFO] Zeppelin: Apache Cassandra interpreter .......... SUCCESS
[4:53.121s]
[INFO] Zeppelin: Elasticsearch interpreter ............. SUCCESS
[2:27.213s]
[INFO] Zeppelin: BigQuery interpreter .................. SUCCESS
[38.911s]
[INFO] Zeppelin: Alluxio intekrpreter .................. SUCCESS
[2:07.707s]
[INFO] Zeppelin: web Application ....................... SUCCESS
[11:16.111s]
[INFO] Zeppelin: Server ............................... SUCCESS
[2:55.576s]
[INFO] Zeppelin: Packaging distribution ............... SUCCESS [1.701s]
[INFO] ------------------------------------------------------------------
----
[INFO] BUILD SUCCESS
[INFO] ------------------------------------------------------------------
----
[INFO] Total time: 1:01:13.648s
[INFO] Finished at: Sun Oct 02 14:37:48 IST 2016
[INFO] Final Memory: 161M/836M
```

Once built, we can start the Zeppelin daemon using the following command:

```
./bin/zeppelin-daemon.sh start &

Log dir doesn't exist, create /home/padmac/bigdata/zeppelin/logs
Pid dir doesn't exist, create /home/padmac/bigdata/zeppelin/run
Zeppelin start                                          [  OK  ]
```

To stop the daemon, we can use the following command:

```
./bin/zeppelin-daemon.sh stop
Zeppelin stop                                           [  OK  ]
```

Customizing Zeppelin's server and websocket port

Zeppelin runs on port `8080` by default, and it has a websocket port enabled at the +1 port `8081` by default. We can customize the port by copying `conf/zeppelin-site.xml.template` to `conf/zeppelin-site.xml` and changing the ports and various other properties, if necessary. Since the Spark standalone cluster master web UI also runs on `8080`, when we are running Zeppelin on the same machine as the Spark master, we have to change the ports to avoid conflicts:

name	value
zeppelin.server.addr	0.0.0.0
zeppelin.server.port	8180
zeppelin.server.context.path	/
zeppelin.war.tempdir	webapps
zeppelin.notebook.dir	notebook
zeppelin.notebook.homescreen	
zeppelin.notebook.homescreen.hide	false
zeppelin.notebook.storage	org.apache.zeppelin.notebook.repo.VFSNotebookRepo
zeppelin.notebook.one.way.sync	false
zeppelin.interpreter.dir	interpreter

The browser window also shows:

file:///home...lin-site.xml

file:///home/padmac/bigdata/zeppelin/conf/zeppelin-site.xml

Most Visited ▾ · Getting Started · Citrix Access Gateway

For now, let's change the port to `8180` by editing the configuration file shown in the following image. In order for this to take effect, let's restart Zeppelin using `bin/zeppelin-daemon restart`. Now Zeppelin can be viewed on the web browser by visiting the site `http://localhost:8180` and the web browser looks like the following screenshot:

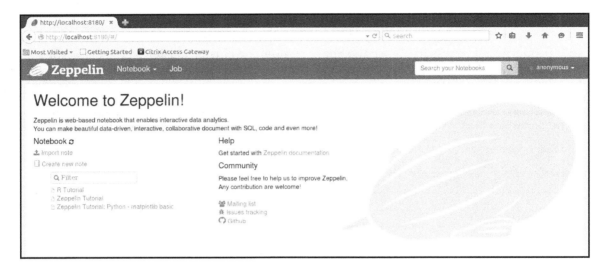

Visualizing data on HDFS – parameterizing inputs

Once we start the service, we can point our browser to `http://localhost:8080` (change the port as per your modified port configuration) to view the Zeppelin UI. Zeppelin organizes its contents as notes and paragraphs. A note is simply a list of all the paragraphs on a single web page.

Using data from HDFS simply means that we point to the HDFS location instead of the local file system location. Before we consume the file from HDFS, let's quickly check the Spark version that Zeppelin uses. This can be achieved by issuing `sc.version` on a paragraph. The `sc` variable is an implicit variable representing the SparkContext inside Zeppelin, which simply means that we need not programmatically create a SparkContext within Zeppelin:

```
sc.version
res0: String = 1.6.0
```

Let's load the sample file `profiles.json`, convert it into a DataFrame, and print the schema and the first 20 rows (show) for verification. Let's also finally register the DataFrame as a table. Just like the implicit variable for SparkContext , SQLContext is represented by the `sqlc` implicit variable inside Zeppelin:

The file is available at the following location:
https://github.com/ChitturiPadma/datasets/blob/master/profiles.json.

Please include the following code in Zeppelin notebook:

```
val profilesJsonRdd = sqlc.jsonFile("hdfs://namenode:9000/profiles.json")
val profileDF=profilesJsonRdd.toDF()
profileDF.printSchema()
profileDF.show(5)
profileDF.registerTempTable("profiles")
```

The output looks like the following screenshot:

```
|-- _id: string (nullable = true)
|-- about: string (nullable = true)
|-- address: string (nullable = true)
|-- age: long (nullable = true)
|-- company: string (nullable = true)
|-- email: string (nullable = true)
|-- eyeColor: string (nullable = true)
|-- favoriteFruit: string (nullable = true)
|-- gender: string (nullable = true)
|-- name: string (nullable = true)
|-- phone: string (nullable = true)

|-- registered: string (nullable = true)
|-- tags: array (nullable = true)
|    |-- element: string (containsNull = true)
```

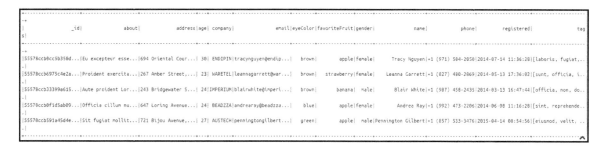

Let's now run a simple query to understand eye colors and their counts for men in the dataset:

```
%sql select eyeColor, count(eyeColor) as count from profiles where
gender='male' group by eyeColor
```

The `%sql` at the beginning of the paragraph indicates to Zeppelin that we are about to execute a Spark SQL query in this paragraph:

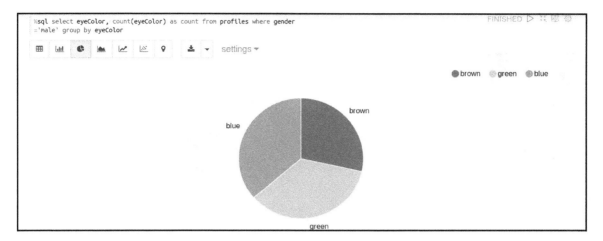

Now, if we wish to share this chart with someone or link it to an external website, we can do so by clicking on the gear icon in this paragraph and then clicking on **Link this paragraph**, as shown in the following screenshot:

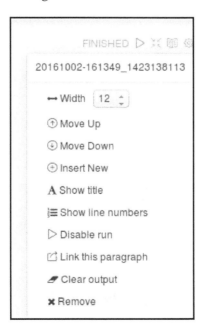

We can actually parameterize the input for gender instead of altering our query every time. This is achieved by the use of `${PARAMETER PLACEHOLDER}`:

```
%sql select eyeColor, count(eyeColor) as count from profiles where
gender="${gender}" group by eyeColor
```

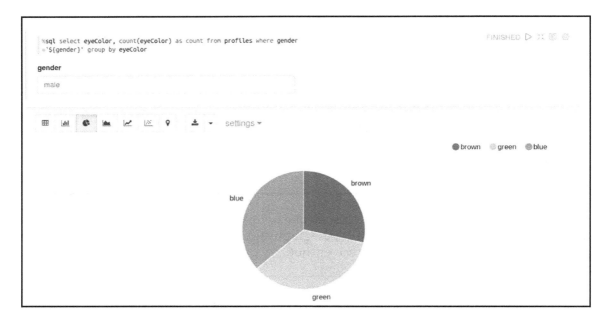

Finally, if parameterizing using free-form text isn't enough, we can use a drop-down list instead:

```
%sql select eyeColor, count(eyeColor) as count from profiles where gender
="${gender=male,male|female}" group by eyeColor
```

Running custom functions

While Spark SQL doesn't support a range of functions as wide as ANSI SQL does, it has an easy and powerful mechanism for registering a normal Scala function and using it inside the SQL context.

Let's say we would like to find out how many profiles fall under each age group. We have a simple function called `ageGroup`. Given an age, it returns a string representing the age group:

```
def fnGroupAge(age: Int, bucket:Int=10) = {
```

```
val buckets = Array("0-10", "11-20", "20-30", "31-40", "41-50", "51-60",
"61-70", "71-80", "81-90", "91-100", ">100")
val bucket = buckets((age-1)/10)
bucket
}
```

Now, in order to register this function to be used inside Spark SQL, all that we need to do is give it a name and call the `register` method of the SQLContext's user-defined function object:

```
sqlc.udf.register("fnGroupAge", (age:Long)=>ageGroup(age.toInt))
```

Let's fire our query and see the use of the function in action:

```
%sql select fnGroupAge(age) as ageGroup, count(gender) as genderTotal from
profiles where gender='${gender=male,male|female}' group by
fnGroupAge(age), gender
```

The following is the output:

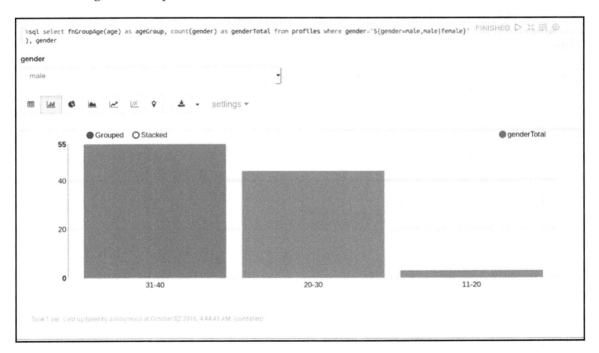

Adding external dependencies to Zeppelin

Sooner or later, we will be depending on external libraries than that don't come bundled with Zeppelin. For instance, we might need, a library for CSV or import or RDBMS data import. Let's see how to load a MySQL database driver and visualize data from a table.

In order to load a `mysql` connector Java driver, we just need to specify the group ID, artifact ID, and version number, and the JAR gets downloaded from the Maven repository. `%dep` indicates that the paragraph adds a dependency, and the `z` implicit variable represents the Zeppelin context:

```
%dep z.load("/home/padmac/bigdata/archives/mysql-connector-java-5.1.21.jar")          FINISHED ▷ ⠿ ⌨ @

DepInterpreter(%dep) deprecated. Load dependency through GUI interpreter menu instead.
res0: org.apache.zeppelin.dep.Dependency = org.apache.zeppelin.dep.Dependency@1b583737

Took 7 sec. Last updated by anonymous at October 02 2016, 7:15:02 PM
```

The only thing that we need to watch out for while using `%dep` is that the dependency paragraph should be used before using the libraries that are being loaded. So it is generally advised to load the dependencies at the top of the Notebook.

Once we have loaded the dependencies, we need to construct the options required to connect to the MySQL database:

```
val props = scala.collection.mutable.Map[String,String]();                    FINISHED ▷ ⠿ ⌨ @

props: scala.collection.mutable.Map[String,String] = Map()

Took 32 sec. Last updated by anonymous at October 02 2016, 7:15:42 PM


props+=("driver" -> "com.mysql.jdbc.Driver")                                  FINISHED ▷ ⠿ ⌨ @
props+=("url" -> "jdbc:mysql://localhost/sample?user=root")
props+=("dbtable" -> "(select id, name, marks, grade from sample.Student) as students")
props+=("partitionColumn" -> "id")
props+=("lowerBound" -> "0")
props+=("upperBound" -> "100")
props+=("numPartitions" -> "2")

res0: props.type = Map(driver -> com.mysql.jdbc.Driver)                                           ↲
res1: props.type = Map(driver -> com.mysql.jdbc.Driver, url -> jdbc:mysql://localhost/sample?user=root)
res2: props.type = Map(dbtable -> (select id, name, marks, grade from sample.Student) as students, driver -> com.mysql.j
dbc.Driver, url -> jdbc:mysql://localhost/sample?user=root)
res3: props.type = Map(dbtable -> (select id, name, marks, grade from sample.Student) as students, driver -> com.mysql.j
dbc.Driver, url -> jdbc:mysql://localhost/sample?user=root, partitionColumn -> id)
res4: props.type = Map(dbtable -> (select id, name, marks, grade from sample.Student) as students, driver -> com.mysql.j
dbc.Driver, url -> jdbc:mysql://localhost/sample?user=root, lowerBound -> 0, partitionColumn -> id)
```

We use the connection to create a DataFrame:

```
import scala.collection.JavaConverters._                                          FINISHED ▷ ⠿ 🖿 ⋮
val studentDf = sqlContext.load("jdbc", props.asJava)
studentDf.printSchema()
studentDf.show()
studentDf.registerTempTable("students")

import scala.collection.JavaConverters._                                                        ⌐
warning: there were 1 deprecation warning(s); re-run with -deprecation for details
studentDf: org.apache.spark.sql.DataFrame = [id: string, name: string, marks: double, grade: string]
root
 |-- id: string (nullable = true)
 |-- name: string (nullable = true)
 |-- marks: double (nullable = true)
 |-- grade: string (nullable = true)


+---+------+-----+-----+
| id|  name|marks|grade|
+---+------+-----+-----+
|101| Padma| 67.0|    A|
|102| Varun| 76.0|   A+|
|103|Vishal| 89.0|   A+|
|104| Raghu| 65.0|   B+|
|105| Ramya| 56.0|    B|
|106|Shanti| 59.0|    B|
|107| Kiran| 62.0|    B|
|108|   Sai| 69.0|    A|
|109| Priya| 86.0|   A+|
|110|Kishore| 64.0|  B+|
+---+------+-----+-----+
```

Pointing to an external Spark Cluster

Running Zeppelin with built-in Spark is all good, but in most of our cases, we'll be executing the Spark jobs initiated by Zeppelin on a cluster of workers. Achieving this is pretty simple: we need to configure Zeppelin to point its Spark master property to an external Spark master URL. Let's take for example a simple and standalone external Spark cluster running on my local machine. Please note that we will have to run Zeppelin on a different port because of the Zeppelin UI port's conflict with the Spark standalone cluster master web UI over `8080`.

Let's bring up the Spark Cluster. From inside your Spark source, execute the following:

```
sbin/start-all.sh
```

How to do it...

1. Finally, let's modify `conf/interpreter.json` and `conf/zeppelin-env.sh` to point the `master` property to the host on which the Spark VM is running. In this case, it will be my localhost, with the port being `7077`, which is the default master port:

2. The `conf/interpreter.json` file looks like the following:

```
"2BXPPAVX1": {
"id": "2BXPPAVX1",
"name": "spark",
"group": "spark",
"properties": {
 "spark.executor.memory": "",
 "args": "",
"zeppelin.spark.printREPLOutput": "true",
 "spark.cores.max": "",
 "zeppelin.dep.additionalRemoteRepository": "spark-
  packages,http://dl.bintray.com/spark-packages/maven,false;",
 "zeppelin.spark.importImplicit": "true",
 "zeppelin.spark.sql.stacktrace": "false",
 "zeppelin.spark.concurrentSQL": "false",
 "zeppelin.spark.useHiveContext": "true",
 "zeppelin.pyspark.python": "python",
 "zeppelin.dep.localrepo": "local-repo",
 "zeppelin.interpreter.localRepo": "local-rep",
 "zeppelin.R.knitr": "true",
 "zeppelin.spark.maxResult": "1000",
 "master": "spark://master:7077",
 "spark.app.name": "Zeppelin",
```

3. The `conf/zeppelin-env.sh` file should look like as follows:

```
export MASTER= spark://master:7077
```

Now, when we rerun Spark SQL from Zeppelin, we can see that the job runs on the external Spark instance.

How it works...

In the preceding recipe, we saw how to install Zeppelin, customize ports, visualize data from a distributed filesystem such as HDFS, write custom functions and invoke them from the Notebook, add external dependencies such as MySQL, and lastly, point Zeppelin towards an external Spark Cluster.

There's more...

In the next recipe, let's see how to visualize data using Bokeh.

See also

Please also visit the subsequent recipe *Creating scatter plots with Bokeh-Scala*

Creating scatter plots with Bokeh-Scala

In this section, we'll take a brief look at the most popular visualizing framework in Python, called Bokeh, and use its (also fast-evolving) Scala bindings to the framework. Breeze also has a visualization API called **breeze-viz**, which is built on JFreeChart. Bokeh is backed by a JavaScript visualization library, called **BokehJS**. The Scala bindings library bokeh-scala not only gives an easier way to construct glyphs (lines, circles, and so on) out of Scala objects, but also translates glyphs into a format that is understandable by the BokehJS JavaScript components. The various terms in Bokeh actually mean the following:

- **Glyph**: All geometric shapes that we can think of–circles, squares, lines, and so on – are glyphs. This is just the UI representation and doesn't hold any data. All the properties related to this object just help us modify the UI properties: color, x, y, width and so on.
- **Plot**: A plot is like a canvas on which we arrange various objects relevant to the visualization, such as the legend, *x* and *y* axes, grid, tools and obviously, the core of the graph–the data itself. We construct various accessory objects and finally add them to the list of renderers in the plot object.
- **Document**: The document is the component that does the actual rendering.

The Bokeh-Scala accepts the plot as an argument and when we call the `save` method in the document, it uses all the child renderers in the plot object and constructs a JSON from the wrapped elements. This JSON is eventually read by the BokehJS widgets to render the data in a visually pleasing manner. More than one plot can be rendered in the document by adding it to a grid plot (we'll look at how this is done in the next recipe, *Creating a time series MultiPlot with Bokeh-Scala*).

Getting ready

To step through this recipe, you will need a running Spark Cluster in any one of the modes, that is, local, standalone, YARN, or Mesos. Also, include the Spark MLlib package in the `build.sbt` file so that it downloads the related libraries and the API can be used. Install Hadoop (optionally), Scala and Java.

How to do it...

Initially, specify the following libraries in the `build.sbt` file as follows:

```
libraryDependencies ++= Seq(
    "io.continuum.bokeh" % "bokeh_2.10" % "0.5",
    "org.scalanlp" %% "breeze" % "0.5",
    "org.scalanlp" %% "breeze-viz" % "0.5" )
```

In this recipe, we will be creating a scatter plot using iris data (https://archive.ics.uci.edu/ml/datasets/Iris), which has the length and width attributes of flowers belonging to three different species of the same plant. Drawing a scatter plot on this dataset involves a series of interesting sub steps. For the purpose of representing the iris data in a Breeze matrix, I have naïvely transformed the species categories into numbers:

- Iris setosa: 0
- Iris versicolor: 1
- Iris virginica: 2

This is available in `irisNumeric.csv`. Later, we'll see how we can load the original iris data (`iris.data`) into a Spark DataFrame and use that as a source for plotting. A plot is a composition of multiple widgets/glyphs. This consists of a series of steps:

1. Preparing our data.
2. Creating the plot, a point (marker object), and a renderer for it.
3. Setting the *x* and *y* axes' data range for the plot.

4. Drawing the *x* and *y* axes.
5. Creating the document object and viewing the plot.
6. Adding tools to the plot.
7. Adding grid lines.
8. Adding a legend to the plot.

The following describes the preceding steps:

Preparing our data

Bokeh plots require our data to be in a format that it understands, but it's really easy to do this. All that we need to do is create a new source object that inherits from `ColumnDataSource`. The other options are `AjaxDataSource` and `RemoteDataSource`. So, let's overlay our Breeze data source on `ColumnDataSource` as follows:

```
import breeze.linalg._
import breeze.plot.Figure
import io.continuum.bokeh._
object IrisSource extends ColumnDataSource {
    val colormap = Map[Int, Color](0 -> Color.Red, 1 ->
      Color.Green, 2 -> Color.Blue)
    val iris = csvread(file = new
      File("/home/padmacuser/data/iris.csv"), separator = ',')
    val sepalLength = column(iris(::, 0))
    val sepalWidth = column(iris(::, 1))
    val petalLength = column(iris(::, 2))
    val petalWidth = column(iris(::, 3)) }
```

Creating the plot, a point (marker object) and a renderer for it

Let's have our image's title as `Iris Petal Length vs Width`. Also, create a marker object that marks the data point. There are a variety of marker objects to choose from: `Asterisk`, `Circle`, `CircleCross`, `CircleX`, `Cross`, `Diamond`, `DiamondCross`, `InvertedTriangle`, `PlainX`, `Square`, `SquareCross`, `SquareX` , and `Triangle`. Let's choose `Diamond` for our purposes:

```
object Bokeh_Scala extends  App{
      import
IrisSource.{colormap,sepalLength,sepalWidth,petalLength,petalWidth}
    val plot = new Plot().title("Iris Petal Length vs Width")
    val diamond = new Diamond()
    .x(petalLength)
    .y(petalWidth)
    .fill_color(Color.Blue)
    .fill_alpha(0.5)
```

```
   .size(5)
val dataPointRenderer = new GlyphRenderer().data_source(IrisSource).
   glyph(diamond)
```

While constructing the marker object, other than the UI attributes, we also say what the *x* and the *y* coordinates for it are. Note that we have also mentioned that the color of this marker is `blue`. We'll change that in a while using the color map.

Setting the x and y axes' data range for the plot

The plot needs to know what the *x* and *y* data ranges of the plot are before rendering. Let's do that by creating two DataRange objects and setting them to the plot:

```
val xRange = new DataRange1d().sources(petalLength :: Nil)
val yRange = new DataRange1d().sources(petalWidth :: Nil)
plot.x_range(xRange).y_range(yRange)
```

Drawing the x and the y axes

Let's now draw the axes, set their bounds, and add them to the plot's renderers. We also need to let the plot know which location each axis belongs to:

```
//X and Y Axis
val xAxis = new LinearAxis().plot(plot).axis_label("Petal Length").
   bounds((1.0, 7.0))
val yAxis = new LinearAxis().plot(plot).axis_label("Petal Width").
   bounds((0.0, 2.5))
plot.below <<= (listRenderer => (xAxis :: listRenderer))
plot.left <<= (listRenderer => (yAxis :: listRenderer))
//Add the renderer to the plot
plot.renderers := List[Renderer](xAxis, yAxis, dataPointRenderer)
```

Creating the document object and viewing the plot

Now, create a document object so that we can save the final HTML by the name `IrisBokehBreeze.html`. Since we haven't specified the full path of the target file in the `save` method, the file will be saved in the same directory as the project itself as follows:

```
val document = new Document(plot)
val file =
document.save("/home/padmacuser/data/IrisBokehBreeze.html")
file.view() } // Object Bokeh_Scala ends here
```

The following is the output:

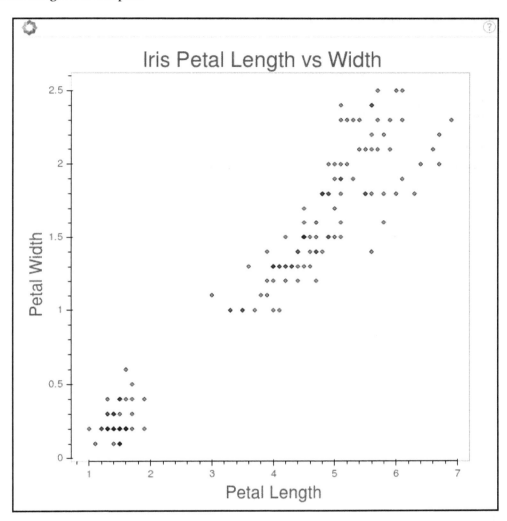

Adding tools to the plot

Let's add some tools to the image. Bokeh has some nice tools that can be attached to the image: BoxSelectTool, BoxZoomTool, CrosshairTool, HoverTool, LassoSelectTool, PanTool, PolySelectTool, PreviewSaveTool, ResetTool, ResizeTool, SelectTool, TapTool, TransientSelectTool and WheelZoomTool.

Let's add some of the tools as follows:

```
val panTool = new PanTool().plot(plot)
val wheelZoomTool = new WheelZoomTool().plot(plot)
val previewSaveTool = new PreviewSaveTool().plot(plot)
val resetTool = new ResetTool().plot(plot)
val resizeTool = new ResizeTool().plot(plot)
val crosshairTool = new CrosshairTool().plot(plot)
plot.tools := List(panTool, wheelZoomTool, previewSaveTool,
resetTool,    resizeTool, crosshairTool)
```

The following is the output:

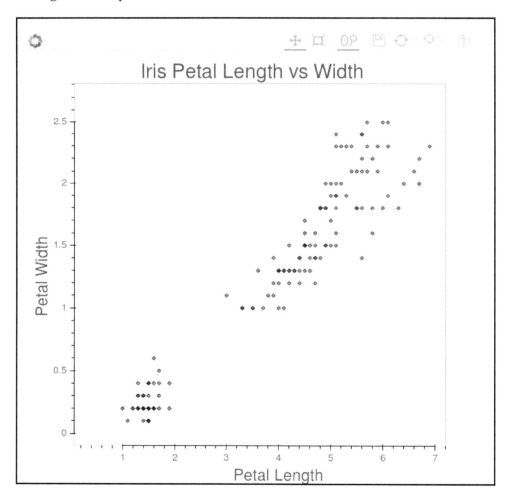

Adding grid lines

While we have the crosshair tool, which helps us locate the exact x and y values of a particular data point, it would be nice to have a data grid too. Let's add two data grids, one for the x axis and one for the y axis as follows:

```
val xgrid = new Grid().plot(plot).axis(xAxis).dimension(0)
val ygrid = new Grid().plot(plot).axis(yAxis).dimension(1)
//Add the renderer to the plot
plot.renderers := List[Renderer](xAxis, yAxis, dataPointRenderer,
xgrid, ygrid)
```

The following is the output:

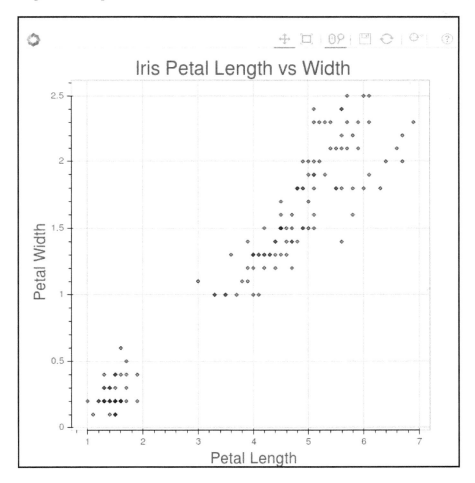

Adding a legend to the plot

This step is a bit tricky in the Scala binding of Bokeh due to the lack of high-level graphing objects, such as scatter. For now, let's cook up our own legend. The `legends` property of the `Legend` object accepts a list of tuples–a label and a `GlyphRenderer` pair. Let's explicitly create three `GlyphRenderer` wrapping diamonds of three colors, which represent the species. We then add them to the plot as follows:

```
//Adding Legend
val setosa = new Diamond().fill_color(Color.Red).size(10).fill_alpha(0.5)
  val setosaGlyphRnd=new GlyphRenderer().glyph(setosa)
  val versicolor = new
Diamond().fill_color(Color.Green).size(10).fill_alpha(0.5)
  val versicolorGlyphRnd=new GlyphRenderer().glyph(versicolor)
  val virginica = new
Diamond().fill_color(Color.Blue).size(10).fill_alpha(0.5)
  val virginicaGlyphRnd=new GlyphRenderer().glyph(virginica)
val legends = List("setosa" -> List(setosaGlyphRnd), "versicolor" ->
List(versicolorGlyphRnd), "virginica" -> List(virginicaGlyphRnd))
  val legend = new
Legend().orientation(LegendOrientation.TopLeft).plot(plot).legends(legends)
  plot.renderers := List[Renderer](xAxis, yAxis, dataPointRenderer, xgrid,
ygrid,   legend, setosaGlyphRnd, virginicaGlyphRnd, versicolorGlyphRnd)
```

The following is the output:

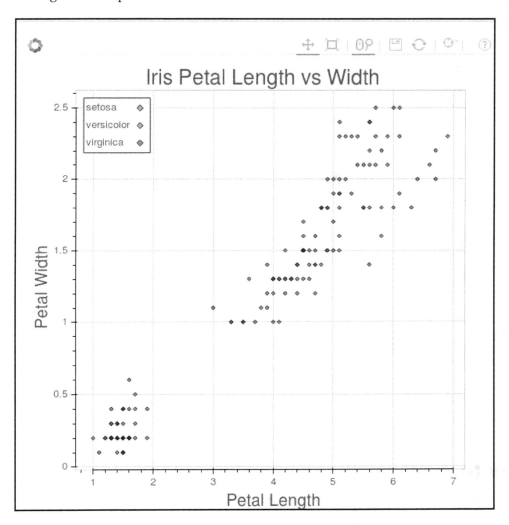

How it works...

In the preceding recipe, we saw the steps in creating scatter plots with Bokeh-Scala, such as preparing data using the Breeze library, creating marker objects (representation for the data points), setting the x and y axes data, creating document objects for viewing the plots, and adding tools, grid lines and legends.

There's more...

In the next recipe, let's see how to create time series plots using Bokeh.

See also

Please visit the *Visualization using Zeppelin* and *Creating scatter plots with Bokeh-Scala* recipes, which show plots from various tools.

Creating a time series MultiPlot with Bokeh-Scala

In this second recipe on plotting using Bokeh, we'll see how to plot a time series graph with a dataset borrowed from `https://archive.ics.uci.edu/ml/datasets/Dow+Jones+Index`. We will also see how to plot multiple charts in a single document.

Getting ready

To step through this recipe, you will need a running Spark Cluster in any one of the modes, that is, local, standalone, YARN, or Mesos. Also, include the Spark MLlib package in the `build.sbt` file so that it downloads the related libraries and the API can be used. Install Hadoop (optionally), Scala, and Java.

How to do it...

Initially, specify the following libraries in the `build.sbt` file as follows:

```
libraryDependencies ++= Seq(
    "io.continuum.bokeh" % "bokeh_2.10" % "0.5",
    "org.scalanlp" %% "breeze" % "0.5",
    "org.scalanlp" %% "breeze-viz" % "0.5" )
```

We'll be using only two fields from the dataset: the closing price of the stock at the end of the week, and the last business day of the week. The dataset is comma separated. Let's take a look at some samples, as shown here:

quarter	stock	date	open	high	low	close	volume	percent_change_price	percent_change_volume_over_last_wk	previous_weeks_volume	next_weeks_open
1	AA	1/7/2011	$15.82	$16.72	$15.78	$16.42	239655616	3.79267			$16.71
1	AA	1/14/2011	$16.71	$16.71	$15.64	$15.97	242963398	-4.42849	1.380223028	239655616	$16.19
1	AA	1/21/2011	$16.19	$16.38	$15.60	$15.79	138428495	-2.47066	-43.02495926	242963398	$15.87
1	AA	1/28/2011	$15.87	$16.63	$15.82	$16.13	151379173	1.63831	9.355500109	138428495	$16.18
1	AA	2/4/2011	$16.18	$17.39	$16.18	$17.14	154387761	5.93325	1.987451735	151379173	$17.33
1	AA	2/11/2011	$17.33	$17.48	$16.97	$17.37	114691279	0.230814	-25.71219489	154387761	$17.39
1	AA	2/18/2011	$17.39	$17.68	$17.28	$17.28	80023895	-0.632547	-30.22669579	114691279	$16.98
1	AA	2/25/2011	$16.98	$17.15	$15.96	$16.68	132981863	-1.76678	66.17769355	80023895	$16.81
1	AA	3/4/2011	$16.81	$16.94	$16.13	$16.58	109493077	-1.36823	-17.66315005	132981863	$16.58
1	AA	3/11/2011	$16.58	$16.75	$15.42	$16.03	114332562	-3.31725	4.419900447	109493077	$15.95
1	AA	3/18/2011	$15.95	$16.33	$15.43	$16.11	130374108	1.00313	14.03060136	114332562	$16.38

Preparing data

In contrast to the previous recipe, where we used the Breeze matrix to construct the Bokeh `ColumnDataSource`, we'll use the Spark DataFrame to construct the source this time. The `getSource` method accepts a ticker (MSFT-Microsoft and CAT-Caterpillar) and a `SQLContext`. It runs a Spark SQL, fetches the data from the table, and constructs a `ColumnDataSource` from it as follows:

```
import org.joda.time.format.DateTimeFormat
import org.apache.spark.sql._
import io.continuum.bokeh._
import org.apache.spark._
object StockSource {
  val formatter = DateTimeFormat.forPattern("MM/dd/yyyy")
  def getSource(ticker: String, sqlContext: SQLContext) = {
    val stockDf = sqlContext.sql(s"select stock, date, close from
stocks where stock= '$ticker'")
    stockDf.cache()
    val dateData: Array[Double] =
stockDf.select("date").collect.map(eachRow =>
formatter.parseDateTime(eachRow.getString(0)).getMillis().toDouble)
    val closeData: Array[Double] =
stockDf.select("close").collect.map(eachRow =>
eachRow.getString(0).drop(1).toDouble)
    object source extends ColumnDataSource {
    val date = column(dateData)
    val close = column(closeData)
    }
    source
  }  }
```

Let's construct the SQLContext and register the DataFrame as a table like this:

```
object TimeSeries_MultiPlot extends App {
  import StockSource.{getSource}
  val conf = new SparkConf()
  .setAppName("TimeSeriesPlot").setMaster("spark://master:7077")
  val sc = new SparkContext(conf)
  val sqlContext = new SQLContext(sc)
  import sqlContext.implicits._
  val stocks= sqlContext.read.format("com.databricks.spark.csv")
    .option("header", "true")
    .option("inferSchema","true").load("hdfs://namenode:9000/
    dow_jones _index.csv")
  stocks.registerTempTable("stocks")
```

Creating a line that joins all the data points

As we saw in the previous recipe with the diamond marker, we'll have to pass the x and the y positions of the data points. Also, we will need to wrap the line glyph into a renderer so that we can add it to the plot as follows:

```
val sourceObject = getSource("AA", sqlContext)
val line = new  Line().x(sourceObject.date).y(sourceObject.close)
.line_color(Color.Blue).line_width(2)
val lineGlyph = new
 GlyphRenderer().data_source(sourceObject).glyph(line)
```

Setting the x and y axes' data range for the plot

The plot needs to know what the x and y data ranges are before rendering. Let's do that by creating two DataRange objects and setting them to the plot as follows:

```
val xdr = new DataRange1d().sources(List(sourceObject.date))
val ydr = new DataRange1d().sources(List(sourceObject.close))
```

Creating the plot

Let's create the plot as follows:

```
//Create Plot
val plot = new Plot().title("Ticker").x_range(xdr).y_range(ydr)
.width(800).height(400)
```

Drawing the axes and the grids

Drawing the axes and the grids is the same as before. We add some labels to the axes, format the display of the x axis and then add them to the plot:

```
//Drawing x-axis and y-axis
val xformatter = new
DatetimeTickFormatter().formats(Map(DatetimeUnits.Months -> List
("%b     %Y")))
val xAxis = new DatetimeAxis().plot(plot).formatter(xformatter)
.axis_label("Month")
val yAxis = new LinearAxis().plot(plot).axis_label("Price")
plot.below <<= (xAxis :: _)
plot.left <<= (yAxis :: _)
val xgrid = new Grid().plot(plot).dimension(0).axis(xAxis)
val ygrid = new Grid().plot(plot).dimension(1).axis(yAxis)
```

Adding tools

Let's add some tools to the image and to the plot:

```
//Tools
val panTool = new PanTool().plot(plot)
val wheelZoomTool = new WheelZoomTool().plot(plot)
val previewSaveTool = new PreviewSaveTool().plot(plot)
val resetTool = new ResetTool().plot(plot)
val resizeTool = new ResizeTool().plot(plot)
val crosshairTool = new CrosshairTool().plot(plot)
plot.tools := List(panTool, wheelZoomTool, previewSaveTool,
    resetTool, resizeTool, crosshairTool)
```

Adding a legend to the plot

Here is the code to add legend to the plot:

```
//Legend
val legends = List("AA" -> List(lineGlyph))
val legend = new Legend().plot(plot).legends(legends)
```

Adding renderer, creating document object and viewing the plot

Here is the code for adding renderer and creating document object:

```
//Add the renderer to the plot
plot.renderers := List[Renderer](xAxis, yAxis, xgrid, ygrid, lineGlyph,
legend)
//Creating document object
val document = new Document(plot)
```

```
    val file =
document.save("/home/padmacuser/data/TimeSeriesMultiPlot.html")
    file.view()
```

The following is the output:

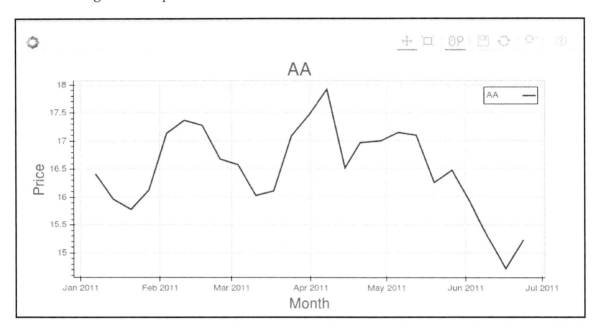

Multiple plots in the document

Creating multiple plots in the same document is child's play. All that we need to do is create all the plots, such as `microsoftPlot`, `bofaPlot`, `caterPillarPlot`, and `mmmPlot`, and then add them into a grid. Finally, instead of passing our individual plot object into the document, we pass in `GridPlot`:

```
val children = List(List(microsoftPlot, bofaPlot),
 List(caterPillarPlot,  mmmPlot))
val grid = new GridPlot().children(children)
val document = new Document(grid)
val html =
document.save("/home/padmac/data/multipleTimeSeriesPlots.html")
```

How it work...

In the preceding recipe, we saw the procedure for creating time series plots in which the data is loaded using Spark. Although the data resides in a distributed system, not all the records can be visualized. We fetched the records pertaining to a specific 'stock' and visualized them using time series plot. While creating multiplots, it is assumed that the user creates the plots `microsoftPlot, bofaPlot, caterPillarPlot` and `mmmPlot` corresponding to specific stock.

There's more...

In the next recipe, let's see how to visualize data using lightning visualization server.

See also

Please visit the earlier recipes *Visualization using Zeppelin* and *Creating scatter plots with Bokeh-Scala*, which show plots from various tools.

Creating plots with the lightning visualization server

Lightning is a framework for interactive data visualization, including a server, visualizations, and client libraries. The lightning server provides API-based access to reproducible, web-based visualizations. It includes a core set of visualization types, but is built for extendibility and customization. It can be deployed in many ways, including Heroku, Docker, a public server, a local app for OS X and even a serverless version well suited to notebooks such as Jupyter.

Lightning can expose a single visualization to all the languages of data science. Client libraries are available in multiple languages, including Python, Scala, JavaScript, and rstats, with many more in future.

Getting ready

To step through this recipe, you will need a running Spark Cluster in any one of the modes, that is, local, standalone, YARN, or Mesos. Install Hadoop (optionally), Scala, and Java. Lightning is designed to support a variety of use cases. The first option is to use a pre-built server, run own server, or use locally without a server. In this recipe, we'll use a public server to generate the visualizations.

How to do it...

1. Install lightning on your local machine as follows.
2. Clone the `git` repository for the `lightning-viz` repository:

```
git clone git@github.com:lightning-viz/lightning.git
npm install
```

3. Install `nvm` as follows:

```
wget -qO-
https://raw.githubusercontent.com/creationix/nvm/v0.32.0/
install.sh | bash
source ~/.bashrc
export NVM_NODEJS_ORG_MIRROR=http://nodejs.org/dist
```

4. Install Node 4.0 as follows:

```
nvm install 4.0
npm install sqlite3
cd lightning/
npm start (starts the lightning server)
```

```
padmac@F01022:~/bigdata/lightning$ npm start

> lightning-server@1.2.1 start /home/padmac/bigdata/lightning
> node bin/lightning-server.js

Lightning started on port: 3000
```

5. Also install the lightning Scala client and build the project as follows:

```
git clone https://github.com/lightning-viz/lightning-scala.git
sbt assembly
```

```
[info] LightningThreeSuite:
[info] - scatter3
[info] LightningSuite:
[info] - create session
[info] LightningImplicitsSuite:
[info] - line (flat)
[info] - line (flat int)
[info] - line (nested int)
[info] LightningStreamingSuite:
[info] - line streaming
[info] - scatter streaming
[info] LightningPlotsSuite:
[info] - line
[info] - line (single)
[info] - force
[info] - force (links)
[info] - force (links and value)
[info] - matrix
[info] - adjacency
[info] - map (states)
[info] - map (countries)
[info] - scatter
[info] - graph
[info] - graph bundled
[info] Run completed in 7 seconds, 120 milliseconds.
[info] Total number of tests run: 19
[info] Suites: completed 5, aborted 0
[info] Tests: succeeded 19, failed 0, canceled 0, ignored 0, pending 0
[info] All tests passed.
[info] Checking every *.class/*.jar file's SHA-1.
[info] Merging files...
[warn] Merging 'META-INF/MANIFEST.MF' with strategy 'discard'
[warn] Merging 'rootdoc.txt' with strategy 'concat'
[warn] Strategy 'concat' was applied to a file
[warn] Strategy 'discard' was applied to a file
[info] SHA-1: 5630d40bb9846aee2c7ca1bfdb39984ecc8a45f9
[info] Packaging /home/padmac/lightning-scala/target/scala-2.10/lightning-scala-assembly-0.1.0-SNAPSHOT.jar ...
[info] Done packaging.
[success] Total time: 61 s, completed 11 Oct, 2016 10:44:08 PM
```

6. Here is the code for creating a visualization on a public server:

```
import org.viz.lightning.types.Make
import org.viz.lightning.{Visualization, Lightning}
object Lightning_Demo {
  def main(args:Array[String]): Unit =
  {
    val lgn = Lightning(host="http://public.lightning-viz.org")
    lgn.createSession("SimpleDemo")
    val viz = lgn.line(Array(Array(1.0,1.0,2.0,3.0,9.0,20.0)))
    println(viz.getPermalinkURL)  }
```

The following is the output:

```
http://public.lightning-viz.org/visualizations/8cd065a6-c416-44ad-addf-
5a0718a5c500
```

Now on visiting the preceding URL by adding/public at the end, that is,
http://public.lightning-viz.org/visualizations/8cd065a6-c416-44ad-addf-
5a0718a5c500/public, the visualization looks like the following:

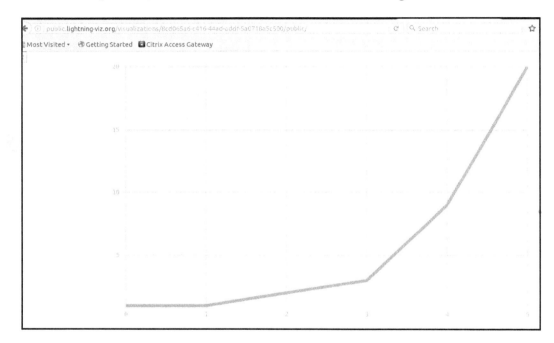

Let's see how to create a scatter streaming plot using Lightning. Here is the code for the same:

```
val lgn = Lightning(host="http://localhost:3000")
lgn.createSession("ScatterStreaming")
val viz = lgn.scatterStreaming(x = Make.gaussian(n = 50, scale = 5),
 y = Make.gaussian(n = 50, scale = 5),
 label = Make.labels(n = 50),
 size = Make.sizes(n = 50),
 alpha = Make.alphas(n = 50))
println(viz.getPermalinkURL)
```

The following is the output:

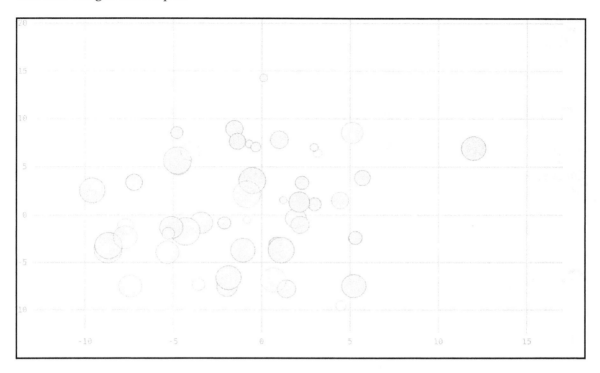

How it works...

In the preceding recipe, we saw how to install the Lightning framework and create line plots as well as streaming plots. When processing the data using RDDs, the data needs to be collected on the driver (since the lightning libraries do not accept RDD as input) in Array format which can be input for the lightning API. This way, the visualization will be on a single node (the driver node) which requires good hardware and software configurations.

There's more...

In the next recipes, let's see how to visualize data using Spark's built-in libraries.

See also

Please visit the earlier recipes *Visualization using Zeppelin, Creating scatter plots with Bokeh-Scala* and *Creating plots with lightning visualization server*, which show plots from various tools.

Visualize machine learning models with Databricks notebook

Databricks provides flexibility to visualize machine learning models using the built-in `display()` command that displays DataFrames as a table and creates convenient one-click plots. In the following recipe we'll, we'll see how to visualize data with Databricks notebook.

Getting ready

To step through this recipe, you will need a running Spark cluster in any one of the modes, that is, local, standalone, YARN, or Mesos. Install Hadoop (optionally), Scala, and Java. Create a user account in Databricks and get access for the Notebook.

How to do it...

The fitted versus residuals plot is available for linear regression and logistic regression models. The Databricks fitted versus residuals plot is analogous to R's residuals versus fitted plot for linear models. Linear regression computes a prediction as a weighted sum of the input variables. The fitted versus residuals plot can be used to assess a linear regression model's goodness of fit. The dataset `diabetes` is default available in the notebook. If not available, please download the dataset from the following location:

```
https://github.com/ChitturiPadma/datasets/blob/master/diabetes.csv
```

Here is the plot:

```
import org.apache.spark._
import org.apache.spark.sql._
import org.apache.spark.ml.regression.LinearRegression
import org.apache.spark.mllib.util.MLUtils
import org.apache.spark.mllib.linalg.Vectors
import org.apache.spark.mllib.regression.LabeledPoint
```

```
import org.apache.spark.mllib.linalg.{Vector, Vectors}
import org.apache.spark.mllib.clustering.{KMeans, KMeansModel}
val data = sqlContext.sql("select * from diabetes")")
val lr = new LinearRegression()
  .setMaxIter(20)
  .setRegParam(0.3)
  .setElasticNetParam(1.0)
val lrModel = lr.fit(data)
> display(lrModel, data, "fittedVsResiduals")
```

The following is the output:

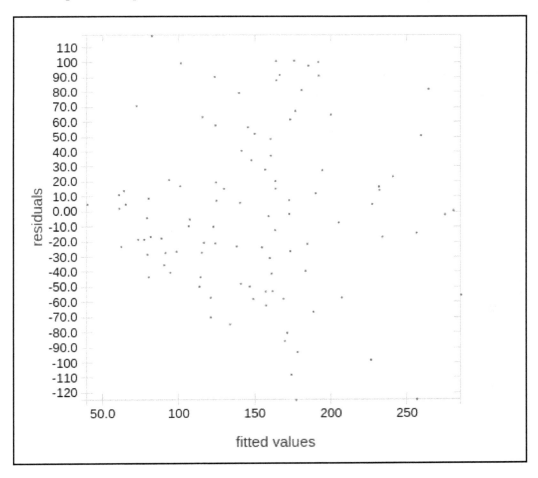

Let's also see how to visualize clusters. K-means tries to separate data points into clusters by minimizing the sum of squared errors between data points and their nearest cluster centers. We can now visualize clusters and plot feature grids to identify trends and correlations. Each plot in the grid corresponds to two features, and data points are colored by their respective cluster labels. The plots can be used to visually assess how well your data has been clustered (the dataset iris is default available in the notebook):

```
val data = sqlContext.sql("select * from iris")")
// The MLLib package requires an RDD[Vector] instead of a dataframe.
We need to   manually extract the vector.
// This is not necessary when using the ml package instead.
val features = data.map(_.getAs[Vector]("features"))
val clusters = KMeans.train(features, 3, 10)
> display(clusters, data)
```

The following is the output:

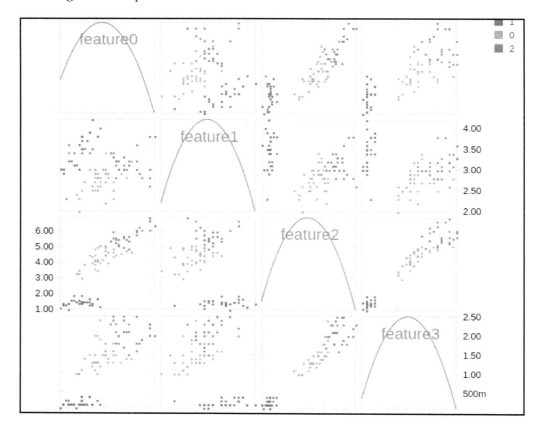

How it works...

In the preceding recipe, we saw how to visualize regression models and clusters using the `display()` built-in command available in Databricks notebook.

There's more...

Although the visualization tools are not fully matured with respect to distributed systems, tools such as Zeppelin, Lightning server and Bokeh are incorporating a lot of features, giving more scope for big data developers to visualize the data.

See also

Please visit the earlier *Creating scatter plots with Bokeh-Scala* and *Creating plots with Lightning Visualization Server* recipes, which show plots from various tools.

9
Deep Learning on Spark

In this chapter, we'll cover the following recipes:

- Installing CaffeOnSpark
- Working with CaffeOnSpark
- Running a feed-forward neural network with DeepLearning4j over Spark
- Running an RBM with DeepLearning4j over Spark
- Running a CNN for learning MNIST with DeepLearning4j over Spark
- Installing TensorFlow
- Working with Spark TensorFlow

Introduction

Deep learning is a new area of machine learning which has been introduced with the objective of moving machine learning closer to one of its original goals, which is **Artificial Intelligence (AI)**. It is becoming an important AI paradigm for pattern recognition, image/video processing and fraud detection applications in finance.

Deep learning is the implementation of neural networks with more than a single hidden layer of neurons. The *deep* architectures vary quite considerably, with different implementations being optimized for different tasks or goals. To get familiar with neural networks, please get acquainted with the fundamentals of neural networks at http://www.analyticsvidhya.com/blog/2016/03/introduction-deep-learning-fundamen tals-neural-networks/ and http://neuralnetworksanddeeplearning.com/. The deep networks use many layers of non-linear information processing that are hierarchical in nature.

The deep models are capable of extracting useful, high-level, structured representations which in turn extract complex statistical dependencies from high-dimensional sensory input and effectively learn the representations by reusing and combining intermediate concepts, allowing these models to generalize well across a wide variety of tasks. These learned high-level representations give state-of-the-art results in challenging problems, including visual object recognition, information retrieval, natural language processing and speech perception. The list of complex models includes deep belief networks, deep Boltzmann machines, deep auto-encoders and sparse coding-based methods.

Apart from addressing computationally intensive problems, deep neural networks can also take precious time and resources to train. Hence, leveraging the existing distributed data processing frameworks such as Hadoop or Spark would parallelize the training phase of the network and reduce the training time. As Spark offers in-memory processing power, it is ideal for iterative workloads. Since the deep network includes training over the same dataset iteratively, Spark would be a great fit when taking advantage of distributed data processing frameworks.

Installing CaffeOnSpark

Caffe is a fully open source deep learning framework which provides access to deep architectures. The code is written in C++ with CUDA used for GPU computation and supports bindings to Python/NumPy and MATLAB. In Caffe, multimedia scientists and practitioners have an orderly and extensible toolkit for state-of-the-art deep learning algorithms. It provides a complete toolkit for training, testing, fine-tuning and deploying models. It offers expressive architecture, modularity, Python and MATLAB bindings. Caffe also provides reference models for visual tasks.

Getting ready

To step through this recipe, you need Ubuntu 14.04 (Linux flavor) installed on the machine. Also, have Apache Hadoop 2.6 and Apache Spark 1.6.0 installed.

How to do it...

1. Before installing CaffeOnSpark, install the caffe prerequisites as follows:

```
sudo apt-get install libprotobuf-dev libleveldb-dev libsnappy-dev
libopencv-dev libhdf5-serial-dev protobuf-compiler
sudo apt-get install --no-install-recommends libboost-all-dev
```

2. Also install the dependent packages gflags, glogs, lmdb and atlas as follows:

```
sudo apt-get install libgflags-dev libgoogle-glog-dev liblmdb-dev
```

3. Now, clone the CaffeOnSpark code as follows:

```
git clone https://github.com/yahoo/CaffeOnSpark.git -recursive
```

4. Add the environment variable CAFFE_ON_SPARK in the .bashrc file as follows:

```
export CAFFE_ON_SPARK=$(pwd)/CaffeOnSpark
```

5. Create CaffeOnSpark/caffe-public/Makefile.config as follows:

```
pushd ${CAFFE_ON_SPARK}/caffe-public
cp Makefile.config.example Makefile.config
echo "INCLUDE_DIRS += ${JAVA_HOME}/include"
>> Makefile.config
```

6. Now, in Makefile.config, uncomment the line CPU_ONLY := 1 as we'll run Caffe on a CPU. Now, build CaffeOnSpark as follows:

```
pushd ${CAFFE_ON_SPARK}
make build
```

7. If the build fails with any dependency issue in numpy packages, re-install numpy as follows:

```
sudo apt-get install python-numpy
```

8. The build may also require Maven; hence, install Maven and add the environment variable M2_HOME in .bashrc as follows:

```
export M2_HOME=$(pwd)/apache-maven-3.2.1
export PATH = $PATH:$M2_HOME/bin
```

9. Once Apache Hadoop 2.6 and Apache Spark 1.6.0 have been installed, load `mnist` and `cifar10` datasets into HDFS as follows:

    ```
    hadoop fs -mkdir -p /projects/machine_learning/image_dataset
    ${CAFFE_ON_SPARK}>./scripts/setup-mnist.sh
    ```

    This will download the `mnist_test_lmdb` and `mnist_train_lmdb` datasets.

    ```
    ${CAFFE_ON_SPARK}>./scripts/setup-cifar10.sh
    ```

    This downloads the `cifar10_train_lmdb` and `cifar10_test_lmdb` datasets.

10. Now move both the preceding datasets into HDFS as follows:

    ```
    hadoop fs -put -f ${CAFFE_ON_SPARK}/data/mnist_*_lmdb
    hdfs:/projects/machine_learning/image_dataset/
    hadoop fs -put -f ${CAFFE_ON_SPARK}/data/cifar10_*_lmdb
    hdfs:/projects/machine_learning/image_dataset/
    ```

    Also, change the solver mode in the `data/lenet_memory_solver.prototxt` and `data/cifar10_quick_solver.prototxt` files as follows:

    ```
    solver_mode: CPU
    ```

How it works...

The preceding commands install the Caffe prerequisites, build the `CaffeOnSpark` package, and download the related `mnist` and `cifar10` datasets. If there are any dependency issues with `numpy`, install the `python-numpy` package and proceed.

There's more...

The Hadoop and Spark installation can be done from `CaffeOnSpark` as it contains `local-setup-hadoop.sh` and `local-setup-spark.sh` which downloads the Hadoop and Spark archived `.tar` files. Extract these TAR files and set the `HADOOP_HOME`, `YARN_CONF_DIR` and `SPARK_HOME` variables.

See also

Please refer to `Chapter 1`, *Big Data Analytics with Spark* to get familiar with Spark. Also, refer to `http://deeplearning.net/tutorial/` and `http://neuralnetworksanddeeplearning.com/` for details on deep learning.

Working with CaffeOnSpark

CaffeOnSpark brings deep learning to Hadoop and Spark clusters. By combining salient features from the deep learning framework Caffe and Big DataFrame works such as Apache Spark and Apache Hadoop, CaffeOnSpark enables distributed deep learning on a cluster of GPU and CPU servers. As a distributed extension of Caffe, CaffeOnSpark supports neural network model training, testing and feature extraction.

This is a Spark deep learning package. The API supports DataFrames so that the application can interface with a training dataset that was prepared using a Spark application and extract the predictions from the model or features from intermediate layers for results and data analysis using MLlib or SQL.

Getting ready

To step through this recipe, you will need a running Spark Cluster either in pseudo distributed mode or in one of the distributed modes, that is, standalone, YARN, or Mesos and CaffeOnSpark ready to be run on a Spark/YARN cluster.

How to do it...

1. A deep learning neural network can be trained using `CaffeOnSpark` with two Spark executors with an Ethernet connection as follows:
2. Edit the `~/.bashrc` file and copy the following lines:

```
export SPARK_WORKER_INSTANCES=2
export DEVICES=1
```

3. Now submit the application to train the DNN as follows:

```
spark-submit --master spark://master:7077 \
--num-executors ${SPARK_WORKER_INSTANCES} \
--files /PATH/CaffeOnSpark/data/lenet_memory_solver.prototxt, \
/PATH/CaffeOnSpark/data/lenet_memory_train_test.prototxt \
--conf spark.driver.extraLibraryPath="${LD_LIBRARY_PATH}" \
--conf spark.executorEnv.LD_LIBRARY_PATH="${LD_LIBRARY_PATH}" \
--class com.yahoo.ml.caffe.CaffeOnSpark \
/PATH/CaffeOnSpark/caffe-grid/target/caffe-grid-0.1-SNAPSHOT-
jar-with-dependencies.jar
-train \
-features accuracy,loss -label label \
-conf lenet_memory_solver.prototxt \
-devices ${DEVICES} \
-connection ethernet \
-model hdfs://<namenode>:54310/models \
-output hdfs://<namenode>:54310/mnist_features_result
```

4. The training will produce a model and various snapshots as follows:

```
-rw-r--r--   3 root supergroup    1725052 2016-04-08 00:57
/mnist_lenet.model
-rw-r--r--   3 root supergroup    1725052 2016-04-08 00:57
/mnist_lenet_iter_10000.caffemodel
-rw-r--r--   3 root supergroup    1724462 2016-04-08 00:57
/mnist_lenet_iter_10000.solverstate
-rw-r--r--   3 root supergroup    1725052 2016-04-08 00:56
/mnist_lenet_iter_5000.caffemodel
-rw-r--r--   3 root supergroup    1724461 2016-04-08 00:56
/mnist_lenet_iter_5000.solverstate
```

5. The feature result file looks as follows:

```
{"SampleID":"00009597","accuracy":[1.0],"loss":
    [0.028171852],"label":  [2.0]}
{"SampleID":"00009598","accuracy":[1.0],"loss":
    [0.028171852],"label":  [6.0]}
{"SampleID":"00009599","accuracy":[1.0],"loss":
    [0.028171852],"label":  [1.0]}
{"SampleID":"00009600","accuracy":[0.97],"loss":
    [0.0677709],"label":  [5.0]}
{"SampleID":"00009601","accuracy":[0.97],"loss":
    [0.0677709],"label":  [0.0]}
{"SampleID":"00009602","accuracy":[0.97],"loss":
    [0.0677709],"label":  [1.0]}
{"SampleID":"00009603","accuracy":[0.97],"loss":
    [0.0677709],"label":  [2.0]}
```

```
{"SampleID":"00009604","accuracy":[0.97],"loss":
   [0.0677709],"label":  [3.0]}
{"SampleID":"00009605","accuracy":[0.97],"loss":
   [0.0677709],"label":  [4.0]}
```

6. Here is the Spark application which uses `CaffeOnSpark` to train a dataset on HDFS and MLlib to perform non-deep learning, that is, logistic regression for classification:

```
val conf = new SparkConf()
.setMaster("spark://master:7077")
.setAppName("Caffe_Spark_Application")
val sc = new SparkContext(conf)
val cos = new CaffeOnSpark(sc)
val config = new Config(sc,args)
val dl_train_source = DataSource.getSource(config, true)
cos.train(dl_train_source)
val lr_raw_source  = DataSource.getSource(config, false)
val extracted_df = cos.features(lr_raw_source)
val lr_input_df = extracted_df.withColumn("Label",
  cos.floatarray2doubleUDF(extracted_df(config.label)))
  .withColumn("Feature",
  cos.floatarray2doublevectorUDF(extracted_df(config.features(0)
  )))

//Learn a LogisticRegression model via Apache MLlib
val lr = new LogisticRegression()
    .setLabelCol("Label")
    .setFeaturesCol("Feature")
val lr_model = lr.fit(lr_input_df)

//save the LogisticRegression classification model onto HDFS
lr_model.write.overwrite().save(config.outputPath)
```

7. The preceding code is submitted to the Spark cluster as follows:

```
spark-submit \   -files
caffenet_train_solver.prototxt,caffenet_train_net.prototxt \   -
num-executors 2 \   -class
com.yahoo.ml.caffe.examples.MyMLPipeline \
caffe-grid-0.1-SNAPSHOT-jar-with-dependencies.jar \
-features fc8 \   -label label \   -conf
caffenet_train_solver.prototxt \   -model
hdfs:///sample_images.model   \   -output
hdfs:///image_classifier_model \   -devices 2
```

How it works...

Initially, `CaffeOnSpark` is used to train the deep learning network with two spark executors and stores the model onto HDFS. It also uses the configuration files for solvers and neural networks as in standard Caffe. The second application uses `CaffeOnSpark` and MLlib. First, the Spark context is initialized and creates `CaffeOnSpark` and a configuration object `caffe.Config`. Next, `CaffeOnSpark` conducts DNN training with the training dataset on HDFS. The learned DL model is applied to extract features from a feature dataset on HDFS. MLlib uses the extracted features to perform non-deep learning. In the preceding example, logistic regression trains the model on extracted features and the classification model is saved onto HDFS.

There's more...

Deep learning (DL) is a critical capability demanded by many Yahoo products. Yahoo's Flickr team applied deep learning for scene detection, object recognition, and computational aesthetics. To benefit from the capabilities of DL on large scale data, it has been introduced into Hadoop clusters. When DL is conducted on Hadoop clusters, unnecessary movement between Hadoop clusters and deep learning clusters is avoided. DL can be made to run on GPU/CPU nodes in Hadoop clusters. When launched using Spark, each executor is given a partition of HDFS-based training data and launches multiple Caffe-based training threads. Each training thread is executed by a particular GPU/CPU.

After back-propagation in processing of a batch of training examples, the training threads exchange the gradients of model parameters. The exchanged gradient is carried out in an MPI Allreduce fashion across all GPUs on multiple servers. Caffe is also enhanced to use multiple GPUs on a server and benefit from RDMA to synchronize DL models.

See also

Please refer to `Chapter 1`, *Big Data Analytics with Spark* to get familiar with Spark. Also, refer to `http://deeplearning.net/tutorial/` and `http://neuralnetworksanddeeplearning.com/` for details on deep learning.

Running a feed-forward neural network with DeepLearning 4j over Spark

DeepLearning4j (**DL4J**) is an open source deep learning library written in Java and Scala and which is used in business environments. This can be easily integrated with GPU and scaled on Hadoop or Spark. It supports a stack of neural networks for image recognition, text analysis and speech to text. Hence, it has implementations for algorithms such as binary and continuous restricted Boltzmann machines, deep belief networks, de-noising auto-encoders, convolutional networks and recursive neural tensor networks.

Getting ready

To step through this recipe, you will need a running Spark cluster either in pseudo distributed mode or in one of the distributed modes, that is, standalone, YARN, or Mesos. Also, get familiar with ND4S, that is, n-dimensional arrays for Scala (Scala bindings for ND4J). ND4J and ND4S are scientific computing libraries for the JVM. Please visit `http://nd4j.org/` for details. The pre-requisites to be installed are Java 7, IntelliJ, and the Maven or SBT build tool.

How to do it...

1. Start an application named `FeedForwardNetworkWithSpark`. Initially, specify the following libraries in the `build.sbt` file as follows:

```
libraryDependencies ++= Seq(
"org.apache.spark" %% "spark-core" % "1.6.0",
"org.apache.spark" %% "spark-mllib" % "1.6.0",
"org.deeplearning4j" % "deeplearning4j-core" % "0.4-rc3.8",
"org.deeplearning4j" % "deeplearning4j-nlp" % "0.4-rc3.8",
"org.deeplearning4j" % "dl4j-spark" % "0.4-rc3.8",
"org.nd4j" % "nd4j-x86" % "0.4-rc3.8",
"org.nd4j" % "nd4j-jcublas-7.0" % "0.4-rc3.8",
"org.nd4j" % "nd4j-api" % "0.4-rc3.8",
"org.nd4j" % "canova-api" % "0.0.0.14"
  )
```

2. Now take the iris dataset, which consists of the measurements of four attributes of 150 iris flowers from three types of irises. The sample iris dataset looks as follows:

```
5.1,3.5,1.4,0.2,Iris-setosa
4.9,3.0,1.4,0.2,Iris-setosa
7.0,3.2,4.7,1.4,Iris-versicolor
6.4,3.2,4.5,1.5,Iris-versicolor
```

3. To have a look at the dataset, please visit the following site: `https://archive.ics.uci.edu/ml/datasets/Iris`. Now the normalized dataset looks as follows:

```
0.194444444,0.625,0.101694915,0.208333333,0
0.444444444,0.416666667,0.694915254,0.708333333,2
0.694444444,0.416666667,0.762711864,0.833333333,2
0.277777778,0.708333333,0.084745763,0.041666667,0
0.083333333,0.583333333,0.06779661,0.083333333,0
0.416666667,0.291666667,0.491525424,0.458333333,1
```

In the preceding sample, the final attribute 0, 1 ,2... represents the label. We can download the normalized iris dataset from the preceding specified location:

4. Here is the code for a feed-forward network which use the normalized iris dataset for classification:

```
import scala.collection.mutable.ListBuffer
import org.apache.spark.SparkConf
import org.apache.spark.SparkContext
import org.canova.api.records.reader.RecordReader
import org.canova.api.records.reader.impl.CSVRecordReader
import org.deeplearning4j.nn.api.OptimizationAlgorithm
import org.deeplearning4j.nn.conf.MultiLayerConfiguration
import org.deeplearning4j.nn.conf.NeuralNetConfiguration
import org.deeplearning4j.nn.conf.layers.DenseLayer
import org.deeplearning4j.nn.conf.layers.OutputLayer
import org.deeplearning4j.nn.multilayer.MultiLayerNetwork
import org.deeplearning4j.nn.weights.WeightInit
import org.deeplearning4j.spark.impl.multilayer.
SparkDl4jMultiLayer
import org.nd4j.linalg.io.ClassPathResource
import org.nd4j.linalg.lossfunctions.LossFunctions
```

```
object FeedForwardNetworkWithSpark {
def main(args:Array[String]): Unit ={
val recordReader:RecordReader = new CSVRecordReader(0,",")
val conf = new SparkConf()
.setMaster("spark://master:7077")
.setAppName("FeedForwardNetwork-Iris")
val sc = new SparkContext(conf)
val numInputs:Int = 4
val outputNum = 3
val iterations =1
val multiLayerConfig:MultiLayerConfiguration = new
  NeuralNetConfiguration.Builder()
  .seed(12345)
  .iterations(iterations)
 .optimizationAlgo(OptimizationAlgorithm
                    .STOCHASTIC_GRADIENT_DESCENT)
  .learningRate(1e-1)
  .l1(0.01).regularization(true).l2(1e-3)
  .list(3)
  .layer(0, new DenseLayer.Builder().nIn(numInputs).nOut(3)
  .activation("tanh")
  .weightInit(WeightInit.XAVIER)
  .build())
  .layer(1, new DenseLayer.Builder().nIn(3).nOut(2)
  .activation("tanh")
  .weightInit(WeightInit.XAVIER)
  .build())
  .layer(2, new
   OutputLayer.Builder(LossFunctions.LossFunction.MCXENT)
    .weightInit(WeightInit.XAVIER)
    .activation("softmax")
    .nIn(2).nOut(outputNum).build())
    .backprop(true).pretrain(false)
    .build
val network:MultiLayerNetwork = new
MultiLayerNetwork(multiLayerConfig)
network.init
network.setUpdater(null)
val sparkNetwork:SparkDl4jMultiLayer = new
SparkDl4jMultiLayer(sc,network)
val nEpochs:Int = 6
val listBuffer = new ListBuffer[Array[Float]]()
(0 until nEpochs).foreach{i =>
val net:MultiLayerNetwork =
sparkNetwork.fit("file:///<path>/
iris_shuffled_normalized_csv.txt",4,recordReader)
listBuffer +=(net.params.data.asFloat().clone())
}
```

```
        println("Parameters vs. iteration Output: ")
        (0 until listBuffer.size).foreach{i =>
        println(i+"\t"+listBuffer(i).mkString)}
    }
}
```

How it works...

The preceding example shows how to use a feed-forward network for classifying the `Iris` dataset. At first, `SparkConf` and `SparkContext` are initialized and then the configuration parameters such as `numInputs`, `outputNum` and `iterations` have been initialized. The `val multiLayerConfig:MultiLayerConfiguration = new NeuralNetConfiguration.Builder()` line runs a builder pattern useful for many parameter objects, on a `NeuralNetConfiguration` (it can create a single layer if needed). The `NeuralNetConfiguration` object can construct many layers and these in turn make a deeper neural network.

The line `.seed(12345)` is used for weight initialization. The line `.iterations(iterations)` specifies the maximum number of iterations the training algorithm will train. The `learningRate(1e-1)` specifies the learning rate, which is the size of the adjustments made to weights with each iteration. A too high or too low learning rate could affect negatively the convergence of the training process. The `.optimizationAlgo(OptimizationAlgorithm.STOCHASTIC_GRADIENT_DESCENT)` line specifies the optimization algorithm as stochastic gradient descent. Next, the regularization parameter is set to `true` and L2 regularization is chosen. The line `.list(3)` specifies the number of neural net layers . We are specifying the layers as `DenseLayer` and the setting `.nIn(numInputs).nOut(3)` sets the number of input nodes as `numInputs` and output nodes as 3 for a layer. The `.activation("tanh")` line sets the activation function to a `tanh` function and the `.weightInit(WeightInit.XAVIER)` line initializes the weights. Also, back-propagation is set to true as `.backprop(true)` and pre-training is set to `false` as `.pretrain(false)`.

The line `.build` builds the configuration settings and this is passed as parameter to the instance of the `MultiLayerNetwork` model. The settings `network.init` and `network.setUpdater(null)` initialize the network and then set the updater to null. Next, `SparkDl4jMultiLayer` is initialized and the `sparkNetwork.fit("file:///home/padma/data/iris_shuffled_normalized_csv.txt",4, recordReader)` line makes the neural network learn on the dataset.

There's more...

In the preceding code, we worked with a feed-forward neural network. Using the `NeuralNetConfiguration` object, we can create a **Convolutional Neural Network (CNN)** as well as **Restricted Boltzmann Machines (RBMs)**. A `NeuralNetConfiguration` object is the fundamental one to construct deeper layers. Datasets are transformed as they are processed by each layer – before and after each layer, they undergo additional pre- or post-processing such as normalization. When initializing the seed, suppose the algorithm is run many times, as new random weights get initialized each time the network's F1 score varies, leading to different local minima of the error scape. When weights are kept the same, the effect of adjusting hyper-parameters is clearly seen.

The `iterations` parameter specifies the number of times the algorithm trains to classify samples with a corrected weight update. An iteration is applicable to an `epoch` (a completed pass through a dataset). Too few iterations might truncate the learning and too many might slow down the learning. When specifying the learning rate, it is essential to initialize the optimal rate, because a high learning rate causes the network to traverse the error scape and it is prone to overshoot the minima, whereas with a lower learning rate, the training doesn't converge. In the case of regularization, L1 and L2 are two ways to avoid over-fitting by decreasing the size of the model's weights.

Also, when initializing weights, `Xavier initialization` keeps weights from becoming too small or too large. Xavier initializes a given neuron's weight by making the variance of that weight equal to one over the number of neurons feeding into it. Apart from training the model, it is also essential to evaluate the model and display statistics such as accuracy and F1 score. F1 score is the metric which determines how well a classifier works. It's between 0 and 1 and explains how well network performed during the training. It is basically the probability that the network guesses are correct.

See also

Please refer to `Chapter 1`, *Big Data Analytics with Spark* to get familiar with Spark. Also, refer to `http://deeplearning.net/tutorial/` and `http://neuralnetworksanddeeplearning.com/` for details on deep learning.

Running an RBM with DeepLearning4j over Spark

In this recipe, we'll see how to run a restricted Boltzmann machine for classifying the iris dataset.

Getting ready

To step through this recipe, you will need a running Spark cluster either in pseudo distributed mode or in one of the distributed modes, that is, standalone, YARN, or Mesos. Also, get familiar with ND4S, that is, n-dimensional arrays for Scala (Scala bindings for ND4J). ND4J and ND4S are scientific computing libraries for the JVM. Please visit http://nd4j.org/ for details. The pre-requisites to be installed are Java 7, IntelliJ, and the Maven or SBT build tool.

How to do it...

1. Start an application named RBMWithSpark. Initially, specify the following libraries in the build.sbt file:

```
libraryDependencies ++= Seq(
"org.apache.spark" %% "spark-core" % "1.6.0",
"org.apache.spark" %% "spark-mllib" % "1.6.0",
"org.deeplearning4j" % "deeplearning4j-core" % "0.4-rc3.8",
"org.deeplearning4j" % "deeplearning4j-nlp" % "0.4-rc3.8",
"org.deeplearning4j" % "dl4j-spark" % "0.4-rc3.8",
"org.nd4j" % "nd4j-x86" % "0.4-rc3.8",
"org.nd4j" % "nd4j-jcublas-7.0" % "0.4-rc3.8",
"org.nd4j" % "nd4j-api" % "0.4-rc3.8",
"org.nd4j" % "canova-api" % "0.0.0.14"
)
```

2. Here is the code for a restricted Boltzmann machine which uses the iris dataset for classification:

```
import org.deeplearning4j.datasets.iterator.impl.
IrisDataSetIterator
import org.deeplearning4j.eval.Evaluation
import org.deeplearning4j.nn.api.{Layer, OptimizationAlgorithm}
import org.deeplearning4j.nn.conf.{Updater,
NeuralNetConfiguration}
```

```scala
import org.deeplearning4j.nn.conf.layers.{OutputLayer, RBM}
import org.deeplearning4j.nn.multilayer.MultiLayerNetwork
import org.deeplearning4j.nn.weights.WeightInit
import org.nd4j.linalg.factory.Nd4j
import org.nd4j.linalg.lossfunctions.LossFunctions

object RBM_IrisDataset {
def main(args: Array[String]) {
Nd4j.MAX_SLICES_TO_PRINT = -1
Nd4j.MAX_ELEMENTS_PER_SLICE = -1
Nd4j.ENFORCE_NUMERICAL_STABILITY = true
val inputNum = 4
var outputNum = 3
var numSamples = 150
var batchSize = 150
var iterations = 1000
var seed = 321
var listenerFreq = iterations / 5
val learningRate = 1e-6
println("Loading data....")
val iter = new IrisDataSetIterator(batchSize, numSamples)
val iris = iter.next()
iris.shuffle()
iris.normalizeZeroMeanZeroUnitVariance()
val testAndTrain = iris.splitTestAndTrain(0.80)
val train = testAndTrain.getTrain
val test = testAndTrain.getTest
println("Building model....")
val RMSE_XENT = LossFunctions.LossFunction.RMSE_XENT
val conf = new NeuralNetConfiguration.Builder()
  .seed(seed)
  .iterations(iterations)
  .learningRate(learningRate)
  .l1(1e-1).regularization(true).l2(2e-4)
  .optimizationAlgo(OptimizationAlgorithm
  .CONJUGATE_GRADIENT)
  .useDropConnect(true)
  .list(2)
  .layer(0, new RBM.Builder(RBM.HiddenUnit.RECTIFIED,
RBM.VisibleUnit.GAUSSIAN)
  .nIn(inputNum).nOut(3).k(1).activation("relu")
  .weightInit(WeightInit.XAVIER).lossFunction(RMSE_XENT)
    .updater(Updater.ADAGRAD).dropOut(0.5)
    .build())
    .layer(1, new OutputLayer.Builder(LossFunctions
        .LossFunction.MCXENT)
    .nIn(3).nOut(outputNum).activation("softmax").build())
    .build()
```

```
val model = new MultiLayerNetwork(conf)
model.init()
println("Train the model....")
model.fit(train.getFeatureMatrix)
println("Evaluating the model....")
val eval = new Evaluation(outputNum)
val output = model.output(test.getFeatureMatrix,
                          Layer.TrainingMode.TEST)
(0 until output.rows()).foreach { i =>
val actual = train.getLabels.getRow(i).toString.trim()
val predicted = output.getRow(i).toString.trim()
println("actual " + actual + " vs predicted " + predicted)
}
eval.eval(test.getLabels, output)
println(eval.stats())
  }
}
```

3. The output looks as follows:

```
Evaluate model....
actual [ 1.00, 0.00, 0.00] vs predicted [ 0.39, 0.32, 0.29]
actual [ 1.00, 0.00, 0.00] vs predicted [ 0.35, 0.34, 0.31]
actual [ 1.00, 0.00, 0.00] vs predicted [ 0.35, 0.34, 0.30]
actual [ 1.00, 0.00, 0.00] vs predicted [ 0.34, 0.34, 0.31]
actual [ 0.00, 0.00, 1.00] vs predicted [ 0.36, 0.35, 0.28]
actual [ 1.00, 0.00, 0.00] vs predicted [ 0.35, 0.34, 0.31]
actual [ 0.00, 1.00, 0.00] vs predicted [ 0.35, 0.35, 0.30]
actual [ 1.00, 0.00, 0.00] vs predicted [ 0.35, 0.34, 0.31]
.
.
.
Examples labeled as 0 classified by model as 0: 5 times
Examples labeled as 1 classified by model as 0: 11 times
Examples labeled as 2 classified by model as 0: 14 times
Warning: class 1 was never predicted by the model. This class
was excluded from the average precision
Warning: class 2 was never predicted by the model. This class
was excluded from the average precision
==========================Scores=================
  Accuracy:  0.1667
  Precision: 0.1667
  Recall:    0.3333
  F1 Score:  0.2222
=================================================
```

How it works...

The Iris flower dataset is widely used in machine learning to test classification techniques. Here, the same is used for testing the effectiveness of a restricted Boltzmann machine. Initially, the configuration parameters such as `inputNum`, `outputNum`, `numSamples`, `batchSize`, `seed` and `iterations` have been initialized. The dataset is available as a CSV file. The `IrisDataSetIterator` is used to traverse the dataset. The `val iris = iter.next()` line assigns each data point to a `DataSet` object with which the neural network trains. Next, the `iris.splitTestAndTrain(0.80)` line splits the dataset into training and testing samples.

The `val conf= new NeuralNetConfiguration.Builder()` line runs a builder pattern useful for many parameter objects, on a `NeuralNetConfiguration` (it can create a single layer if needed). The `NeuralNetConfiguration` object can construct many layers and these in turn make a deeper neural network. Once the `NeuralNetConfiguration` object is created, various configuration parameters such as `seed`, `iterations`, `learningRate`, `regularization` and `optimizationAlgo` are specified. The `.useDropConnect(true)` line ensures that the `DropConnect` is used (a regularization technique which randomly sets to zero a subset of activations within each layer). The `.list(2)` line specifies the number of neural net layers. We are specifying the layers as RBM which is instantiated as new `RBM.Builder(RBM.HiddenUnit.RECTIFIED, RBM.VisibleUnit.GAUSSIAN)` and the setting `.nIn(inputNum).nOut(3)` sets the number of input nodes as `inputNum` and output nodes as 3 for a layer. The `.activation("relu")` line sets the activation function to a rectified linear transform. The `LossFunctions.LossFunction.MCXENT` line sets the loss function.

When all the layers are instantiated, the `.build()` line calls build on the configuration and this instance is passed as a parameter to the `MultiLayerNetwork`. The `model.init` initializes the model. The `model.fit(train.getFeatureMatrix)` line makes the neural network learn by passing the training set. Finally, the model is evaluated and the output displays how well the samples are labeled by each classification. The output also displays the accuracy and F1 score.

There's more...

In the preceding code, we worked with an RBM. Using the `NeuralNetConfiguration` object, we can create a CNN as well. A `NeuralNetConfiguration` object is the fundamental one to construct deeper layers. The `DataSetIterator` fetches one or more examples with each iteration and loads these examples into a `DataSet` object. The `DataSetIterator` takes two parameters – `batchSize` (specifies the number of examples to be fetched with each step) and `numSamples` (the total number of input data examples). After the `DataSet` is created, it is normalized to another scale, which is likely known as feature-scaling. The neural net learns on the training set and it verifies the guessed labels against the ground truth of the test set. When initializing the seed, suppose the algorithm is run many times, as new random weights get initialized each time the network's F1 score varies leading to different local minima of the error scape. When the weights are kept the same, the effect of adjusting hyper-parameters is clearly seen.

The `iterations` parameter specifies the number of times the algorithm trains to classify samples with a corrected weight update. An iteration is applicable to an epoch (a completed pass through a dataset). Too few iterations might truncate the learning and too many might slow down the learning rate. When specifying the learning rate, it is essential to initialize the optimal rate, because a high learning rate causes the network to traverse the errorscape and is prone to overshoot the minima, whereas a lower learning rate doesn't converge. In the case of regularization, L1 and L2 are two ways to avoid over-fitting by decreasing the size of the model's weights.

Also, DropConnect allows a neural network to generalize from training data by randomly cancelling out the interlayer edges between nodes. The layer is an RBM which is a shallow, building-block layer that is stacked to become a deep belief network. A Gaussian transform is applied and the Gaussian white noise is applied to normalize a distribution of continuous data. The **Rectified Linear Unit** (**ReLU**) creates more robust activations and this also improves the F1 score. ReLU applies fixed offset to the bias of each node. Apart from training the it is also essential to evaluate the model and display statistics such as accuracy and F1 score. F1 score is the metric which determines how well a classifier works. It's between 0 and 1 and explains how well the network performed during the training. It is basically the probability that the network guesses are correct.

See also

Please refer to `Chapter 1`, *Big Data Analytics with Spark* to get familiar with Spark. Also, refer to `http://deeplearning.net/tutorial/` and `http://neuralnetworksanddeeplearning.com/` for details on deep learning.

Running a CNN for learning MNIST with DeepLearning4j over Spark

In this recipe, we'll see how to run a CNN for classifying the iris dataset.

Getting ready

To step through this recipe, you will need a running Spark cluster either in pseudo distributed mode or in one of the distributed modes, that is, standalone, YARN, or Mesos. Also, get familiar with ND4S, that is, n-dimensional arrays for Scala (Scala bindings for ND4J). ND4J and ND4S are scientific computing libraries for the JVM. Please visit `http://nd4j.org/` for details. The prerequisites to be installed are Java 7, IntelliJ, and the Maven or SBT build tool.

How to do it...

1. The MNIST database is a large set of handwritten digits used to train neural networks and other algorithms in image recognition. This dataset has 60,000 images in its training set and 10,000 in its test set. Each image is a 28X28 pixel.

2. Here is the code for a convolutional neural network which uses the MNIST dataset for digit recognition:

```
object CNN_MNIST {

  def main(args:Array[String]): Unit ={
    val nCores =2
    val conf = new SparkConf()
    .setMaster("spark://master:7077")
    .setAppName("MNIST_CNN")
    .set(SparkDl4jMultiLayer.AVERAGE_EACH_ITERATION,
    String.valueOf(true))
    val sc = new SparkContext(conf)
```

```
val nChannels = 1
val outputNum = 10
val numSamples = 60000
val nTrain = 50000
val nTest = 10000
val batchSize = 64
val iterations = 1
val seed = 123
val mnistIter = new MnistDataSetIterator(1,numSamples, true)
val allData = new ListBuffer[DataSet]()
while(mnistIter.hasNext) allData.+=(mnistIter.next)
new Random(12345).shuffle(allData)
  val iter = allData.iterator
  var c =0
  val train = new ListBuffer[DataSet]()
  val test = new ListBuffer[DataSet]()
while(iter.hasNext) {
  if(c <= nTrain) {
    train.+=(iter.next)
    c +=1
  }
  else test.+=(iter.next)
}
val sparkDataTrain = sc.parallelize(train)
sparkDataTrain.persist(StorageLevel.MEMORY_ONLY)
println("Building model ....")
val builder = new NeuralNetConfiguration.Builder()
.seed(seed)
.iterations(iterations)
.regularization(true).l2(0.0005)
.learningRate(0.01)
.optimizationAlgo(OptimizationAlgorithm
.STOCHASTIC_GRADIENT_DESCENT)
.updater(Updater.ADAGRAD)
.list(6)
.layer(0, new ConvolutionLayer.Builder(5, 5)
.nIn(nChannels)
.stride(1, 1)
.nOut(20)
.weightInit(WeightInit.XAVIER)
.activation("relu")
.build())
.layer(1, new SubsamplingLayer.Builder(SubsamplingLayer
.PoolingType.MAX, Array(2, 2))
.build())
.layer(2, new ConvolutionLayer.Builder(5, 5)
.nIn(20)
.nOut(50)
```

```
.stride(2,2)
.weightInit(WeightInit.XAVIER)
.activation("relu")
.build())
.layer(3, new
SubsamplingLayer.Builder(SubsamplingLayer.PoolingType.MAX,
Array(2, 2))
.build())
.layer(4, new DenseLayer.Builder().activation("relu")
.weightInit(WeightInit.XAVIER)
.nOut(200).build())
.layer(5, new OutputLayer.Builder
(LossFunctions.LossFunction.NEGATIVELOGLIKELIHOOD)
.nOut(outputNum)
.weightInit(WeightInit.XAVIER)
.activation("softmax")
.build())
.backprop(true).pretrain(false);
new ConvolutionLayerSetup(builder,28,28,1);
val multiLayerConf:MultiLayerConfiguration= builder.build()
val net:MultiLayerNetwork = new
MultiLayerNetwork(multiLayerConf)
net.init()
net.setUpdater(null)
val sparkNetwork = new SparkDl4jMultiLayer(sc, net)
val nEpochs = 5
(0 until nEpochs).foreach{i =>
val network = sparkNetwork.fitDataSet(sparkDataTrain,
nCores*batchSize)
//Evaluate the model
val eval = new Evaluation()
for(ds <- test)
    {
  val output = network.output(ds.getFeatureMatrix)
        eval.eval(ds.getLabels, output)
        }
    println("Statistics..."+eval.stats())
  }
 }
}
```

How it works...

The preceding code shows how to use a convolutional neural network for recognizing the handwritten digits in the MNIST dataset. Initially, the configuration parameters such as `nChannels`, `outputNum`, `numSamples`, `nTrain`, `nTest`, `batchSize`, `seed` and `iterations` have been initialized. The `MnistDataSetIterator` initializes the MNIST dataset and this dataset is split into training and testing sets.

The `val builder= new NeuralNetConfiguration.Builder()` line runs a builder pattern useful for many parameter objects, on a `NeuralNetConfiguration` (it can create a single layer if needed). The `NeuralNetConfiguration` object can construct many layers and these in turn make a deeper neural network. Once the `NeuralNetConfiguration` object is created, various configuration parameters such as `seed`, `iterations`, `learningRate`, `regularization` and `optimizationAlgo` are specified.

We are have specified six layers, in which the input layer is `ConvolutionalLayer`, initialized as `-new ConvolutionLayer.Builder(5, 5)`, three hidden layers are initialized as sub-sampling layers `new SubsamplingLayer.Builder(SubsamplingLayer.PoolingType.MAX, Array(2, 2),` and a 4th layer is initialized as `new DenseLayer.Builder().activation("relu"))`. The output layer is initialized as new `OutputLayer.Builder(LossFunctions.LossFunction.NEGATIVELOGLIKELIHOOD)`.

The setting `.nIn(20).nOut(50)` sets the number of input nodes as 20 and output nodes as 50 for a layer. The line `.activation("relu")` sets the activation function to a rectified linear transform. The `LossFunctions.LossFuncti.NEGATIVELOGLIKELIHOOD` line sets the loss function. The `.weightInit(WeightInit.XAVIER)` line initializes the weights. For the output layer, the activation function is softmax. Also, backpropagation-propogation is set to `true` as `.backprop(true)` and pre-training is set to `false` as `.pretrain(false)`.

The `.build` line builds the configuration settings and this is passed as parameter to the instance of `MultiLayerNetwork` model. The settings `network.init` and `network.setUpdater(null)` initialize the network and then set the updater to null. Next, `SparkDl4jMultiLayer` is initialized and the line `sparkNetwork.fitDataSet(sparkDataTrain,nCores*batchSize)` makes the neural network learn on the dataset. Finally, the model is evaluated and the output displays how well the samples are labeled by each classification. The output displays the statistics.

There's more...

Using the `NeuralNetConfiguration` object, we created a CNN (convolutional neural network). A `NeuralNetConfiguration` object is the fundamental one to construct deeper layers. Convolutional networks perform object recognition with images. They can identify faces, individuals, street signs, and many other aspects of visual data. These networks overlap with character recognition; they are also useful when analyzing words as discrete textual units.

The efficiency of convolutional nets `ConvNets` in image recognition is one of the main reasons why the world has up to deep learning. They are powering major advances in machine vision, which has obvious applications for self-driving cars, robotics, drones, and treatments for the visually impaired. Convolutional nets ingest and process images as tensors and tensors are matrices of numbers with additional dimensions. Tensors are formed by arrays nested within arrays, and that nesting can go on infinitely, accounting for an arbitrary number of dimensions far greater than what we can visualize spatially.

Convolutional networks perceive images as volumes, that is, three-dimensional objects, rather than flat canvases to be measured only by width and height. That's because digital color images have a **red-blue-green** (**RGB**) encoding, mixing those three colors to produce the color spectrum humans perceive. A convolutional network ingests such images as three separate strata of color stacked one on top of the other. To know more about convolutional neural networks, please visit `http://ufldl.stanford.edu/tutorial/supervised/ConvolutionalNeuralNetwork/` and `http://deeplearning.net/tutorial/lenet.html`.

See also

Please refer to `Chapter 1`, *Big Data Analytics with Spark* to get familiar with Spark. Also, refer to `http://deeplearning.net/tutorial/` and `http://neuralnetworksanddeeplearning.com/` for details on deep learning.

Installing TensorFlow

TensorFlow is an interface for expressing machine learning algorithms, and it's an implementation for executing such algorithms. The TensorFlow computation can be expressed with little or no change on a wide variety of heterogeneous systems, such as mobile phones, tablets, and large-scale distributed systems of hundreds of machines. It is flexible and can express a wide variety of algorithms, such as training and inference algorithms for deep neural network models. It is also used for deploying machine learning systems into production across many areas, such as speech recognition, computer vision, robotics, information retrieval, natural language processing, geographic information extraction, and so on.

The application of tensors and their networks is a relatively new (but fast-evolving) approach in machine learning. Tensors, if you recall your algebra classes, are simply n-dimensional data arrays (so a scalar is a 0th order tensor, a vector is 1st order, and a matrix 2nd order). A simple practical example of this is a color image's RGB layers (essentially three 2D matrices combined into a 3rd order tensor). Or a more business-minded example – if your data source generates a table (a 2D array) every hour, you can look at the full dataset as a 3rd order tensor–time being the extra dimension.

Getting ready

To step through this recipe, you will need a running Spark Cluster either in pseudo distributed mode or in one of the distributed modes, that is, standalone, YARN, or Mesos.

Python comes pre-installed. `python --version` gives the version of the Python installed. If the version seems to be 2.6.x, upgrade it to Python 2.7 as follows:

```
sudo apt-get install python2.7
```

How to do it...

1. Install pip as follows:

```
sudo apt-get install python-pip python-dev
```

2. Install TensorFlow as follows:

```
sudo pip install --upgrade
https://storage.googleapis.com/tensorflow/linux/cpu/tensorflow-
0.8.0rc0-cp27-none-linux_x86_64.whl
Downloading/unpacking
https://storage.googleapis.com/tensorflow/linux/cpu/tensorflow-
0.8.0rc0-cp27-none-linux_x86_64.whl
Downloading tensorflow-0.8.0rc0-cp27-none-linux_x86_64.whl
(22.2MB): 22.2MB downloaded
Requirement already up-to-date: protobuf==3.0.0b2 in
/usr/local/lib/python2.7/dist-packages (from
tensorflow==0.8.0rc0)
Requirement already up-to-date: wheel in
/usr/local/lib/python2.7/dist-packages (from
tensorflow==0.8.0rc0)
Requirement already up-to-date: numpy>=1.8.2 in
/usr/local/lib/python2.7/dist-packages (from
tensorflow==0.8.0rc0)
Requirement already up-to-date: six>=1.10.0 in
/usr/local/lib/python2.7/dist-packages (from
tensorflow==0.8.0rc0)
Installing collected packages: tensorflow
Successfully installed tensorflow
Cleaning up...
```

3. Once TensorFlow is installed, try the following code from the command line to ensure that it is working:

```
python
Python 2.7.6 (default, Mar 22 2014, 22:59:56)
[GCC 4.8.2] on linux2
Type "help", "copyright", "credits" or "license" for more
information.
>>> import tensorflow as tf
>>> hello = tf.constant('Hello, TensorFlow!')
>>> sess = tf.Session()
>>> print(sess.run(hello))
Hello, TensorFlow!
>>> a = tf.constant(10)
>>> b = tf.constant(32)
```

```
>>> print(sess.run(a + b))
42
```

4. The TensorFlow package will be available at the following location:
   `/usr/local/lib/python2.7/dist-packages/tensorflow`

5. Now, from the preceding location, run the model for classifying handwritten digits from the MNIST dataset available in the sub-directory `models/image/mnist/convolutional.py` as follows:

```
$ cd models/image/mnist
/<TensorFlow_Package_Path>/models/image/mnist$ python
convolutional.py
Extracting data/train-images-idx3-ubyte.gz
Extracting data/train-labels-idx1-ubyte.gz
Extracting data/t10k-images-idx3-ubyte.gz
Extracting data/t10k-labels-idx1-ubyte.gz
Initialized!
Step 0 (epoch 0.00), 4.4 ms
Minibatch loss: 12.054, learning rate: 0.010000
Minibatch error: 90.6%
Validation error: 84.6%
Step 100 (epoch 0.12), 401.4 ms
Minibatch loss: 3.289, learning rate: 0.010000
Minibatch error: 6.2%
Validation error: 7.0%
Step 200 (epoch 0.23), 404.5 ms
```

How it works...

Initially, the installation commands install the pip and TensorFlow packages. The basic TensorFlow program initializes a string constant as `tf.constant('Hello, TensorFlow!')`. The `sess = tf.Session()` line creates the TensoFlow session and then `print(sess.run(hello))` starts the TensorFlow session and displays the constant string message. Then, for other constants a and b, the sum is calculated and the result is displayed.

Next, the TensorFlow demo model runs the simple convolutional neural network which makes the network learn the MNIST data. It achieves a validation error of 7.0%.

There's more...

TensorFlow is the dataflow graph representing computations. Nodes represent operations and the edges represent tensors (multi-dimensional arrays, the backbone of TensorFlow). The entire dataflow graph is a complete description of computations which occur within a session, and are executed on devices such as CPUs or GPUs. TensorFlow supports the Python API where tensors are represented as NumPy `ndarray` objects. It also has support for C++ API.

Graphs are constructed from nodes that don't require input which then pass their output to further operations, which in turn performing computations on these output tensors. These operations are performed asynchronously and optionally in parallel.

For more details, please visit: `https://www.tensorflow.org/`.

See also

Please refer to `Chapter 1`, *Big Data Analytics with Spark* to get familiar with Spark. Also, refer to `http://deeplearning.net/tutorial/` and `http://neuralnetworksanddeeplearning.com/` for details on deep learning.

Working with Spark TensorFlow

As Spark offers distributed computation, it can be used to perform neural network training on large data and the model deployment could be done at scale. The distributed training cuts down the training time, improves accuracy and also speeds up the model validation over a single-node model validation. The ability to scale model selection and neural network tuning by adopting tools such as Spark and TensorFlow may be a boon for the data science and machine learning communities because of the increasing availability of cloud computing and parallel resources to a wider range of engineers.

Getting ready

To step through this recipe, you will need a running Spark cluster either in pseudo distributed mode or in one of the distributed modes, that is, standalone, YARN, or Mesos. Also, have *Installing TensorFlow* recipe for details on the installation.

How to do it...

1. Here is the Python code to run TensorFlow in distributed mode:

```python
import numpy as np
import tensorflow as tf
import os
from tensorflow.python.platform import gfile
import os.path
import re
import sys
import tarfile
from subprocess import Popen, PIPE, STDOUT
from pyspark import SparkContext
def run(cmd):
p = Popen(cmd, shell=True, stdin=PIPE, stdout=PIPE,
    stderr=STDOUT, close_fds=True)
return p.stdout.read()
model_dir = '/tmp/imagenet'
image_file = ""
num_top_predictions = 5
DATA_URL =
'http://download.tensorflow.org/models/image/imagenet/inception-
2015-12-05.tgz'
IMAGES_INDEX_URL = 'http://image-
net.org/imagenet_data/urls/imagenet_fall11_urls.tgz'
```

2. The number of images to process is as follows:

```python
image_batch_size = 3
max_content = 1000L
sc = SparkContext("local", "Distributed_tensorFlow")
def read_file_index():
from six.moves import urllib
content = urllib.request.urlopen(IMAGES_INDEX_URL)
data = content.read(max_content)
tmpfile = "/tmp/imagenet.tgz"
with open(tmpfile, 'wb') as f:
f.write(data)
run("tar -xOzf %s > /tmp/imagenet.txt" % tmpfile)
with open("/tmp/imagenet.txt", 'r') as f:
lines = [l.split() for l in f]
input_data = [tuple(elts) for elts in lines if len(elts) == 2]
return [input_data[i:i+image_batch_size] for i in
range(0,len(input_data),
image_batch_size)]
class NodeLookup(object):
```

```
def __init__(self,
             label_lookup_path=None,
             uid_lookup_path=None):
    if not label_lookup_path:
     label_lookup_path = os.path.join(
        model_dir, 'imagenet_2012_challenge_label_map_proto.pbtxt')
    if not uid_lookup_path:
    uid_lookup_path = os.path.join(
         model_dir, 'imagenet_synset_to_human_label_map.txt')
    self.node_lookup = self.load(label_lookup_path,
                       uid_lookup_path)

def load(self, label_lookup_path, uid_lookup_path):
    if not gfile.Exists(uid_lookup_path):
      tf.logging.fatal('File does not exist %s', uid_lookup_path)
    if not gfile.Exists(label_lookup_path):
      tf.logging.fatal('File does not exist %s', label_lookup_path)
```

3. Loads mapping from string UID to human-readable string:

```
proto_as_ascii_lines = gfile.GFile(uid_lookup_path).readlines()
    uid_to_human = {}
    p = re.compile(r'[n\d]*[ \S,]*')
    for line in proto_as_ascii_lines:
    parsed_items = p.findall(line)
    uid = parsed_items[0]
    human_string = parsed_items[2]
    uid_to_human[uid] = human_string
```

4. Loads mapping from string UID to integer node ID:

```
node_id_to_uid = {}
proto_as_ascii = gfile.GFile(label_lookup_path).readlines()
for line in proto_as_ascii:
  if line.startswith('  target_class:'):
    target_class = int(line.split(': ')[1])
  if line.startswith('  target_class_string:'):
    target_class_string = line.split(': ')[1]
node_id_to_uid[target_class] = target_class_string[1:-2]
```

5. Loads the final mapping of integer node ID to human-readable string:

```
node_id_to_name = {}
    for key, val in node_id_to_uid.items():
      if val not in uid_to_human:
      tf.logging.fatal('Failed to locate: %s', val)
      name = uid_to_human[val]
      node_id_to_name[key] = name
```

```
    return node_id_to_name
def id_to_string(self, node_id):
if node_id not in self.node_lookup:
  return ''
return self.node_lookup[node_id]
def create_graph():
with gfile.FastGFile(os.path.join(
  model_dir, 'classify_image_graph_def.pb'), 'rb') as f:
graph_def = tf.GraphDef()
graph_def.ParseFromString(f.read())
_ = tf.import_graph_def(graph_def, name='')
def run_inference_on_image(image):
if not gfile.Exists(image):
tf.logging.fatal('File does not exist %s', image)
image_data = gfile.FastGFile(image, 'rb').read()
create_graph()
with tf.Session() as sess:
softmax_tensor = sess.graph.get_tensor_by_name('softmax:0')
predictions = sess.run(softmax_tensor,
                      {'DecodeJpeg/contents:0': image_data})
predictions = np.squeeze(predictions)
```

6. Creates `node ID --> English` string lookup:

```
node_lookup = NodeLookup()
top_k = predictions.argsort()[-num_top_predictions:][::-1]
for node_id in top_k:
  human_string = node_lookup.id_to_string(node_id)
  score = predictions[node_id]
  print('%s (score = %.5f)' % (human_string, score))
  def maybe_download_and_extract():
  from six.moves import urllib
  dest_directory = model_dir
  if not os.path.exists(dest_directory):
    os.makedirs(dest_directory)
  filename = DATA_URL.split('/')[-1]
  filepath = os.path.join(dest_directory, filename)
  if not os.path.exists(filepath):
    filepath2, _ = urllib.request.urlretrieve(DATA_URL, filepath)
    print("filepath2", filepath2)
    statinfo = os.stat(filepath)
    print('Succesfully downloaded', filename, statinfo.st_size,
          'bytes.')
    tarfile.open(filepath, 'r:gz').extractall(dest_directory)
    else:
     print('Data already downloaded:', filepath,
     os.stat(filepath))
maybe_download_and_extract()
```

```
batched_data = read_file_index()
label_lookup_path = os.path.join(model_dir,
  'imagenet_2012_challenge_label_map_proto.pbtxt')
uid_lookup_path = os.path.join(model_dir,
 'imagenet_synset_to_human_label_map.txt')
def load_lookup():
if not gfile.Exists(uid_lookup_path):
    tf.logging.fatal('File does not exist %s', uid_lookup_path)
if not gfile.Exists(label_lookup_path):
    tf.logging.fatal('File does not exist %s', label_lookup_path)
```

7. The following code loads mapping from string UID to human-readable string:

```
proto_as_ascii_lines = gfile.GFile(uid_lookup_path).readlines()
uid_to_human = {}
p = re.compile(r'[n\d]*[ \S,]*')
for line in proto_as_ascii_lines:
  parsed_items = p.findall(line)
  uid = parsed_items[0]
  human_string = parsed_items[2]
  uid_to_human[uid] = human_string
```

8. The following code loads mapping from string UID to integer node ID:

```
node_id_to_uid = {}
proto_as_ascii = gfile.GFile(label_lookup_path).readlines()
for line in proto_as_ascii:
  if line.startswith('  target_class:'):
    target_class = int(line.split(': ')[1])
  if line.startswith('  target_class_string:'):
    target_class_string = line.split(': ')[1]
  node_id_to_uid[target_class] = target_class_string[1:-2]
```

9. The following code loads the final mapping of integer node ID to human-readable string:

```
node_id_to_name = {}
for key, val in node_id_to_uid.items():
  if val not in uid_to_human:
    tf.logging.fatal('Failed to locate: %s', val)
  name = uid_to_human[val]
  node_id_to_name[key] = name
return node_id_to_name
node_lookup = load_lookup()
node_lookup_bc = sc.broadcast(node_lookup)
model_path = os.path.join(model_dir,
'classify_image_graph_def.pb')
with gfile.FastGFile(model_path, 'rb') as f:
```

```
model_data = f.read()
model_data_bc = sc.broadcast(model_data)
def run_image(sess, img_id, img_url, node_lookup):
from six.moves import urllib
from urllib2 import HTTPError
try:
  image_data = urllib.request.urlopen(img_url,
              timeout=1.0).read()
  except HTTPError:
  return (img_id, img_url, None)
  except:
  return (img_id, img_url, None)
  scores = []
  softmax_tensor = sess.graph.get_tensor_by_name('softmax:0')
  predictions = sess.run(softmax_tensor,
                    {'DecodeJpeg/contents:0': image_data})
  predictions = np.squeeze(predictions)
  top_k = predictions.argsort()[-num_top_predictions:][::-1]
  scores = []
  for node_id in top_k:
  if node_id not in node_lookup:
    human_string = ''
  else:
    human_string = node_lookup[node_id]
  score = predictions[node_id]
  scores.append((human_string, score))
  return (img_id, img_url, scores)
  def apply_batch(batch):
  with tf.Graph().as_default() as g:
  graph_def = tf.GraphDef()
  graph_def.ParseFromString(model_data_bc.value)
  tf.import_graph_def(graph_def, name='')
  with tf.Session() as sess:
    labelled = [run_image(sess, img_id, img_url,
        node_lookup_bc.value) for (img_id, img_url) in batch]
    return [tup for tup in labelled if tup[2] is not None]
urls = sc.parallelize(batched_data)
labelled_images = urls.flatMap(apply_batch)
local_labelled_images = labelled_images.collect()
local_labelled_images
```

How it works...

The constants `model_dir`, `image_file`, `num_top_predictions`, `DATA_URL` and `IMAGES_INDEX_URL` are initialized before start of the program. The `read_file_index` function reads the images, writes them to a temporary file, and returns the images and image batch size. The `NodeLookup` class contains related methods which convert integer node IDs to human-readable labels. The `__init__` method initializes the `label_lookup_path` from `model_dir` and also initializes `uid_lookup_path`. The `load` method loads a human-readable English name for each softmax node. The `create_graph` method creates a graph from the saved `GraphDef` file and returns it. The `run_inference_on_image` method loads the image from file and creates a graph out of it by invoking the `create_graph` method and runs the softmax tensor by feeding the `image_data` as input to the graph. The `maybe_download_and_extract` method downloads and extracts the modelTAR file.

The model is first distributed to the workers of the clusters, using Spark's built-in broadcasting mechanism, as `model_data_bc =sc.broadcast(model_data)`. The model is loaded on each node and applied to images by invoking the `apply_batch(image_url)` method. The `labelled_images = urls.flatMap(apply_batch)` line applies the model to each image. Finally, the outcome is returned to the driver using `labelled_images.collect()`.

There's more...

Spark is excellent for iterated MapReduce problems, but training neural networks is something different from the MapReduce paradigm. In the `Spark_TensorFlow` architecture, downpourSGD is a data-parallel setup, which means each worker has the entire model and is operating on data different from the other workers (data-parallel) instead of having different parts of the model on different machines (model-parallelism). The gradient descent method is taken and is split into two *Compute Gradient* followed by *Apply Gradients (Descent)* and insert a network boundary between them.

The Spark workers are computing gradients asynchronously, periodically sending their gradients back to the driver (parameter server), which combines all the worker's gradients and sends the resulting parameters back to the workers as the workers ask for them. The current implementation of Spark-TensorFlow is best for large datasets and small models, since the model size is linearly related to network overhead. Future work will involve model parallelism and model compression to improve performance.

See also

Please refer to `Chapter 1`, *Big Data Analytics with Spark* to get familiar with Spark. Also, refer to `http://deeplearning.net/tutorial/` and `http://neuralnetworksanddeeplearning.com/` for details on deep learning.

10
Working with SparkR

In this chapter, we'll cover the following recipes:

- Introduction
- Installing R
- Interactive analysis with the SparkR shell
- Creating a SparkR standalone application from RStudio
- Creating SparkR DataFrames
- SparkR DataFrame operations
- Applying user-defined functions in SparkR
- Running SQL queries from SparkR and caching DataFrames
- Machine learning with SparkR

Introduction

R is a flexible, open source, and powerful statistical programming language. It is preferred by many professional statisticians and researchers in a variety of fields. It has extensive statistical and graphical capabilities. R combines the aspects of functional and object-oriented programming. One of the key features of R is implicit looping, which yields compact, simple code and frequently leads to faster execution. It provides a command-line interpreted statistical computing environment with built-in scripting language.

R is an integrated suite of software facilities for data manipulation, calculation, and graphical display. Its key strengths are effective data handling and storage facility, and a collection of tools for data analysis. It provides a number of extensions that support data processing and machine learning tasks. However, interactive analysis in R is limited as the runtime is single-threaded and can only process datasets that fit in a single machine's memory.

The SparkR project was started in the AMPLab as an effort to explore different techniques to integrate the usability of R with the scalability of Spark. Based on these efforts, the first developer preview was open sourced in January 2014. The project was then developed in the AMPLab for the next year and many performance and usability improvements were made through open source contributions. It is an R package that offers flexibility to use Apache Spark from R. From 1.6.0, SparkR provides distributed DataFrames and the related operations on large datasets and it also supports distributed machine learning using MLlib.

Installing R

In this recipe, we will see how to install R on Linux.

Getting ready...

To step through this recipe, you need Ubuntu 14.04 (Linux flavor) installed on the machine.

How to do it...

Here are the steps in the installation of R:

1. The **Comprehensive R Archive Network** (**CRAN**) contains precompiled binary distributions of the base system and contributed packages. It also contains source code for all the platforms. Add the security key as follows:

   ```
   sudo apt-key adv --keyserver
   keyserver.ubuntu.com --recv-keys
   E084DAB9
   ```

2. Add the CRAN repository to the end of `/etc/apt/sources.list`:

   ```
   deb https://cran.cnr.berkeley.edu/bin/linux/ubuntu trusty/
   ```

3. Install R as follows:

   ```
   sudo apt-get update
   sudo apt-get install r-base r-base-dev
   ```

This will install R and the recommended packages, and additional packages can be installed using `install.packages("<package>")`. The packages on CRAN are updated on a regular basis and the most recent versions will usually be available within a couple of days of their release. The advantage of using the CRAN repository is that older versions of packages are available.

How it works...

The preceding commands install the R package. If the installation fails with unmet dependencies, install the required dependencies. The instructions for installing R in Debian are similar to Ubuntu. Append the CRAN repository to the Debian list to update the available R version as follows:

```
sudo sh -c 'echo "deb
http://cran.rstudio.com/bin/linux/debianlenny-cran/"
>> /etc/apt/sources.list
```

There's more...

In order to get R running on RHEL 6, we'll need to add an additional repository that allows us to install the new package EPEL. This is done as follows: `su -c 'rpm -Uvh http://download.fedoraproject.org/pub/epel/5/i386/epel-release-5.4.noarch.rpm'` and `sudo yum install R`. Search for additional R packages in the terminal as follows: `yum list R-\*`. We can also install Rstudio on Fedora/RHEL/CentOS as follows: `sudo yum install http://download1.rstudio.org/rstudio-0.97.320-x86_64.rpm`. If installation through the terminal fails, download the package from the Rstudio website. Open the file in the Ubuntu software center. Click **Install** and it will be done.

See also

Please refer to `Chapter 2`, *Tricky Statistics with Spark* and `Chapter 6`, *NLP with Spark* to learn how to work with Pandas and about using NLTK, OpenNLP on the Spark framework. Similarly, refer to `Chapter 1`, *Big Data Analytics with Spark* to get familiar with Spark.

Interactive analysis with the SparkR shell

The entry point into SparkR is the SparkContext which connects the R program to a Spark Cluster. When working with the SparkR shell, SQLContext and SparkContext are already available. SparkR's shell provides a simple way to learn the API, as well as a powerful tool to analyze data interactively.

Getting ready

To step through this recipe, you will need a running Spark Cluster either in pseudo distributed mode or in one of the distributed modes, that is, standalone, YARN, or Mesos.

How to do it...

In this recipe, we'll see how to start SparkR interactive shell using Spark 1.6.0:

1. Start the SparkR shell by running the following in the SparkR package directory:

```
/bigdata/spark-1.6.0-bin-hadoop2.6$ ./bin/sparkR --master
spark://192.168.0.118:7077
R version 3.2.3 (2015-12-10) -- "Wooden Christmas-Tree"
Copyright (C) 2015 The R Foundation for Statistical Computing
Platform: x86_64-pc-linux-gnu (64-bit)
R is free software and comes with ABSOLUTELY NO WARRANTY.
You are welcome to redistribute it under certain conditions.
Type 'license()' or 'licence()' for distribution details.
Natural language support but running in an English locale
R is a collaborative project with many contributors.
Type 'contributors()' for more information and
'citation()' on how to cite R or R packages in publications.
Type 'demo()' for some demos, 'help()' for on-line help, or
'help.start()' for an HTML browser interface to help.
Type 'q()' to quit R.
Launching java with spark-submit command
/home/padmac/bigdata/spark-1.6.0-bin-hadoop2.6/bin/spark-submit
```

```
"sparkr-shell" /tmp/RtmpKBOXGW/backend_port125f6707fc13
16/03/18 10:04:40 INFO spark.SparkContext: Running Spark version
1.6.0
16/03/18 10:04:40 WARN util.NativeCodeLoader: Unable to load
native-hadoop library for your platform... using builtin-java
classes where applicable
16/03/18 10:04:41 INFO spark.SecurityManager: Changing view acls
to: padmac
16/03/18 10:04:41 INFO spark.SecurityManager: Changing modify
acls to: padmac
16/03/18 10:04:41 INFO spark.SecurityManager: SecurityManager:
authentication disabled; ui acls disabled; users with view
permissions: Set(padmac); users with modify permissions:
Set(padmac)
16/03/18 10:04:41 INFO util.Utils: Successfully started service
'sparkDriver' on port 54515.
16/03/18 10:04:42 INFO slf4j.Slf4jLogger: Slf4jLogger started
16/03/18 10:04:42 INFO Remoting: Starting remoting
16/03/18 10:04:42 INFO Remoting: Remoting started; listening on
addresses [akka.tcp://sparkDriverActorSystem@172.16.171.91:48197]
16/03/18 10:04:42 INFO util.Utils: Successfully started service
'sparkDriverActorSystem' on port 48197.
16/03/18 10:04:42 INFO spark.SparkEnv: Registering
MapOutputTracker
16/03/18 10:04:42 INFO spark.SparkEnv: Registering
BlockManagerMaster
16/03/18 10:04:42 INFO storage.DiskBlockManager: Created local
directory at /tmp/blockmgr-f178c98f-125f-4607-8748-a80e5d1e5a08
16/03/18 10:04:42 INFO storage.MemoryStore: MemoryStore started
with capacity 511.5 MB
16/03/18 10:04:42 INFO spark.SparkEnv: Registering
OutputCommitCoordinator
16/03/18 10:04:42 INFO server.Server: jetty-8.y.z-SNAPSHOT
16/03/18 10:04:42 INFO server.AbstractConnector: Started
SelectChannelConnector@0.0.0.0:4040
16/03/18 10:04:42 INFO util.Utils: Successfully started service
'SparkUI' on port 4040.
16/03/18 10:04:42 INFO ui.SparkUI: Started SparkUI at
http://172.16.171.91:4040
16/03/18 10:04:43 INFO executor.Executor: Starting executor ID
driver on host localhost
16/03/18 10:04:43 INFO util.Utils: Successfully started service
'org.apache.spark.network.netty.NettyBlockTransferService' on port
36055.
16/03/18 10:04:43 INFO netty.NettyBlockTransferService: Server
created on 36055
16/03/18 10:04:43 INFO storage.BlockManagerMaster: Trying to
register BlockManager
```

```
16/03/18 10:04:43 INFO storage.BlockManagerMasterEndpoint:
Registering block manager localhost:36055 with 511.5 MB RAM,
BlockManagerId(driver, localhost, 36055)
16/03/18 10:04:43 INFO storage.BlockManagerMaster: Registered
BlockManager
Welcome to
```

```
      ____              __
     / __/__  ___ _____/ /__
    _\ \/ _ \/ _ `/ __/  '_/
   /__ / .__/\_,_/_/ /_/\_\   version 1.6.0
      /_/
```

Spark context is available as sc, SQL context is available as sqlContext

2. Spark's primary abstraction is a distributed collection of items called a **Resilient Distributed Dataset** (**RDD**). Let's make a new RDD from the text of the readme file in the SparkR-pkg source directory as follows:

```
> textfile = SparkR:::textFile(sc, "~/<path to spark>/spark-
1.6.0-bin- hadoop2.6/README.md")
> count(textfile)
[1] 95
> take(textfile,1)
[[1]]
[1] "# Apache Spark"
```

3. We will use the filterRDD transformation to return a new RDD with a subset of the items in the file as follows:

```
> linesWithSpark <- filterRDD(textFile, function(line){
grepl("Spark",    line)})
> count(linesWithSpark)
[1] 17
```

4. We can chain together transformations and actions as follows:

```
>count(SparkR:::filterRDD(textfile, function(line){
  grepl("Spark", line)}))
16/03/18 11:02:39 INFO SparkContext: Starting job: collect at
NativeMethodAccessorImpl.java:-2
16/03/18 11:02:39 INFO DAGScheduler: Got job 3 (collect at
NativeMethodAccessorImpl.java:-2) with 2 output partitions
16/03/18 11:02:39 INFO DAGScheduler: Final stage: ResultStage 3
(collect at NativeMethodAccessorImpl.java:-2)
16/03/18 11:02:39 INFO DAGScheduler: Parents of final stage:
List()
16/03/18 11:02:39 INFO DAGScheduler: Missing parents: List()
```

```
16/03/18 11:02:39 INFO DAGScheduler: Submitting ResultStage 3
(RRDD[4] at RDD at RRDD.scala:36), which has no missing parents
16/03/18 11:02:39 INFO MemoryStore: Block broadcast_4 stored as
values in memory (estimated size 16.1 KB, free 216.9 KB)
16/03/18 11:02:39 INFO MemoryStore: Block broadcast_4_piece0
stored as bytes in memory (estimated size 5.2 KB, free 222.1 KB)
16/03/18 11:02:39 INFO BlockManagerInfo: Added
broadcast_4_piece0 in memory on localhost:46499 (size: 5.2 KB,
free: 511.5 MB)
16/03/18 11:02:39 INFO SparkContext: Created broadcast 4 from
broadcast at DAGScheduler.scala:1006
16/03/18 11:02:39 INFO DAGScheduler: Submitting 2 missing tasks
from ResultStage 3 (RRDD[4] at RDD at RRDD.scala:36)
16/03/18 11:02:39 INFO TaskSchedulerImpl: Adding task set 3.0
with 2 tasks16/03/18 11:02:39 INFO TaskSetManager: Starting task
0.0 in stage 3.0 (TID 5, localhost, partition 0,PROCESS_LOCAL,
2163 bytes)
16/03/18 11:02:39 INFO TaskSetManager: Starting task 1.0 in
stage
3.0 (TID 6, localhost, partition 1,PROCESS_LOCAL, 2163 bytes)
16/03/18 11:02:39 INFO Executor: Running task 0.0 in stage 3.0
(TID 5)
16/03/18 11:02:39 INFO Executor: Running task 1.0 in stage 3.0
(TID 6)
16/03/18 11:02:39 INFO HadoopRDD: Input split:
file:/home/padmac/bigdata/spark-1.6.0-bin-
hadoop2.6/README.md:0+1679
16/03/18 11:02:39 INFO HadoopRDD: Input split:
file:/home/padmac/bigdata/spark-1.6.0-bin-
hadoop2.6/README.md:1679+1680
16/03/18 11:02:39 INFO RRDD: Times: boot = 0.011 s, init = 0.004
s, broadcast = 0.001 s, read-input = 0.000 s, compute = 0.002
s, write-output = 0.001 s, total = 0.019 s
16/03/18 11:02:39 INFO Executor: Finished task 1.0 in stage 3.0
(TID 6). 2077 bytes result sent to driver
16/03/18 11:02:39 INFO TaskSetManager: Finished task 1.0 in
stage
3.0 (TID 6) in 32 ms on localhost (1/2)
16/03/18 11:02:39 INFO RRDD: Times: boot = 0.010 s, init = 0.011
s, broadcast = 0.000 s, read-input = 0.000 s, compute = 0.003 s,
write-output = 0.001 s, total = 0.025 s
16/03/18 11:02:39 INFO Executor: Finished task 0.0 in stage 3.0
(TID 5). 2077 bytes result sent to driver
16/03/18 11:02:39 INFO TaskSetManager: Finished task 0.0 in
stage
3.0 (TID 5) in 40 ms on localhost (2/2)
16/03/18 11:02:39 INFO TaskSchedulerImpl: Removed TaskSet 3.0,
whose tasks have all completed, from pool
```

```
16/03/18 11:02:39 INFO DAGScheduler: ResultStage 3 (collect at
NativeMethodAccessorImpl.java:-2) finished in 0.042 s
16/03/18 11:02:39 INFO DAGScheduler: Job 3 finished: collect at
NativeMethodAccessorImpl.java:-2, took 0.052781 s
[1] 17
```

5. RDD actions and transformations can be used for more complex computations. Let's say we want to find the line with the most words:

```
> SparkR:::reduce( SparkR:::lapply( textfile, function(line) {
length(strsplit(unlist(line), " ")[[1]])}), function(a, b) { if
(a > b) { a } else { b }})
[1] 14
```

6. We can define a max function to make this code easier to understand:

```
>  max <- function(a, b) {if (a > b) { a } else { b }}
> SparkR:::reduce(SparkR:::map(textfile, function(line) {
length(strsplit(unlist(line), " ")[[1]])}), max)
[1] 14
```

7. Now, let's define the word count program using the `flatMap`, `lapply`, and `reduceByKey` transformations as follows:

```
> words <- SparkR:::flatMap(textfile,
function(line){
strsplit(line," ")[[1]]  })
wordCount <- SparkR:::lapply(words, function(word){
list(word,   1L)
})
counts <- SparkR:::reduceByKey(wordCount, "+", 2L)
```

8. To collect the word counts in our shell, we can use the collect action:

```
output <- collect(counts)
> for (wordcount in output) {
    cat(wordcount[[1]], ": ", wordcount[[2]], "\n")
    }
how :  2
Thriftserver :   1
detailed :   2
its :  1
other :  1
Alternatively, :   1
refer :  2
"yarn" :  1
runs. :  1
start :  1
[...]
```

How it works...

Spark RDDs can be created from Hadoop `InputFormats` (HDFS files) or by transforming other RDDs. `SparkR:::textFile` makes a new RDD from the text of the README file in the SparkR-package source directory. The actions such as count and take return values. The `filterRDD` transformation returns a new RDD with a subset of the items in the file. We have also seen how we chain transformations and actions together. The complex computation `SparkR:::reduce( SparkR:::lapply( textfile, function(line) { length(strsplit(unlist(line), " ")[[1]])})`, `function(a, b) { if (a > b) { a } else { b }})` works as the inner function `lapply` maps a line to an integer value, creating a new RDD. The outer function reduce is invoked on the new RDD to find the largest line count. In this case, the arguments to both functions are passed as anonymous functions. We also defined R functions such as max beforehand and passed them as arguments to RDD functions.

When performing a word count, we combined the `flatMap`, `lapply`, and `reduceByKey` transformations to compute the per-word counts in the file as an RDD of (`string`, `int`) pairs. We used the collect action to get the word counts.

There's more...

The preceding code snippet shows the use of the SparkR shell for interactive data analysis. We can also write and execute a standalone application in SparkR, which is shown in the coming recipes. The central component in SparkR is the SparkR DataFrame, a distributed DataFrame implemented on top of Spark. The SparkR DataFrames API is similar to R DataFrames but it can scale to large datasets using support for distributed computation in Spark. There is also support for caching datasets, which allows the data to be accessed repeatedly. The upcoming release of SparkR will offer extensive support for running high-level machine learning algorithms and SQL queries over SparkR DataFrames.

See also

Please refer to `Chapter 1`, *Big Data Analytics with Spark* to get familiar with Spark.

Creating a SparkR standalone application from RStudio

In this recipe, we'll look at the process of writing and executing a standalone application in SparkR.

Getting ready

To step through this recipe, you will need a running Spark Cluster either in pseudo distributed mode or in one of the distributed modes, that is, standalone, YARN, or Mesos. Also, install RStudio. Please refer to the *Installing R* recipe for details on the installation of R.

How to do it...

In this recipe, we'll create standalone application using Spark-1.6.0 and Spark-2.0.2:

1. Before working with SparkR, make sure that SPARK_HOME is set in environment as follows:

```
if (nchar(Sys.getenv("SPARK_HOME")) < 1) {
Sys.setenv(SPARK_HOME = "/home/padmac/bigdata/spark-1.6.0-bin-
hadoop2.6")
}
```

2. Now, load the SparkR package and invoke sparkR.init as follows:

```
library(SparkR, lib.loc = c(file.path(Sys.getenv("SPARK_HOME"),
"R", "lib")))
sc <- sparkR.init(master = "spark://192.168.0.118:7077",
sparkEnvir =   list(spark.driver.memory="2g"))
```

3. Here is the word count example written in a standalone application:

```
lines <- SparkR:::textFile(sc,
"hdfs://<namenode>:9000/data/README.md")
words <- SparkR:::flatMap(lines, function(line){
  strsplit(line," ")[[1]]
})
wordCount <- SparkR:::lapply(words, function(word){
  list(word,1L)
})
counts <- SparkR:::reduceByKey(wordCount,"+",numPartitions = 2)
output <- collect(counts)
for (wordcount in output) {
  cat(wordcount[[1]], ": ", wordcount[[2]], "\n")
}
how :  2
Thriftserver :  1
detailed :  2
its :  1
other :  1
Alternatively, :  1
refer :  2
"yarn" :  1
runs. :  1
start :  1
[...]
```

4. Here is another example:

```
SampleApp.R
if (nchar(Sys.getenv("SPARK_HOME")) < 1) {
  Sys.setenv(SPARK_HOME = "/home/padmac/bigdata/spark-1.6.0-bin-
hadoop2.6")
}
library(SparkR, lib.loc = c(file.path(Sys.getenv("SPARK_HOME"),
"R", "lib")))
sc <- sparkR.init(master = "spark://192.168.0.118:7077",
sparkEnvir =   list(spark.driver.memory="2g"))
logFile <- "hdfs://<namenode>:9000/<path>/README.md"
logData <- cache(SparkR:::textFile(sc, logFile))
numAs <- count(SparkR:::filterRDD(logData, function(s) {
grepl("a",   s) }))
numBs <- count(SparkR:::filterRDD(logData, function(s) {
grepl("b",   s) }))
paste("Lines with a: ", numAs, ", Lines with b: ", numBs, sep="")
[1] "Lines with a: 58, Lines with b: 26"
```

5. Let's see how to create a standalone using Spark 2.0.2. Here is the code for the same –

```
if (nchar(Sys.getenv("SPARK_HOME")) < 1) {
Sys.setenv(SPARK_HOME = "/home/padmac/bigdata/spark-2.0.2-bin-
hadoop2.6")
}
library(SparkR, lib.loc = c(file.path(Sys.getenv("SPARK_HOME"),
"R", "lib")))
sparkR.session(master = "spark://master:7077", sparkConfig =
list(spark.driver.memory = "2g"))
```

The following is the output:

```
Attaching package: 'SparkR'
The following objects are masked from 'package:stats':cov, filter, lag,
na.omit, predict, sd, var, window
The following objects are masked from 'package:base':
as.data.frame, colnames, colnames<-, drop, endsWith, intersect, rank,
rbind, sample, startsWith, subset, summary, transform, union
> if (nchar(Sys.getenv("SPARK_HOME")) < 1) {
+ Sys.setenv(SPARK_HOME = "/home/padmac/bigdata/spark-2.0.2-bin-hadoop2.6")
+ }
> library(SparkR, lib.loc = c(file.path(Sys.getenv("SPARK_HOME"),
"R","lib")))
> sparkR.session(master = "spark://master:7077", sparkConfig =
list(spark.driver.memory = "2g"))
Spark package found in SPARK_HOME: /home/padmac/bigdata/spark-2.0.2-bin-
```

```
hadoop2.6
Launching java with spark-submit command /home/padmac/bigdata/spark-2.0.2-
bin- hadoop2.6/bin/spark-submit --driver-memory "2g" sparkr-shell
/tmp/Rtmpg7HYyp/backend_port258d105c19c0
Using Spark's default log4j profile: org/apache/spark/log4j-
defaults.properties
Setting default log level to "WARN".
To adjust logging level use sc.setLogLevel(newLevel).
16/11/20 21:34:09 WARN NativeCodeLoader: Unable to load native-hadoop
library for your platform... using builtin-java classes where applicable
16/11/20 21:34:09 WARN Utils: Your hostname, F01022 resolves to a loopback
address:127.0.0.1; using 192.168.0.5 instead (on interface wlan3)
16/11/20 21:34:09 WARN Utils: Set SPARK_LOCAL_IP if you need to bind to
another address
Java ref type org.apache.spark.sql.SparkSession id 1
```

How it works...

The preceding code snippet shows how to write a standalone application in `SparkR`. Initially, `Sys.getenv` checks whether `SPARK_HOME` is set in the environment. The module `library` is used to load the `SparkR` package. `sparkR.init` is used to initialize the `SparkContext`. It also takes Spark driver properties as parameters using `sparkEnvir`. We combined `flatMap`, `lapply`, and `reduceByKey` transformations to compute the per word counts in the file.

The program `SampleApp.R` counts the number of lines containing `a` and the number containing `b` in a text file and returns the counts as a string on the command line. We can pass R functions to Spark, where they are automatically serialized along with any variables they reference.

We also saw how to create standalone application using Spark 2.0.2. The `sparkR.session(master = "spark://master:7077", sparkConfig = list(spark.driver.memory = "2g"))` line creates Spark Session which is used in operations such as creating DataFrames from local DataFrames, various data sources such as CSV, JSON, Parquet and also from Hive.

There's more...

There is also support for caching datasets, which allows the data to be accessed repeatedly. Similar to R DataFrames, SparkR provides distributed DataFrames which can be constructed from a variety of sources, such as structured data files, Hive tables, databases, and R DataFrames. In the coming recipes, we'll see how to work with DataFrames created from a variety of data sources.

See also

Please refer to Chapter 1, *Big Data Analytics with Spark* to get familiar with Spark. Also, see the *Installing R* recipe to learn the installation details of R.

Creating SparkR DataFrames

A DataFrame is a distributed collection of data organized into named columns. It is conceptually equivalent to a table in a relational database or a DataFrame in R, but with rich optimizations. SparkR DataFrames scale to large datasets using the support for distributed computation in Spark. In this recipe, we'll see how to create SparkR DataFrames from different sources, such as JSON, CSV, local R DataFrames, and Hive tables.

Getting ready

To step through this recipe, you will need a running Spark Cluster either in pseudo distributed mode or in one of the distributed modes, that is, standalone, YARN, or Mesos. Also, install RStudio. Please refer to the *Installing R* recipe for details on the installation of R. Please refer to the *Creating a SparkR standalone application from Rstudio* recipe for details on working with the SparkR package.

How to do it...

In this recipe, we'll see how to create SparkR data frames in Spark 1.6.0 as well as Spark 2.0.2:

1. Use createDataFrame to pass a local R DataFrame and create a SparkR DataFrame:

   CreateSparkRDataFrame.R

```
if (nchar(Sys.getenv("SPARK_HOME")) < 1) {
Sys.setenv(SPARK_HOME = "/home/padmac/bigdata/spark-1.6.0-bin-
hadoop2.6")
}
library(SparkR, lib.loc = c(file.path(Sys.getenv("SPARK_HOME"),
"R", "lib")))
sc <- sparkR.init(master = "local[*]", sparkEnvir =
list(spark.driver.memory="2g"))
sqlContext <- sparkRSQL.init(sc)
df <- createDataFrame(sqlContext, iris)
head(df)
```

The following is the output:

```
16/03/19 15:20:14 INFO Executor: Finished task 0.0 in stage 4.0
(TID 5). 1794    bytes result sent to driver
16/03/19 15:20:14 INFO TaskSetManager: Finished task 0.0 in stage
4.0 (TID 5) in   765 ms on localhost (1/1)
16/03/19 15:20:14 INFO DAGScheduler: ResultStage 4 (dfToCols at
NativeMethodAccessorImpl.java:-2) finished in 0.765 s
16/03/19 15:20:14 INFO TaskSchedulerImpl: Removed TaskSet 4.0,
whose tasks have   all completed, from pool
16/03/19 15:20:14 INFO DAGScheduler: Job 4 finished: dfToCols at
NativeMethodAccessorImpl.java:-2, took 0.781704 s
  Sepal_Length Sepal_Width Petal_Length Petal_Width Species
1        5.1         3.5         1.4          0.2     setosa
2        4.9         3.0         1.4          0.2     setosa
3        4.7         3.2         1.3          0.2     setosa
4        4.6         3.1         1.5          0.2     setosa
5        5.0         3.6         1.4          0.2     setosa
6        5.4         3.9         1.7          0.4     setosa
```

2. Now, create a DataFrame from a JSON file. The sample JSON file `people.json` contains the following content:

```
{"name":"Michael"}
{"name":"Andy", "age":30}
{"name":"Justin", "age":19}
```

3. Here is the code snippet for creating a DataFrame from JSON content for `ReadingJSON.R`:

```
if (nchar(Sys.getenv("SPARK_HOME")) < 1) {
   Sys.setenv(SPARK_HOME = "~/bigdata/spark-1.6.0-bin-hadoop2.6")
}
library(SparkR, lib.loc = c(file.path(Sys.getenv("SPARK_HOME"),
"R", "lib")))
sc <- sparkR.init(master = "local[*]", sparkEnvir =
list(spark.driver.memory="2g"))
sqlContext <- sparkRSQL.init(sc)
people <- read.df(sqlContext, "~/<path>/people.json","json")
head(people)
```

The following is the output:

```
Launching java with spark-submit command
/home/padmac/bigdata/spark-1.6.0-bin-  hadoop2.6/bin/spark-submit
--driver-memory "2g" sparkr-shell
/tmp/Rtmphk0btR/backend_portad92e8be16e
log4j:WARN No appenders could be found for logger
(io.netty.util.internal.logging.InternalLoggerFactory).
log4j:WARN Please initialize the log4j system properly.
log4j:WARN See
http://logging.apache.org/log4j/1.2/faq.html#noconfig for more
info.
Using Spark's default log4j profile: org/apache/spark/log4j-
defaults.properties
16/03/19 15:09:17 INFO SparkContext: Running Spark version 1.6.0
16/03/19 15:09:17 WARN NativeCodeLoader: Unable to load native-
hadoop library for  your platform... using builtin-java classes
where applicable
[...]
> head(people)
16/03/19 15:09:21 INFO MemoryStore: Block broadcast_2 stored as
values in memory (estimated size 86.4 KB, free 338.3 KB)
16/03/19 15:09:21 INFO MemoryStore: Block broadcast_2_piece0
stored as bytes in memory (estimated size 19.3 KB, free 357.6 KB)
16/03/19 15:09:21 INFO BlockManagerInfo: Added broadcast_2_piece0
in memory on localhost:55348 (size: 19.3 KB, free: 1247.6 MB)
16/03/19 15:09:21 INFO SparkContext: Created broadcast 2 from
dfToCols at NativeMethodAccessorImpl.java:-2
16/03/19 15:09:22 INFO MemoryStore: Block broadcast_3 stored as
values in memory (estimated size 225.7 KB, free 583.3 KB)
16/03/19 15:09:22 INFO MemoryStore: Block broadcast_3_piece0
stored as bytes in memory (estimated size 19.4 KB, free 602.8 KB)
16/03/19 15:09:22 INFO BlockManagerInfo: Added broadcast_3_piece0
in memory on localhost:55348 (size: 19.4 KB, free: 1247.6 MB)
```

```
16/03/19 15:09:22 INFO SparkContext: Created broadcast 3 from
dfToCols at NativeMethodAccessorImpl.java:-2
16/03/19 15:09:22 INFO FileInputFormat: Total input paths to
process : 1
16/03/19 15:09:22 INFO SparkContext: Starting job: dfToCols at
NativeMethodAccessorImpl.java:-2
16/03/19 15:09:22 INFO DAGScheduler: Got job 1 (dfToCols at
NativeMethodAccessorImpl.java:-2) with 1 output partitions
16/03/19 15:09:22 INFO DAGScheduler: Final stage: ResultStage 1
(dfToCols at NativeMethodAccessorImpl.java:-2)
16/03/19 15:09:22 INFO DAGScheduler: Parents of final stage:
List()
16/03/19 15:09:22 INFO DAGScheduler: Missing parents: List()
16/03/19 15:09:22 INFO DAGScheduler: Submitting ResultStage 1
(MapPartitionsRDD[9] at dfToCols at
NativeMethodAccessorImpl.java:-2), which has no missing parents
[...]
   age    name
1  NA Michael
2  30     Andy
3  19   Justin
```

4. Let's create SparkR DataFrames from Hive tables. The `students.txt` file contains the following content:

```
101   padma
102   priya
103   chitturi
```

5. Here is the code snippet for creating DataFrames from Hive tables:

```
CreatingDFHive.R
if (nchar(Sys.getenv("SPARK_HOME")) < 1) {
Sys.setenv(SPARK_HOME = "/home/padmac/bigdata/spark-1.6.0-bin-
hadoop2.6")
 }
library(SparkR, lib.loc = c(file.path(Sys.getenv("SPARK_HOME"),
"R", "lib")))
sc <- sparkR.init(master = "local[*]", sparkEnvir =
list(spark.driver.memory="2g"))
hiveContext <- sparkRHive.init(sc)
sql(hiveContext, "CREATE TABLE IF NOT EXISTS Student (id INT,
name STRING)")
sql(hiveContext, "LOAD DATA LOCAL INPATH '~/<path>/students.txt'
INTO TABLE Student")
results <- sql(hiveContext, "FROM src SELECT key, value")
head(results)
```

The following is the output:

```
id      name
101     padma
102   priya
103   chitturi
```

6. Let's try to read a CSV file as follows:

```
library(SparkR, lib.loc = c(file.path(Sys.getenv("SPARK_HOME"),
"R", "lib")))
sc <- sparkR.init(master = "local[*]", sparkEnvir =
list(spark.driver.memory="2g"),
sparkPackages="com.databricks:spark-  csv_2.10:1.4.0")
sqlContext <- sparkRSQL.init(sc)
people <- read.df(sqlContext, "~/<path>/people.csv", "csv")
head(people)
```

The following is the output:

```
age     name
1  NA       Michael
2  30       Andy
3  19       Justin
```

7. Now, let's see how to create SparkDataFrame using Spark 2.0.2 in the following ways:

```
#Create SparkDateFrame from a local data frame
df <- as.DataFrame(faithful)
head(df)
#From Data Sources
people <- read.df("/home/padmac/bigdata/spark-2.0.2-bin-
hadoop2.6/examples/src/main/resources/people.json","json")
head(people)
printSchema(people)
```

The following is the output:

```
> #Create SparkDateFrame from a local data frame
> df <- as.DataFrame(faithful)
> head(df)
eruptions waiting
1 3.600 79
2 1.800 54
3 3.333 74
4 2.283 62
5 4.533 85
```

```
6 2.883 55
>
> #From Data Sources
> people <- read.df("/home/padmac/bigdata/spark-2.0.2-
  binhadoop2.6/examples/src/main/resources/people.json","json")
> head(people)

age name
1 NA Michael
2 30 Andy
3 19 Justin
> printSchema(people)
 root
|-- age: long (nullable = true)
|-- name: string ( nullable = true)
```

8. Let's also see how to create SparkDataFrame from csv and parquet files as below. Please download the csv file from the location: https://github.com/ChitturiPa dma/datasets/blob/master/Breast_CancerData.csv:

```
#Reading CSV File
df <- read.df("/home/padmac/cookbook/Problems/
Breast_CancerData.csv", "csv", header = "true", inferSchema =
"true", na.strings = "NA")
head(subset(df, select=c("clump_thickness","label")))
#Write SparkDataFrame in parquet format
write.df(people, path = "people.parquet", source = "parquet",
mode = "overwrite")
```

The following is the output:

```
> #Reading CSV File
> df <-read.df("/home/padmac/cookbook/Problems
/Breast_CancerData.csv", "csv", header = "true", inferSchema =
"true", na.strings = "NA")
> head(subset(df, select=c("clump_thickness","label")))
clump_thickness label
1               5           B
2               5           B
3               3           B
4               6           B
5               4           B
6               8           M
> #Write SparkDataFrame in parquet format
> write.df(people, path =
"/home/padmac/cookbook/output/people.parquet", source =
"parquet", mode = "overwrite")
```

9. We can also create SparkDataFrames from Hive tables. For this, we need to create a SparkSession with Hive support which can access tables in the Hive MetaStore:

```
sparkR.session()
sql("CREATE TABLE IF NOT EXISTS src (key INT, value STRING)")
sql("LOAD DATA LOCAL INPATH 'examples/src/main/resources/kv1.txt'
INTO TABLE src")
# Queries can be expressed in HiveQL.
results <- sql("FROM src SELECT key, value")
# results is now a SparkDataFrame
head(results)
```

The following is the output:

```
  key   value
1   238   val_238
2   86    val_86
3   311   val_311
```

How it works...

The preceding code snippets show how to create SparkR DataFrames from a variety of data sources. Initially, `sqlContext <- sparkRSQL.init(sc)` initializes the SQLContext. Using `createDataFrame`, a SparkR DataFrame is created from the existing dataset iris available in R. Next, we saw how to create DataFrames using `read.df`. It takes SQLContext and the path for the file to load and the type of data source as parameters. For reading a CSV file, we specified the packages with the packages argument while initializing SparkContext.

Also, we have seen how to create SparkR DataFrames from hive tables. For this, we initialized HiveContext, using which tables can be accessed in the Hive Metastore. To initialize HiveContext, Spark must be built with Hive support.

As in Spark 2.0.2, we created Spark Session which is used for creating SparkDataFrame from local data frames (available in R), from JSON, CSV and Hive tables. The statement `write.df(people, path = "/home/padmac/cookbook/output/people.parquet", source = "parquet", mode = "overwrite")` writes the SparkDataFrame in the specified file format.

There's more...

SparkR supports operating on a variety of data sources, such as JSON, Parquet, and Avro files natively through Spark packages (`http://spark-packages.org/`). We can find data source connectors for popular file formats such as CSV and Avro. These can be added by specifying packages with `spark-submit` or `sparkR` commands, or can be specified with the packages argument while initializing `SparkContext` using `init`. Also, while creating DataFrames from Hive tables, Spark must be built with Hive support (`https://spark.apache.org/docs/1.6.0/building-spark.html#building-with-hive-and -jdbc-support`). The upcoming release of SparkR will have support for other sets of data sources as well.

See also

Please refer to `Chapter 1`, *Big Data Analytics with Spark* to get familiar with Spark. Also, visit the *Interactive analysis with the SparkR shell* recipe to get familiar with SparkR.

SparkR DataFrame operations

SparkR DataFrames support a number of operations to do structured data processing. In this recipe, we'll see a good number of examples, such as selection, grouping, aggregation, and so on.

Getting ready

To step through this recipe, you will need a running Spark Cluster either in pseudo distributed mode or in one of the distributed modes, that is, standalone, YARN, or Mesos. Also, install RStudio. Please refer to the *Installing R* recipe for details on the installation of R and the *Creating SparkR DataFrames* recipe to get acquainted with the creation of DataFrames from a variety of data sources.

How to do it...

In this recipe, we'll see how to perform various operations SparkR data frames:

1. Let's see how to select a column from a DataFrame:

```
library(SparkR, lib.loc = c(file.path(Sys.getenv("SPARK_HOME"),
"R", "lib")))
sc <- sparkR.init(master = "local[*]", sparkEnvir =
list(spark.driver.memory="2g"))
sqlContext <- sparkRSQL.init(sc)
df <- createDataFrame(sqlContext, faithful)
head(select(df, df$eruptions))
[...]
16/03/19 21:52:11 INFO TaskSchedulerImpl: Adding task set 4.0
with 1 tasks
16/03/19 21:52:11 INFO TaskSetManager: Starting task 0.0 in stage
4.0 (TID 4,   localhost, partition 0,PROCESS_LOCAL, 12976 bytes)
16/03/19 21:52:11 INFO Executor: Running task 0.0 in stage 4.0
(TID 4)
16/03/19 21:52:11 INFO Executor: Finished task 0.0 in stage 4.0
(TID 4). 1522   bytes   result sent to driver
16/03/19 21:52:11 INFO TaskSetManager: Finished task 0.0 in stage
4.0 (TID 4) in   27 ms on localhost (1/1)
16/03/19 21:52:11 INFO TaskSchedulerImpl: Removed TaskSet 4.0,
whose tasks have   all completed, from pool
16/03/19 21:52:11 INFO DAGScheduler: ResultStage 4 (dfToCols at
NativeMethodAccessorImpl.java:-2) finished in 0.029 s
16/03/19 21:52:11 INFO DAGScheduler: Job 4 finished: dfToCols at
NativeMethodAccessorImpl.java:-2, took 0.041186 s
   eruptions
1     3.600
2     1.800
3     3.333
4     2.283
5     4.533
6     2.883
```

2. We can also select a column by passing the column name as a string as follows:

```
head(select(df, "eruptions"))
```

3. Next, filter the DataFrame to retain rows with wait times shorter than 50 minutes:

```
head(filter(df, df$waiting < 50))
  eruptions waiting
1    1.750      47
2    1.750      47
3    1.867      48
4    1.750      48
5    2.167      48
6    2.100      49
```

4. Now we'll see how to group and perform aggregations over data:

```
waiting_counts <- summarize(groupBy(df, df$waiting), count =
n(df$waiting))
head(waiting_counts)
```

The following is the output:

```
waiting count
1 81 13
2 60 6
3 93 2
4 68 1
5 47 4
6 80 8
```

5. Next, sort the output from the preceding aggregated results as follows:

```
head(arrange(waiting_counts, desc(waiting_counts$count)))
  waiting count
1      78     15
2      83     14
3      81     13
4      77     12
5      82     12
6      84     10
```

6. Here is how to apply arithmetic functions on columns:

```
df$waiting_secs <- df$waiting * 60
   eruptions waiting waiting_secs
1      3.600      79         4740
2      1.800      54         3240
3      3.333      74         4440
4      2.283      62         3720
5      4.533      85         5100
6      2.883      55         3300
```

How it works...

The preceding code snippets show how to perform various DataFrame operations. The lines `select(df, df$eruptions)` and `select(df, "eruptions")` select the `eruptions` column. The line `filter(df, df$waiting < 50)` filters the DataFrame such that it contains rows with wait times shorter than 50 minutes. The line `summarize(groupBy(df, df$waiting), count = n(df$waiting))` groups the rows in the DataFrame by waiting time and counts the number of times each waiting time appears.

Now, `arrange(waiting_counts, desc(waiting_counts$count))` sorts the output from the aggregation to get the most common waiting times. We have also seen how to apply arithmetic functions on columns for data processing and during aggregation.

The grouping and aggregation operations are same in Spark 2.0.2 as well except that we have to create spark session as `sparkR.session(master = "spark://master:7077", sparkConfig = list(spark.driver.memory = "2g"))`.

There's more...

There is also support for SparkR DataFrames to be registered as tables which allows to run SQL queries over the data. The SQL queries return results as a DataFrame. In the coming recipe, we'll see how to apply user-defined functions, SQL queries and also machine learning libraries over SparkR.

See also

Please refer to `Chapter 1`, *Big Data Analytics with Spark* to get familiar with Spark. Also, visit the *Interactive analysis with the SparkR shell* and *Creating SparkR DataFrames* recipes to get familiar with SparkR.

Applying user-defined functions in SparkR

In this recipe we'll see how to apply the functions such as dapply, gapply and lapply over the Spark DataFrame.

Getting ready

To step through this recipe, you will need a running Spark Cluster either in pseudo distributed mode or in one of the distributed modes that is, standalone, YARN, or Mesos. Also, install RStudio. Please refer the *Installing R* recipe for details on the installation of R and *Creating SparkR DataFrames* recipe to get acquainted with the creation of DataFrames from a variety of data sources.

How to do it...

In this recipe, we'll see how to apply the user defined functions available as of Spark 2.0.2.

1. Here is the code which applies `dapply` on the Spark DataFrame.

```
schema <- structType(structField("eruptions", "double"),
structField("waiting", "double"), structField("waiting_secs",
"double"))
df1 <- dapply(df, function(x) { x <- cbind(x, x$waiting * 60) },
schema)
head(collect(df1))
```

The following is the output:

```
  eruptions waiting waiting_secs
1 3.600 79 4740
2 1.800 54 3240
3 3.333 74 4440
4 2.283 62 3720
5 4.533 85 5100
6 2.883 55 3300
```

2. Let's see how to use `dapplyCollect`:

```
ldf <- dapplyCollect(
df,
function(x){ x <- cbind(x, "waiting_secs" = x$waiting * 60)
})
head(ldf,4)
```

The following is the output:

```
  eruptions waiting waiting_secs
1 3.600 79 4740
2 1.800 54 3240
3 3.333 74 4440
4 2.283 62 3720
```

3. Let's see how to use `gapply` and `gapplyCollect`:

```
#gapply
schema <- structType(structField("waiting", "double"),
structField("max_eruption", "double"))
result <- gapply(
df,
"waiting",
function(key, x) {
y <- data.frame(key, max(x$eruptions))
}, schema)
print("gapply output:")
head(collect(arrange(result, "max_eruption", decreasing = TRUE)))
print("gapplyCollect output:")
result <- gapplyCollect( df, "waiting",
function(key, x) {
y <- data.frame(key, max(x$eruptions))
colnames(y) <- c("waiting", "max_eruption")
y })
head(result[order(result$max_eruption, decreasing = TRUE), ])
```

The following is the `gapply` output:

```
  waiting max_eruption
1 96 5.100
2 76 5.067
3 77 5.033
4 88 5.000
5 86 4.933
6 82 4.900
```

The following is the `gapply` Collect output:

```
   waiting max_eruption
10  96  5.100
49  76  5.067
15  77  5.033
4   88  5.000
12  86  4.933
29  82  4.900
```

4. Now, let's see the code which runs `lapply` over a list of elements:

```
print("lapply")
families <- c("gaussian", "poisson")
train <- function(family) {
model <- glm(Sepal.Length ~ Sepal.Width + Species, iris, family
= family)
summary(model) }
# Return a list of model's summaries
model.summaries <- spark.lapply(families, train)
# Print the summary of each model
print(model.summaries)
```

The following is the output:

```
[[1]]
Call:
glm(formula = Sepal.Length ~ Sepal.Width + Species, family =
family, data = iris)
Deviance Residuals:
Min 1Q Median 3Q Max
-1.30711 -0.25713 -0.05325 0.19542 1.41253
Coefficients:
Estimate Std. Error t value Pr(>|t|)
(Intercept) 2.2514 0.3698 6.089 9.57e-09 ***
Sepal.Width 0.8036 0.1063 7.557 4.19e-12 ***
Speciesversicolor 1.4587 0.1121 13.012 < 2e-16 ***
Speciesvirginica 1.9468 0.1000 19.465 < 2e-16 ***
---
Signif. codes: 0 '***' 0.001 '**' 0.01 '*' 0.05 '.' 0.1 ' ' 1
(Dispersion parameter for gaussian family taken to be
 0.1918059)
Null deviance: 102.168 on 149 degrees of freedom
Residual deviance: 28.004 on 146 degrees of freedom
AIC: 183.94
Number of Fisher Scoring iterations: 2
[[2]]
Call:
```

```
glm(formula = Sepal.Length ~ Sepal.Width + Species, family =
family, data = iris)
Deviance Residuals:
Min 1Q Median 3Q Max
-0.52652 -0.10966 -0.01230 0.07755 0.56101
Coefficients:
Estimate Std. Error z value Pr(>|z|)
(Intercept) 1.13033 0.35454 3.188 0.001432 **
Sepal.Width 0.13971 0.10119 1.381 0.167361
Speciesversicolor 0.26277 0.10901 2.410 0.015931 *
Speciesvirginica 0.33842 0.09587 3.530 0.000416 ***
---
Signif. codes: 0 '***' 0.001 '**' 0.01 '*' 0.05 '.' 0.1 ' ' 1
(Dispersion parameter for poisson family taken to be 1)
Null deviance: 17.3620 on 149 degrees of freedom
Residual deviance: 4.5202 on 146 degrees of freedom
AIC: Inf
Number of Fisher Scoring iterations: 3
```

How it works...

In the preceding code snippets, we applied various user-defined functions over the Spark DataFrame df (created from the R DataFrame `faithful`). The `schema <- structType(structField("eruptions", "double"), structField("waiting", "double"), structField("waiting_secs", "double"))` line creates schema and the function `dapply` is applied to each partition of the Spark DataFrame. The function defined as `function(x) { x <- cbind(x, x$waiting * 60) }` takes one parameter which is applied to each partition and the schema specifies the row format of the resulting `SparkDataFrame`. Next, `dapplyCollect` is also applied on each partition and the results are collected back on the driver.

The `gapply` function is applied to each group of the `SparkDataFrame` which takes two parameters: grouping key and `Rdata.frame` corresponding to that key. The groups are chosen from `SparkDataFrame` column(s). The output of the function should be a `data.frame`. Schema specifies the row format of the resulting `SparkDataFrame`. The `gapplyCollect` function works the same as `gapply`, but doesn't require schema to be passed as parameter and collects the result back to `Rdata.frame`. Similar to `lapply` in R, `spark.lapply` runs a function over a list of elements and distributes the computations with Spark. It also applies a function in a manner that is similar to `doParallel` or `lapply` to elements of a list.

There's more...

When applying `dapplyCollect` and `gapplyCollect` functions over the Spark DataFrame, they can fail if the output of UDF execution on all the partitions cannot fit in the driver memory. Also when running `lapply`, if the results of all the computations do not fit in a single machine, create DataFrame from the list as `dfcreateDataFrame(list)` and then use `dapply`.

There is also support for SparkR DataFrame to be registered as table and allows to run SQL queries over its data. The SQL queries return results as a DataFrame. In the coming recipe, we'll see how to apply SQL queries and machine learning libraries over SparkR.

See also

Please refer to `Chapter 1`, *Big Data Analytics with Spark* to get familiar with Spark. Also, visit the *Interactive analysis with the SparkR shell* , *Creating SparkR DataFrames* and *SparkR DataFrame operations* recipes to get familiar with SparkR and to learn the type by operations performed of Spark DataFrames.

Running SQL queries from SparkR and caching DataFrames

In this recipe, we'll see how to run SQL queries over SparkR DataFrames and cache the datasets.

Getting ready

To step through this recipe, you will need a running Spark Cluster either in pseudo distributed mode or in one of the distributed modes, that is, standalone, YARN, or Mesos. Also, install RStudio. Please refer to the Installing R recipe for details on the installation of R and the *Creating SparkR DataFrames* recipe to get acquainted with the creation of DataFrames from a variety of data sources.

How to do it...

The following code shows how to apply SQL queries over SparkR data frames using Spark 1.6.0. As per Spark 2.0.2, the methods would remain same except that spark session is used instead of SQLContext:

1. Let's create a DataFrame from a JSON file. The sample JSON file `people.json` contains the following content:

```
{"name":"Michael"}
{"name":"Andy", "age":30}
{"name":"Justin", "age":19}
Here is the code snippet for creating a data frame from JSON
content:
ReadingJSON.R
if (nchar(Sys.getenv("SPARK_HOME")) < 1) {
  Sys.setenv(SPARK_HOME = "~/bigdata/spark-1.6.0-bin-hadoop2.6")
}
library(SparkR, lib.loc = c(file.path(Sys.getenv("SPARK_HOME"),
"R", "lib")))
sc <- sparkR.init(master = "local[*]", sparkEnvir =
list(spark.driver.memory="2g"))
sqlContext <- sparkRSQL.init(sc)
people <- read.df(sqlContext, "~/<path>/people.json","json")
```

2. Next, run SQL queries on the DataFrame as follows:

```
registerTempTable(people, "people")
teenagers <- sql(sqlContext, "SELECT name, age FROM people WHERE
age >= 10)
head(teenagers)
16/03/20 21:05:12 INFO TaskSchedulerImpl: Adding task set 26.0
with 1 tasks
16/03/20 21:05:12 INFO TaskSetManager: Starting task 0.0 in stage
26.0 (TID 37, localhost, partition 1,PROCESS_LOCAL, 2193 bytes)
16/03/20 21:05:12 INFO Executor: Running task 0.0 in stage 26.0
(TID 37)
16/03/20 21:05:12 INFO HadoopRDD: Input split:
file:/home/padmac/bigdata/spark-  1.6.0-bin-
hadoop2.6/examples/src/main/resources/people.json:36+37
16/03/20 21:05:12 INFO Executor: Finished task 0.0 in stage 26.0
(TID 37). 2638   bytes result sent to driver
16/03/20 21:05:12 INFO TaskSetManager: Finished task 0.0 in stage
26.0 (TID 37) in   15 ms on localhost (1/1)
16/03/20 21:05:12 INFO TaskSchedulerImpl: Removed TaskSet 26.0,
whose tasks have   all completed, from pool
16/03/20 21:05:12 INFO DAGScheduler: ResultStage 26 (dfToCols at
```

```
NativeMethodAccessorImpl.java:-2) finished in 0.016 s
16/03/20 21:05:12 INFO DAGScheduler: Job 26 finished: dfToCols at
NativeMethodAccessorImpl.java:-2, took 0.025842 s
     name age
1   Andy  30
2 Justin  19
```

3. Here is the code snippet to cache the DataFrame:

```
cache(teenagers)
  system.time(count(teenagers))
```

How it works...

In the preceding code snippet, a SparkR DataFrame is registered as a temporary table in Spark SQL so that SQL queries can be run over the data. The `registerTempTable` function registers the DataFrame as a table. The `sql` method is used to run `sql` statements over the DataFrame. We have also seen that cache (teenagers) is used to cache the DataFrame so that it can be used repeatedly. In order to run the code using Spark 2.0.2, please refer the recipe, *Creating SparkR standalone application from RStudio* for details on creating Spark session.

There's more...

Apart from running SQL queries over DataFrames, as Dataset is the new interface added in Spark 1.6, the upcoming versions of SparkR will also integrate with the DataSet API. In the coming recipe, we'll see how to run machine learning models over DataFrames.

See also

Please refer to `Chapter 1`, *Big Data Analytics with Spark* to get familiar with spark. Also, visit the *Interactive analysis with the SparkR* shell and *Creating SparkR DataFrames* recipes to get familiar with SparkR.

Machine learning with SparkR

SparkR is integrated with Spark's MLlib machine learning library so that algorithms can be parallelized seamlessly without specifying manually which part of the algorithm can be run in parallel. MLlib is one of the fastest-growing machine learning libraries; hence, the ability to use R with MLlib will create a huge number of contributions to MLlib from R users. As of Spark 1.6, there is support for generalized linear models (Gaussian and binomial) over DataFrames and as per Spark 2.0.2, the algorithms such as Naive Bayes and KMeans are available.

Getting ready

To step through this recipe, you will need a running Spark Cluster either in pseudo distributed mode or in one of the distributed modes, that is, standalone, YARN, or Mesos. Also, install RStudio. Please refer to *Installing R* recipe for details on the installation of R and the *Creating SparkR DataFrames* recipe to get acquainted with the creation of DataFrames from a variety of data sources.

How to do it...

Here let's see how to apply gaussian linear model and Kmeans model as per Spark 2.0.2:

1. Let's use a Gaussian linear model over the SparkR DataFrame as follows:

```
GLMExample.R
if (nchar(Sys.getenv("SPARK_HOME")) < 1) {
Sys.setenv(SPARK_HOME = "/home/padmac/bigdata/spark-2.0.2-bin-
hadoop2.6")
}
library(SparkR, lib.loc = c(file.path(Sys.getenv("SPARK_HOME"),
"R", "lib")))
sparkR.session(master = "spark://master:7077", sparkConfig =
list(spark.driver.memory = "2g"))
irisDF <- as.DataFrame(iris)
# Fit a generalized linear model of family "gaussian" with
#spark.glm
 gaussianDF <- irisDF
 gaussianTestDF <- irisDF
 gaussianGLM <- spark.glm(gaussianDF, Sepal_Length ~ Sepal_Width
+ Species, family = "gaussian")
 #Model summary
 summary(gaussianGLM)
```

```
# Prediction
gaussianPredictions <- predict(gaussianGLM, gaussianTestDF)
showDF(gaussianPredictions,5)

# Fit a generalized linear model of family "binomial" with
# spark.glm
binomialDF <- filter(irisDF, irisDF$Species != "setosa")
binomialTestDF <- binomialDF
binomialGLM <- spark.glm(binomialDF, Species ~ Sepal_Length +
Sepal_Width, family = "binomial")

# Model summary
summary(binomialGLM)

# Prediction
binomialPredictions <- predict(binomialGLM, binomialTestDF)
showDF(binomialPredictions,5)
```

The following is the output:

```
> #Model summary
> summary(gaussianGLM)
Deviance Residuals:
(Note: These are approximate quantiles with relative error <=
0.01)
Min 1Q Median 3Q Max
-1.30711 -0.26011 -0.06189 0.19111 1.41253

Coefficients:
Estimate Std. Error t value Pr(>|t|)
(Intercept) 2.2514 0.36975 6.0889 9.5681e-09
Sepal_Width 0.80356 0.10634 7.5566 4.1873e-12
Species_versicolor 1.4587 0.11211 13.012 0
Species_virginica 1.9468 0.10001 19.465 0

(Dispersion parameter for gaussian family taken to be 0.1918059)

Null deviance: 102.168 on 149 degrees of freedom
Residual deviance: 28.004 on 146 degrees of freedom
AIC: 183.9

Number of Fisher Scoring iterations: 1

> # Prediction
> gaussianPredictions <- predict(gaussianGLM, gaussianTestDF)
> showDF(gaussianPredictions,5)
+------------+----------+-----------+-----------+-------+-----+
```

```
|Sepal_Length|Sepal_Width|Petal_Length|Petal_Width|Species|label |
+------------+-----------+------------+-----------+-------+------+
| 5.1        | 3.5       | 1.4        | 0.2       | setosa| 5.1  |
| 4.9        | 3.0       | 1.4        | 0.2       | setosa| 4.9  |
| 4.7        | 3.2       | 1.3        | 0.2       | setosa| 4.7  |
| 4.6        | 3.1       | 1.5        | 0.2       | setosa| 4.6  |
| 5.0        | 3.6       | 1.4        | 0.2       | setosa| 5.0  |
+------------+-----------+------------+-----------+-------+------+


+------------------+
|prediction        |
+------------------+
|5.063856384860281 |
|4.662075934441678 |
|4.82278811460912  |
|4.7424320245253995|
|5.144212474944002 |
+------------------+


> # Fit a generalized linear model of family "binomial" with spark.glm
> binomialDF <- filter(irisDF, irisDF$Species != "setosa")
> binomialTestDF <- binomialDF
> binomialGLM <- spark.glm(binomialDF, Species ~ Sepal_Length +
Sepal_Width, family = "binomial")
16/11/30 18:10:14 WARN WeightedLeastSquares: regParam is zero, which
might cause numerical instability and overfitting.
16/11/30 18:10:14 WARN WeightedLeastSquares: regParam is zero, which
might cause numerical instability and overfitting.
16/11/30 18:10:14 WARN WeightedLeastSquares: regParam is zero, which
might cause numerical instability and overfitting.
16/11/30 18:10:14 WARN WeightedLeastSquares: regParam is zero, which
might cause numerical instability and overfitting.
16/11/30 18:10:14 WARN WeightedLeastSquares: regParam is zero, which
might cause numerical instability and overfitting.
16/11/30 18:10:15 WARN WeightedLeastSquares: regParam is zero, which
might cause numerical instability and overfitting.
>
> # Model summary
> summary(binomialGLM)

Deviance Residuals:
(Note: These are approximate quantiles with relative error <= 0.01)
Min 1Q Median 3Q Max
-1.87365 -0.93236 -0.35150 0.96084 2.35669

Coefficients:
Estimate Std. Error t value Pr(>|t|)
(Intercept) -13.046 3.0974 -4.2119 2.5319e-05
```

```
 Sepal_Length 1.9024 0.51692 3.6802 0.00023303
 Sepal_Width 0.40466 0.86283 0.46899 0.63908
(Dispersion parameter for binomial family taken to be 1)

Null deviance: 138.63 on 99 degrees of freedom
 Residual deviance: 110.33 on 97 degrees of freedom
 AIC: 116.3

Number of Fisher Scoring iterations: 5
 >
 > # Prediction
 > binomialPredictions <- predict(binomialGLM, binomialTestDF)
 > showDF(binomialPredictions,5)


+------------+-----------+------------+----------+----------+----+
|Sepal_Length|Sepal_Width|Petal_Length|Petal_Width| Species label|
+------------+-----------+------------+----------+----------+----+
| 7.0        | 3.2       | 4.7        | 1.4      |versicolor|0.0 |
| 6.4        | 3.2       | 4.5        | 1.5      |versicolor|0.0 |
| 6.9        | 3.1       | 4.9        | 1.5      |versicolor|0.0 |
| 5.5        | 2.3       | 4.0        | 1.3      |versicolor|0.0 |
| 6.5        | 2.8       | 4.6        | 1.5      |versicolor|0.0 |
+------------+-----------+------------+----------+----------+-----

+--------------------+
| prediction         |
+--------------------+
|0.8271421517601683  |
| 0.6044595910412891 |
| 0.7916340858282183 |
| 0.16080518180591663|
|0.6112229217050481  |
+--------------------+
```

2. Now, let's see how to run Kmeans over the SparkDataFrame:

```
#Run KMeans
kmeansDF <- irisDF
kmeansTestDF <- irisDF
kmeansModel <- spark.kmeans(kmeansDF, ~ Sepal_Length +
Sepal_Width +Petal_Length + Petal_Width,k = 3)
# Model summary
summary(kmeansModel)
# Get fitted result from the k-means model
showDF(fitted(kmeansModel),5)
# Prediction
kmeansPredictions <- predict(kmeansModel, kmeansTestDF)
showDF(kmeansPredictions,5)
```

The following is the output:

```
> #Run KMeans
> kmeansDF <- irisDF
> kmeansTestDF <- irisDF
> kmeansModel <- spark.kmeans(kmeansDF, ~ Sepal_Length +
Sepal_Width +Petal_Length+ Petal_Width, k = 3)
16/11/30 18:29:35 WARN KMeans: The input data is not directly
cached, which may hurt performance if its parent RDDs are also
uncached.
16/11/30 18:29:38 WARN KMeans: The input data was not directly
cached, which may hurt performance if its parent RDDs are also
uncached.
[Stage 184:===================================> (124 + 5) / 200]
[Stage 184:========================================> (166 + 4)
/ 200] >
> # Model summary
> summary(kmeansModel)
$coefficients
Sepal_Length Sepal_Width Petal_Length Petal_Width
1 5.006 3.428 1.462 0.246
2 6.853846 3.076923 5.715385 2.053846
3 5.883607 2.740984 4.388525 1.434426

$size
$size[[1]]
[1] 50
$size[[2]]
[1] 39
$size[[3]]
[1] 61
$cluster
SparkDataFrame[prediction:int]
$is.loaded
[1] FALSE


>
> # Get fitted result from the k-means model
> showDF(fitted(kmeansModel),5)
```

Sepal_Length	Sepal_Width	Petal_Length	Petal_Width	Species	prediction
5.1	3.5	1.4	0.2	setosa	0
4.9	3.0	1.4	0.2	setosa	0
4.7	3.2	1.3	0.2	setosa	0
4.6	3.1	1.5	0.2	setosa	0
5.0	3.6	1.4	0.2	setosa	0

```
>
> # Prediction
> kmeansPredictions <- predict(kmeansModel, kmeansTestDF)
> showDF(kmeansPredictions,5)
+------------+-----------+------------+-----------+-------+---------+
|Sepal_Length|Sepal_Width|Petal_Length|Petal_Width|Species|prediction
+------------+-----------+------------+-----------+-------+---------+
|  5.1       |  3.5      |   1.4      |   0.2     | setosa| 0       |
|  4.9       |  3.0      |   1.4      |   0.2     | setosa| 0       |
|  4.7       |  3.2      |   1.3      |   0.2     | setosa| 0       |
|  4.6       |  3.1      |   1.5      |   0.2     | setosa| 0       |
|  5.0       |  3.6      |   1.4      |   0.2     | setosa| 0       |
+------------+-----------+------------+-----------+-------+---------+
```

How it works...

The preceding code snippets show how to fit generalized Gaussian and binomial linear models over DataFrames. The Gaussian GLM model returns a list with `devianceResiduals` and `coefficients` components. `devianceResiduals` gives the min/max deviance residuals of the estimation; `coefficients` gives the estimated coefficients and their estimated standard errors, t-values and p-values. (This is only available when the model is fitted by a normal solver.) The binomial GLM also returns `devianceResiduals` and `coefficients` components similar to gaussian GLM.

Similarly we applied k-means over the SparkDataFrame. The `kmeansModel <-` `spark.kmeans(kmeansDF, ~ Sepal_Length + Sepal_Width + Petal_Length +` `Petal_Width, k = 3)` line generates the k-means model by running k-means over the SparkDataFrame with k=3. The `summary(kmeansModel)` line display the model summary that is, the centroids of the clusters and size of each cluster (number of data points in each cluster). Once the model is ready, the `kmeansPredictions <- predict(kmeansModel,` `kmeansTestDF)` line predicts the cluster for each data point in the `kmeansTestDF`.

There's more...

SparkR implements the interpretation of R model formulas as an MLlib feature transformer (http://spark.apache.org/docs/latest/ml-guide.html#transformers), and provides integration with the ML pipelines API. The RFormula transformer provides a convenient way to specify feature transformations as in R. In Spark 2.0.2, there is additional support for more advanced features of R model formulas, including feature interactions, more model families, link functions, and better summary support.

See also

Please refer to Chapter 1, *Big Data Analytics with Spark* to get familiar with Spark. Also, visit the *Interactive analysis with the SparkR shell, Creating SparkR DataFrames*, and *SparkR DataFrame operations* recipes to get familiar with SparkR.

Index

implementing, Pandas used 68, 69
URL 69
crime detection application
implementing 238, 239, 243, 248

D

data
loading 22, 24, 25
sampling 43, 44
saving 22, 24, 25
visualizing, on HDFS 258, 262, 267
Databricks notebook
machine learning models, visualizing 286
DataFrame
about 30, 60, 338
complex operations 73, 74
creating 31, 32, 33
creating, over Spark 60, 62, 64
filtering, over Spark 64, 67
grouping, over Spark 64, 67
operations, concatenating 70, 71, 72
operations, merging 70
slicing, over Spark 64, 67
sorting, over Spark 64, 67
splitting, over Spark 64, 67
Dataset 33
decision trees
implementing 174, 177
URL 177
deep learning (DL)
about 298
with airlines data 234, 237
with weather data 234, 237
DeepLearning4j (DL4J)
about 299
CNN, executing for MNIST database 309, 312, 313
feed-forward neural network, executing over Spark 299, 302, 303
restricted Boltzmann machine (RBM), executing 304, 307, 308
descriptive statistics
about 47
obtaining 48, 51
diabetes dataset

URL 286
Directed Acyclic Graph (DAG) 186

E

en-sent.bin model
URL 209

F

feed-forward neural network
executing, with DeepLearning4j (DL4J) 299, 300, 303
frequency tables
generating 51, 53, 54

H

H2O
about 217
downloading, on Spark 218, 223
features 218
installing, on Spark 218, 223
URL 223, 227, 237, 249, 252
used, for executing SVM 249, 251, 252
used, for implementing k-means clustering 223, 227
H2OFrame 227
Hadoop InputFormat
URL 25
HDFS
custom functions, running 262
data, visualizing 258, 262, 267
external dependencies, adding to Zeppelin 264
external Spark cluster, pointing to 265
Hidden Markov Model (HMM) 202

I

IPython
for Named Entity Recognition (NER), over Spark 199, 202
using, with PySpark 58, 60
Iris dataset
URL 268, 300

J

Jackson library
  URL 24
JSON libraries
  URL 24

K

k-means clustering
  implementing, with H2O over Spark 223, 227
key value (KV) storage 218

L

labeled point
  URL 174
lemmatization
  about 210
  applying, with stanford NLP over Spark 210, 212
lightning visualization server
  plots, creating 281, 283, 285
linear classification model 141
Linux
  Anaconda, installing 191, 192
  Natural Language ToolKit (NLTK), installing 188, 190
  Pandas, installing 54, 56
load prediction data
  URL 43, 47, 51, 92
local vector
  URL 174
logistic regression
  applying 153, 155
  applying, on bank marketing data 141
  data exploration, performing 144, 147
  feature engineering, applying 148, 151, 153
  implementing, with Spark ML pipelines 181, 185
  variables, identifying 141, 144

M

machine learning (ML)
  about 169
  with SparkR 356
machine learning models
  visualizing, with Databricks notebook 286, 288, 289

mathematical functions
  reference link 69
matrix factorization 177
Maximum Entropy Classifier (MEC) 202
median absolute deviation (MAD) 102
micro-batch architecture 37
missing value
  fixing, for analysis 91, 95
MLlib feature transformer
  URL 361
MovieLens dataset
  analyzing 107, 111
  URL 107, 178

N

Naive Bayes' classification
  implementing 171
  URL 171
Named Entity Recognition (NER) 188
  about 199
  with IPython, over Spark 199, 202
Natural Language Processing (NLP)
  reference link 199, 202
Natural Language ToolKit (NLTK)
  about 188
  applications 188
  installing, on Linux 188, 190
ND4J
  about 299, 304
  URL 299, 304, 309
neural networks
  reference link 291
noun phrase (NP) 206
NSL-KDD dataset
  URL 157

O

openNLP-chunker
  implementing, over Spark 203, 206
openNLP-sentence detector
  implementing, over Spark 207, 210
Ordinary Least Squares Regression (OLSR) 140, 156
outliers
  detecting 96, 106

www.ingramcontent.com/pod-product-compliance
Lightning Source LLC
Chambersburg PA
CBHW062037050326
40690CB00016B/2971